SERMONS, SAYINGS AND SUCH

Ben Scott

This book was printed in the United States of America.

FWB Publications
Columbus, Ohio 43207
Alton.loveless@prodigy.net

Table Of Contents

FORWARD

In my lifetime I have known many great preachers who have become mentors for me and the one of whom this book is about was one of them.

Ben Scott's grandfather, father, brother and three sons and grandson are all ministers of the gospel. I am not at all sure as to how many ministers that was in his family tree, and that of his wife's family. I am aware of at least four families of which he were a part that all had ministers. For example, the Scott family, the Smith family, the Vandivort and Postlewaites.

We have shared so much in common. We both served the same churches at different times in our ministries, both pastored in Arkansas and Missouri. We have served as denominational officers from time to time.

He and his wife were always active in areas where my wife and I could share sound advice.

He and his wife, Genelle, have three sons all of whom are Free Will Baptist ministers and have followed in the steps of their parents as active ministers in this denomination.

--Alton E. Loveless

INTRODUCTION

This is a simple collection of paragraphs from the pen of a preacher who has spent more than forty years as pastor and evangelist.

The illustrations are taken from actual experiences. Nothing is made up or artificial. Most of the short articles have been published before in the *Mid-Week News* while serving as pastor of the North Little Rock First FWB Church.

The sermons and sermon excerpts are taken from recordings and are given as preached from the pulpit, except for some deletions and minor changes.

This is in no way intended to be a stimulant to deep Theological thinking; nor is it designed to be a doctrinal dissertation. It is simply what the title implies ...a collection of *Sermons, Sayings, & such.*

"I Remember Mama" and "I Remember Papa" are feeble attempts to honor the cherished memory of old-fashioned, God-fearing, hard-working South Missouri Ozarks parents. Papa was a preacher from the early '20s until his death in 1957.

Mama was everything that a family of eight children could ever expect or hope for in a mother. Maybe someone will see in these lines something of your own parents and be blessed with the memory.

DEDICATION

To
Ben Scott
For The
Amazing history you have left.

Feb. 23, 1924 – May 20, 2010

To
The Greater Family
Who Have Plowed The Hard Rows,
So We Could Have A Greater Ministry.

To
A denomination
That Has Allowed Us To Preach A Saving Gospel
And
Work In To Fulfill Your Call On We All.

Genelle Smith Scott
Ben's wife and Women's leader

Randy Scott, Pastor
Sutton Free Will Baptist, Pocahontas, Arkansas

Fred Scott, Pastor
Gardner Free Will Baptist Church, Gardner, N.C.

Len Scott, Pastor
Pardue Church, Clarksville, Tennessee

BRIEF AUTOBIOGRAPHY OF BEN SCOTT'S FATHER

George William Scott
1890-1957

March 20, in 1952
1904 South Central Ave.
Oklahoma city, Oklahoma

I, George William Scott, son of the late F. F. Scott or Forster Fleming Scott and Nancy Howe Wilson Scott was born November 18, 1890 about 4 miles northwest of Huggins, Missouri in a log house my father had built.

My father was a son of Fleming Scott and Phoebe Scott whose maiden name was James. My grandfather Fleming Scott was a minister of the gospel, a member of the Christian church, but not like the Christian church of today. Their faith and practice was the same as Free Will Baptists. Grandfather Scott is buried at Ava, Missouri. Grandmother Scott is buried somewhere in Arkansas.

My father's maiden name was Wilson, the daughter of Jim and Tanny Wilson. Grandfather was the son of Harrison Wilson buried in the Concord graveyard at Roubidoux north of Huggins, Missouri. Grandmother Wilson's name was Smith— her father was Thomas Smith who is buried in the Denlow graveyard on Fox Creek in Douglas County.

My father and mother were Christians when I was born. Father was in ordained deacon in a Free Will Baptist Church. One of the first things I can remember is that I used to stand at my mother's knee and ask for the butter spoon when she would churn.

I have a faint remembrance of my father moving into Indian Territory and then back to Arkansas in Washington County, from there to Ava, Missouri. I remember very well on January 30, 1895. My brother John, was four years old that day and it and Ed Perry was hung in Ava that day for helping kill the Sower family. We lived east of Ava on the Joe stall farm. We then moved back to Texas County. On our way my little sister took sick and died just north of Mansfield, Missouri. Cora May is buried in the Dennis graveyard.

When I was eight years old, I went to school about 10 months of schooling. I was in the fourth reader. I hold no ill will toward my parents. They did teach me to believe in God. When I was 13 years old my father moved to Ceiling, Oklahoma. In 1903 —another one of my baby sisters died there and is buried in the Ceiling graveyard. Her name was Sarah Elizabeth.

We moved back to Texas County Missouri on a farm north of Number One Free Will Baptist Church. Then, to a farm west of Huggins near Graff, Missouri. It was there I met Oma L Rattlerree and fell in love with her and on September 21, 1910 we were married. She was 18 and I was 19. We were both Christians and members of the Union Chapel Church. I possibly was not too well settled, but I worked hard and we love to go to church. We lost our first baby prematurely. Then, we had two little girls—Anna Isabel and Bessie Jane and another baby boy that lived just a week. We then went to North Missouri near Tarkio. I worked up there on a Rankin ranch. We came back to our home and that winter I made and hauled railroad ties all winter. The next June, 1917 on the third Sunday I preached my first sermon at

Union Chapel Church. I was licensed by The Union Association that same year and was ordained in 1918 at the Pleasant Hill Church. I accepted a pastoral care of four churches namely; Pleasant Grove Number One, Oak Grove, Astoria and Cope. Uncle Dick Hutsell was the first one I baptize. Mrs. Cleaver, Bill Cleaver's mother, was the first funeral I had. I have pastored churches in the country and in towns— Hartville and Mountain Grove, Missouri and Oklahoma City, and Oklahoma. At the present time I am in Oklahoma City, March 21, 1952

We're building a new church house. It is block and brick and will cost about $20,000. One of the biggest undertakings I have ever done.

On April 3, 1952 the footing for the new building--56 ½ yards of cement was run. On April 15, 1952 the first block was laid. Contract for the work to Magers— Load Bates Foreman. George W. Scott-backspace, pastor. In all my experiences pastor I have never worked with a more agreeable group of people. So far they have all seemed to want to do what is right. We are having services in it.

September 19, 1952. I am here all alone. Mom is at Turley with Leah Mae and Johnnie, Joey and Mary Susan.

At the present time Adam and family are pastoring in Durham, North Carolina; Benjamin, Genelle and Randy in Third Church, St. Louis, Missouri; Rolla and family at flat River, Missouri; Johnnie and family at Turley, Oklahoma— Herbert is not pastoring at the present time

My whole heart's desire is that we may all live and number as many in heaven as we do here on earth. I dearly love every one of the family and mom does, too. I sure miss her this week, but she is taking care of Bogie. She is our baby, but we would do the same for any one of the rest.

Back to the earlier part of my life and work. We have reared eight children—six girls and two boys. The two boys are both ministers. The girls are all Christians. I am proud of them all. To me they are the best children in the world and I love them.

There is not anything in the world that is right that I wouldn't do for any of them if I could. They were all converted at an early age. I had the privilege of baptizing every one of them.

As I look back over my life I cannot be too faithful to my helpmate and the children. They mean everything to me. Mom and made don't how much of this world's goods, but we feel rich in the Lord. (This brief autobiography was type from the original handwritten manuscript found and grandpa Scott's record book dated 1952. The following was written by Oma's God after the death of her husband.)

"Daddy "had a heart attack September 16, 1955 and wasn't ever well anymore. He was unable to carry on the work of the church and never preached but a few more times after this. He was at this time pastoring the church at Myrtle, Missouri. He resigned and we moved back to Mountain Grove on November 11, 1955.

We rented a house and lived in it for three months. We had already purchased a lot and we had a house built on it during these three months. We moved into the new house on February 7, 1956. We united with the church here and attended when daddy was well enough. He pastored this church for 17 years and it is dear to our hearts. Daddy died just 13 months after we moved here. I am left all alone and no one but the Lord knows how much I miss him and how lonely I am, but I am looking forward to the time I can go to be with him and all the other good people that have gone on before.

Daddy was active in the work of the Lord for 48 years. The first eight years of this ministry we went on a horse back. He worked on a farm to help support his family for 21 years after he started preaching.

The following is a summarize report of his 38 years of preaching just in part. There are many things that he did not that he did not record.

Sermons he preached-six, 064
Conversions Witness-1122
Baptize-641
Received Into The Church-345
Funerals Preached-675
Marriages Performed-59 Couples
Helped Organize Churches
Helped Ordained Preachers And Deacons
Miles Traveled-62,716
Money Received-29,500

Victorious Christian Living
National Association of FWB meeting
in Cobo Hall, Detroit, 1963

It is said that a passenger on a large airliner became disturbed one night while in flight. She walked to the cockpit and asked the pilot, "Where are we now?" To which the pilot replied, "Well, right now we're lost." Then, taking note of the passenger's concerned look, he added, "But we're making good time!"

I believe this presents a true picture of this present generation. We don't know exactly where we are, but I think we all know we're making pretty good time!

The decade in which we live has been described as "The Soaring Sixties." And I think it is! Man has soared higher into space than ever before. Our National debt is higher than it ever was. Our National crime rate is soaring year after year. Our juvenile problems are soaring; the consumption of alcoholic beverages is increasing year after year. These are truly the SOARING SIXTIES.

This is an age that has traded God for gadgets. We, like the men of Jeremiah's day, have forsaken the Fountain of living waters and have hewed us out cisterns, broken cisterns that can hold no water. We have tried to defy the Word of the Lord Jesus Who said, "A man's life consisteth not in the abundance of the things which he possesseth." So far, we have failed to prove Christ wrong. We take more aspirins for our headaches than any generation. In fact, this might well be called the age of the pill. The tranquilizer takes its place on many a medicine cabinet shelf. We take a pill to pep us up; we take a pill to calm us down; we take a pill to put us to sleep; and we take a pill to keep us awake.

But there is something wrong with the world tonight that a pill cannot cure! Morally, we are sick. Spiritually, we are sick. Socially, we are sick. To a great extent, even the church itself is sick. We need a spiritual transfusion of the life that only comes from the Son of God.

Jesus said to His followers, "These things have I spoken unto you, that in ME ye might have peace. In the world ye shall have tribulation; but be of good cheer; I have overcome the world." The question that perplexes a lot of people is: How, in a world like this, can we have VICTORY? How can we live above the clouds? How can we stay on the right road in a world that's lost its way?

In answer to these questions, I offer three imperatives for VICTORIOUS CHRISTIAN LIVING. First, our attitude toward Christ. Second, our relationship with the Holy Spirit. And third, a proper attachment to this present world.

We're living in a day when many religionists are beckoning with open arms and saying, "Come on, fellows, let's all get in the same boat and ride together." And about the only stipulation they make is that we look toward the starry skies and acknowledge that somewhere there is a God Who is the Father of us all. I tell you, it is not enough that we merely believe there is a God. It makes a great deal of difference what we believe about God's Son, the Lord Jesus Christ! There's a man in our town who has told me different times. "The world has twelve saviours." I don't know who they are; I'm not interested. The Bible says there is ONE Saviour.

You'll never know real victory in your soul until you settle it once and for all what you believe about Jesus Christ! Jesus Himself declared, "For if ye believe not that I am He ye shall die in your sins!" And in the same chapter He said, "Where I am ye cannot come." The greatest question facing us today is, "What think ye of Christ? Whose Son is He?" To that question, I hope we'll affirm with all the conviction of our souls. "Thou art the Christ, the Son of the living God."

The Doctrine of Salvation

The National Association of Free Will Baptist
Convened in Ft. Worth, TX, July 1982
Scripture:
Luke 2:25-32

Fundamentals of the Faith...
My particular subject is "Salvation" from the scripture found in Luke 2:25-32.

Simeon, an old servant of the Lord, said these words,
"Lord, now lettest Thy servant depart in peace, according to Thy Word; For mine eyes have seen Thy Salvation."

The Apostle Paul wrote:
"From a child thou hast known the Holy Scriptures which are able to make thee wise unto Salvation."

In dealing with this subject there are three points which I'd like to present. First, the *DESIGN*: second, To us who are saved, the design of Salvation has been revealed for all time to come in the Person of Jesus Christ, Son of God, Who became Son of Man. He was the Person of promise in prophecy, of whom it was written, *"There shall come out of Zion the Deliverer."* The Deliverer DID come! He is the Ark of safety from the flood of God's wrath in And I believe, looking a bit further, he saw the shadow of a cross upon a lonely hill. He saw these little hands that would be stretched out as full-grown Man, nailed to a rugged, cruel cross to complete the plan of God's redemption.

I believe he looked at those little baby feet; and he saw the day when they would walk the by-ways and the streets and the lanes of the cities. But he also saw by the Grace of God the day when these feet would walk up a rugged hill called Calvary; and He would stumble under the weight of the cross as He went to complete the will of the Father.

Simeon looked at that little Baby's head; and I think he saw the day when that head would be beaten; and upon that head there would be placed a crown of thorns. I think he looked into those eyes and foresaw the day when they would be filled with tears because of a Christ-0rejecting world.

Jesus said to Zacchaeus after he had come down from the tree:

"Today is SALVATION come to your house."

After Pentecost, Peter, the converted fisherman, said to a group of religious elitists, concerning Christ:

"This is the Stone that was set at naught of you builders; which is become the Head of the corner; neither is there Salvation in any other; for there is none other Name given under Heaven among men whereby we must be saved."

And I'll tell you friend that culls out an awful lot of folks! "None other Name!" It is the ONLY Name by which a sinner is saved and leaves this world to go to the Paradise of God.

The DESIGN of Salvation is Deity.   It is not man-made. Consequently, it is a perfect plan of Salvation. It is broad enough to include "Whosoever Will."

The *DISCIPLINE* of Salvation.

Somebody said not long ago, "This is the most un-disciplined generation that ever lived." Maybe that is true. We need to be reminded that Jesus said,

"If any man will come after me, let him deny himself and take up his cross and follow me."

Paul wrote in Titus chapter 2

"For the grace of God that bringeth salvation hath appeared unto all men, teaching us that denying ungodliness and worldly lusts, we should live soberly, righteously, in this present world."

That is discipline!

But where is the discipline in our day? Where is the dedication? Where is the cross-bearing? The first-century Christians lived lives that were characterized by discipline and dedication. We desperately need the same in our day!

I grew up under old-fashioned country hill preaching that just scared the day-lights out of me; and I really believe the right kind of preaching ought to scare a fellow a little bit. They made me believe that if I didn't shape up and live right, if I died in my sins I stood in great danger of going to hell. And I'm glad they preached it that way. One of the things they emphasized was that when a fellow got saved he was supposed to act and live like it.

We're living in the generation that says, "I've gotta be me, I did it my way, and don't fence me in."

As a result of this philosophy, we've got churches filled with "Wandering Stars," "Trees with no fruit," "Clouds with no water."

We've got too many births with no labor pains of repentance and conviction. We see sports figures and so-called "celebrities" get religion. They get up and give a testimony and, figuratively, if not literally, they hold the Bible in one hand and the "bottle" in the other.

Entertainment personalities get religion, but they go on entertaining in the night club, or wherever they want to. I read the account of one female entertainer no long ago. She said she really had a problem. She had made a profession of faith in Christ. She had a commitment in Las

Vegas. She said, "I wrestled with the decision, didn't really know what to do; I felt like I ought to get out of it." But she said, "I finally came to this conclusion: I'll go ahead and I'll perform, and I'll conclude my program with a religious hymn." And she went ahead to say that it (the singing of a hymn) was the most popular thing.

But where is the cross? Where is the discipline of the cross? It doesn't make a bit of difference whether it's a sports figure making a million dollars a year, (which is about nine hundred and ninety thousand more than they are worth) or whether it's somebody like you and me who have been called upon to leave the things of the world and follow Christ. There's a cross to bear! Thank God that we still have in our hymn books, the blood and the cross. But we had better have it in more than the lyrics that we sing; we had better have it in the lives that we live!

I've lived in the greatest days of our denomination. I remember in 1952, a young couple, Carlisle and Marie Hanna, took their newly born daughter, Sheila Marie, and went to India. I was pastor of the church in St. Louis where Marie and her parents were members. I'll never forget a few months after they left, a telegram came. Sheila Marie had taken dysentery and suddenly died. Every time I see Carlisle and Marie I cannot help thinking how much they and some others as Foreign Missionaries have been called upon to bear.

Are the demands and discipline of salvation any greater for missionaries than for a church member here in the home-land? I'm speaking to us tonight about things that really matter, I don't have any right to dictate to God where I'll go, or under what conditions I'll serve! But while we send our missionaries to a foreign land for four years at a time, their children can die, their parents can die, conditions can get terrible; and we say to them, "You stay on the mission field for four years." And her in the homeland, we've got multitudes of church members who haven't been in church in FOUR SUNDAYS straight.

There's the discipline of FAITHFULNESS. Do you remember that Jesus, the Captain of our salvation, was made perfect through suffering? Are we, His servants, greater than our Lord? I admonish you and me, beloved, hang in there! The Captain of our Salvation DIED at His post. I want to die where the Lord wants me to die; and I want to be doing when that moment comes what the Lord wants me to be doing!

John chapter six is an interesting chapter. It begins with Meat, Miracles, and a Multitude. You deal in meat and miracles, and you can get a multitude! But when the chapter ends, the meat's played out; the miracles have ceased, the multitude is dispersed, and the Lord Jesus is saying to a handful of Disciples, "Will ye also go away?"

I read the story the other day of Elisha when he was called to follow Elijah. He was ploughing with twelve yoke of oxen. Elisha was a big farmer. Elijah came by and cast the mantle of the prophet upon him. Elisha said, "Let me go and kiss my father and my mother. And then I'll follow you." And he did. Can you imagine Elisha coming home and he embraced his father and his mother and said, "Mother, I won't be seeing you now for a while? Dad, I'm going and I won't be seeing you any time soon." "Where are you going, son?" "I'm just going wherever the Lord wants me to go. The Lord has called and I must go!" he slew a pair of oxen; he built an altar. He forsook his profession. He forsook his possessions. He kissed his dad and mom good-by, and multitudes of people tonight have never kissed anything good-bye! "Must I be carried to the skies on flowery beds of ease, while others fought to win the prize, and sailed through bloody seas?" No!

There is the discipline of DILIGENCE. Free Will Baptist doctrine emphasizes diligence. Peter did, too. He wrote: "Besides this, giving all diligence." He then admonished that we add these Christian graces...Virtue, knowledge, temperance, Godliness, brotherly kindness, charity..."For if these things be in you and abound they make you that ye shall neither be barren nor unfruitful in the knowledge of the Lord. He that lacketh these things is blind and cannot see afar off and has forgotten that he was purged from his old sins."

Now what's the opposite of diligence? I think its neglect. And the writer of Hebrews asks this question, "How shall we escape if we neglect so great Salvation?" Sinners REJECT. Christians NEGLECT. Be diligent! How are we going to escape if we neglect?

There's the discipline of SEPARATION. I don't know how separated we can get. I'm sure that none of us are as much separated from this world as we ought to be. I'm not like they used to say about the Puritans. When ice cream came along they said the Puritans wouldn't eat it. They said nothing could taste that good without being sinful!

The Bible does say, "Be no conformed to this world." And again it is written, "Having these promises dearly beloved, let us cleanse ourselves from all filthiness of the flesh and spirit perfecting holiness in the fear of God."

"The church and the world walked far apart
On the changing shores of time;
    The world was singing a giddy song;
    The church a hymn sublime.
    Come, give me your hand, cried the merry world
    And walk with me this way.
    But the good church hid her snowy hand
    And solemnly answered 'Nay.'

The following verses describe the compromise of the church as she gives in to the allurements and temptations of the world, and the final sad conclusion can be stated like this:
    "The sons of the world and the sons of the church
    Walked closely, hand and heart
    And only the Master Who knoweth all,
    Could tell the two apart."

I'd like to say last of all, a few things about the DESTINY of salvation. God gets kicked around down here. His Name is blasphemed. Jesus Christ is still the Rejected Redeemer. He's ruled out of the class room. He gets a raw deal in the court room by the judge and the jury. Entertainers would be hard-pressed to come up with a line if it were not for "hell" or God, or some vulgarity.

Some of you have heard Dr. R.G. Lee's message, "Pay Day, Some Day." I listen to it every once in a while. Ahab is going on in his sin. The blood of Naboth has not been avenged, and Jezebel is going her merry way, Justice seems to have been aborted.

I can hear this old preacher as he cries out, "Where is God? Where is God? Is He deaf that He cannot hear? Is He blind that He cannot see? Is He paralyzed that He cannot move?"

No, God's not blind, or deaf, or paralyzed. We know where God is. He is still where He's always been. One of these days it is going to all be over down here, and God's going to have His way!

The LAST chapter is the most interesting and exciting! Because when you read the last chapter you know how it's all going to turn out.

A few years ago during one of our Arkansas State Minister's Retreats, I was staying in a motel room with some of our state's younger preachers. During this time, Arkansas' Razorbacks were playing Texas A&M's basketball team in a very important conference game. The game was shown on a delayed telecast. That means the game was already over when the telecast started, and the score was already determined.

I knew what the score was. I already knew who the winner was. The game had been won by one point, and I knew which team had the victory! So I went to bed and went to sleep!

If I didn't know how this thing was going to turn out, I'd have a nervous breakdown. I know! I've read the last chapter. I'm not alarmed about how it's going to turn out. I know who is going to be on the victory side.

I'd like to talk to Daniel for a moment. He seemed to have special insight. Daniel?...He said, "There'll be a time of trouble like there never has been." But he's got more to say than that. How about it, Daniel? Daniels says, "The saints...the saints of the most High shall take the Kingdom and possess the Kingdom...forever, even forever and ever." And I like that!   Jesus said, "Fear not, little flock; it's" your Father's good pleasure to give you the Kingdom."

John, the isle-of-Patmos John? "After this I beheld and lo, a great multitude which no man could number of kindred's and people and tongues stood before the throne and before the Lamb clothed with robes and palms in their hands and cried with a loud voice, SALVATION to our God which sitteth upon the throne, and unto the Lamb."

What's it like, John? John said, "They shall hunger no more, neither thirst any more, neither shall the sun light on them nor any heat; for the Lamb which is in the midst of the throne shall feed them and shall lead them unto fountains of living waters and God shall wipe away all tears from their eyes.

Another look, John, "And I saw Heaven opened, and behold a white horse and He that sat upon him was called FAITHFUL and TRUE. And He hath on His vesture and on His thigh a Name written, KING OF KINGS AND LORD OF LORDS."

The last chapter of this whole thing turns out well. The saints take the Kingdom. Christ reigns as King. God is still the Almighty. The prophets have learned about that Salvation of which they enquired. The Master's minority has become a mighty multitude. We lay down the cross and take up the crown. We quit our sighing and start singing. And we proclaim "Worthy is the Lamb."

I close with this benediction: "Unto Him that loved us and washed us from our sins in His own blood; and hath made us Kings and Priests unto God and His Father, to Him be glory and dominion forever and ever. A-men."

Our Blessed Hope

Two weeks ago, Bob Hope died. He was one hundred years old. Shortly after his death, there were a lot of articles about the century in which he lived. I gleaned a few interesting statistics:

A hundred years ago this year, the Wright Brothers made their first flight at Kitty Hawk, North Carolina. Ford Motor Company was organized in **1903.** Sanka Coffee was put on the market in **1903.** And, the first World Series was played between the Boston Red Sox and the Pirates. If it's any omen, Boston won!

The average life expectancy in the United States a hundred years ago was 47 years. Fourteen percent of homes had a bath tub; the others had a wash tub. Eight percent had a phone. There were **8,000** cars in the United States and 144 miles of paved road.

Average wages were 22 cents an hour. Ninety-five per-cent of the births took place at home. Sugar cost 4 cents a pound, eggs 14 cents a dozen and coffee 15 cents a pound.

Most women washed their hair once a month and used Bo-rax or egg-yokes for shampoo. Population of Las Vegas was 30 and there were 230 total reported murders in the United States in all of that year.

I come before this congregation with an awful lot of emotions. My association with this church goes back a long time. I was a year old preacher in 1945 when I was put on to preach at the association here that summer to be followed by my dad.

I remembered the text that I preached from ... it was in the book of Kings, "If the Lord be God, follow him-, but if Baal, follow him." I done a lot of things wrong in my life, but I've done one thing right. I decided a long time ago that the Lord is God and I have followed Him.

I feel highly honored ... an honor which I do not deserve to be able to stand here this hour. And not only do I stand here in the name of the Lord Jesus Christ, I stand here hoping somehow that I can represent the many pastors this church has been blessed with. Many of them very near and dear to my heart. One hundred years ... anyone who can ap-proach this observance as just another service must be lack-ing in appreciation for the rich heritage of this church and others.

We've survived lots of hour-long sermons. We've sat and squirmed on slat-bottomed pews. We've had night servic-es by light of Coleman lanterns and coal-oil lamps.

We've been cooled by funeral home fans, open windows and open doors. We've been baptized in cold creek or river water. We've washed feet in a dishpan and taken communion from one common cup. We've enjoyed revival meetings, shouts of praise, and we've survived a few business meeting spats. We've carried our new baby with pride and joy. We've rel-ished the "ooo's and awe's." We've enrolled them in Sunday school and watched them graduate from toddlers and beginners class all the way through teen years, courtship, and marriage. We've buried our dead in the church yard cemetery. We've walked the rocky roads with heavy hearts, a lump in our throats, and a tear in our eye. But we've kept coming back to the meeting house singing "I meet you in the morning, just inside the eastern gate." We've heard heaven sounding so sweet and hell sounding so hot and horrible that sinners have trembled and wept under the weight of convic-tion till they found relief at the mourner's bench alter. We've listened to sermons by preachers, many of whom had not been to college, but they had been to Calvary!

In the infancy of this new century, quite different from that of a hundred years ago. What would the old time preachers and church leaders have us preach for this age?

I'm taking my message today based on four points from the "Congregational Crusader" which Bro. Ralph Staten pub-lished for so many years. I remember these words that Bro. Staten put in bold letters across the top of the page.

The Book (with a capital B)
The Blood (meaning the Blood of Christ)
The Bride (meaning the Church)
The Blessed Return

I'd like for us to look at these things for today's message. First of all, The Book. Now we've been reminded of a lot of changes. In the old song "Abide with Me", one verse says "Change and decay, All around I see, Oh Thou who changeth not, Abide with me." I catching myself more and more all the time as the days go by latching on to the things that are unchangeable. There is so much that is transient.

For scripture verses, I want to give you Jeremiah 6:16 and Proverbs 22:28.

Jeremiah 6:16 "Thus saith the LORD, Stand ye in the ways, and see, and ask for the old paths, where is the good way, and walk therein, and ye shall find rest for your souls."

I'm telling you folks, if there ever was a generation that needs to come back to some of the old bed rock truths of the Holy Book of God, this generation needs to do that.

There is so much unrest, so many things that are disturbing our peace and so little that we can really say is good in this day-may God help us to make our way back to the old tried and truth paths of God's Word.

First, The Book

"Remove not the ancient landmark." That was given in Deu-teronomy. It was substantiated in other books. Without go-ing into detail, we understand basically what the "landmark" is. It's a point from which you start. It has something to do with the inheritance. The land was to be handed down from generation to generation. And each succeeding genera-tion was to have a benchmark or a landmark that they could point to and say this is where the property starts and this is what we are going to base our claim upon.

I stand before this wonderful congregation here today and I say this is the starting point of our Christian faith and this is what we are going to hang our faith on. It is not going down. It is going to stand when the world is on fire and darkness fails the sun!

The Word of God-I like some things that are said about the Word of God in the Word of God. (Story) When I was a kid growing up in Brushy Knob community, in Texas County, my sisters who were older than 1, got a wonderful idea one New Year's day, that it would be good for us kids if we would make a resolution to read a chapter in the Bible every day that year. So they conned me into joining them in that reso-lution. It was a good resolution. But, I confess as I looked back, there were a lot of nights I started to go to bed, I hadn't read a chapter. It didn't take me long to start gravitating to Psalms 117. 1 read Psalms 117 an awful lot that year just so I could say I had read a chapter.

I still remember it: "O praise the LORD, all ye nations: praise him, all ye people. For his merciful kindness is great toward us: and the truth of the LORD endureth forever. Praise ye the LORD."

I'm telling you today, beloved, the truth of the Lord endures to all generations. It is unchangeable! I get amazed some-times at the ideas that I hear floating around by so-called "intellects" of our day. What we've got is a bunch of people who are so stupid that they don't know they're stupid.

The Bible is the Word of God! It is true in every generation that every generation needs the Word of God as much as the other generations needed the Word of God.

Psalm 119:89 says, "Forever, O LORD, thy word is settled in heaven." I figure, if the word of God is settled in Heaven, it's going to be mighty hard to disturb it here on earth.

2 Timothy 3:16 - 17 "All scripture is given by inspiration of God, and is profitable for doctrine, for reproof, for correction, for instruction in righteousness, that the man of God may be perfect, thoroughly furnished unto all good works."

2 Peter 1:21 says, "For the prophecy came not in old time by the will of man: but holy men of God spake as they were moved by the Holy Ghost."

Isaiah 40, which our fore fathers loved so much, "The grass withereth, the flower fadeth: but the word of our God shall stand for ever."

And I stand here today not to defend the Book but to pro-claim the Book and the Book will stand. The Bible will stand when this world has passed away. For Jesus said, "Heaven and earth may pass away but my Word shall not pass away."

Years and years ago, I read this story. The skeptic, critic approached Missionary Gladstone and said to the old Missionary, "What would you think if I could tell you that I could produce in an hour arguments that would utterly disprove the Bible?" He said, "I think about the same as I would if I saw an ant crawling up Mount Everest threatening to squash the mighty mountain with its weight."

Can a sparrow drain the ocean dry? Can a man with a wheel barrow move all the sand of the Sahara?

A thousand times- NO! But a sparrow can come near drinking the ocean dry than you can come to disproving the Word of God. It will stand as it has stood.

You understand of course that every one of these points -one of our good ole fashion preachers of other days and this day could preach and hour on each one and could barely touch the surface. I realize I'm getting old. I used to have bad thoughts about old preachers. First, I thought they preached a long time; and some of them did. They all got loud. I thought that was a requirement that a man had to preach a long time. One reason I know I'm getting' old is I stopped out on the parking lot a here while back and looked down and there were two brand new, shiny pennies. And I started to do as I always do, bend over and pick'em up. Got about half way down and decided it's not worth it! They may be laying there, yet.

Couple days later, I was putting gas in my truck, and right at my feet there were a couple of quarters. I said that was a little different. I bent over and picked up those quarters and found a dime down there, too. Put 'em in my pocket; kept on pumping gas, looked down and there were a couple more quarters. I picked them up and put them in my pocket and then, discovered I had a hole in my pocket.

Getting old is not too bad. There's some things about it I don't enjoy, but I'm telling you if you've got your sanity and got your heart in the right place, you know that it's not going to be long until you cross over and you see what's on the other side.

What I hope and pray for this service, oh man, Fannie Cros-by wrote "a foretaste of glory divine." If you've not got your mind made up to go to Heaven, get your mind set toward Heaven. Don't let anything keep you from going.

We're just getting a little sample today. I tell you, I expect to see those old preachers. I expect to see the saints of God. We're getting a little sample of what it will be when we get over to Glory.

Second, The Blood

The second point is The Blood. I look through our hymn books an awful lot. I roll over in my mind the blessed old songs; then, I check them out to see if they're scriptural. For ages, we've been singing "what can wash away my sins? Nothing but the blood of Jesus." We sing "My hope is built on nothing less than Jesus blood and righteousness. I dare not trust the sweetest strain but only lean on Jesus' name." It is the blood we sang with our forefathers "There is a foun-tain filled with blood drawn from Emmanuel's vain. And sin-ners plunge beneath that flood, lose all their guilty stain."

Now I know that somebody that's not familiar with the Bible, might wonder what you are singing about being cleansed by the blood. I'll tell you what we're singing about. We're sing-ing about the blood of the Lamb of God that was sprinkled on the post of the door in the Old Testament. And that night when God went down into Egypt on the most terrible night of all, he said when I see the blood, I will pass over you. That was established as an ordinance. Then, in Leviticus 17:11 "For the life of the flesh is in the blood: and I have given it to you upon the altar to make an atonement for your souls: for it is the blood that maketh an atonement for the soul."

In the New Testament, this practice is carried over in the communion of the Lord's Supper. When we reenact that evening when Jesus took bread and broke it and gave it to His disciples and said this is my body. Then, the cup-He said "drink you this as oft as you do it in remembrance of Me. This is My blood in the New Testament."

I want to tell you my brother   sister, when you stand before God in judgement you'd better have more to recommend you than your good works. That won't cut it! You'd better have more to recommend you than your own recommendation. You need the blood of Christ. And when God sees the blood He'll pass over you. It's not the blood of the Lamb that was taken from the flock. It's the blood of the one that John the Baptist saw that morning and he said "Behold the Lamb of God that takes away the sins of the world."

I would like to hear some of those old preachers preach on this. But we didn't have tape recorders back in those days. You know, preachers have a unique way of getting puffed up momentarily. I remember up at Flat River one time, I preached as late as March or early April. And the pas-tor's little boy came back and stood by me while the closing prayer was going on. As quick as the prayer was closed, he said "Brother Scott that was a tremendous sermon." Well, I started to pat him on the head and say thank you, son. And he broke out and said "Ha! Ha! Ha! ... April Fool!"

I came down to the Byrd church several years ago for a re-vival and here came Brother   Sister Campbell. Bro. Glynn was carrying a tape recorder. You know what thought went through my mind. Bro. Campbell wants to record my ser-mon. Do you know what he brought that for? He had music on it and he was going to sing a solo. Brother, it doesn't pay to get puffed up because God's got a lot of ways to getting us puffed down.

I don't have anything of which to boast. I've wondered about this thought an awful lot. I'm just a sinner saved by grace. I'd like to say that since I got saved that I'm not a sinner. But, I know me too well. So, I stand here and I say that by the grace of God that I'm a sinner saved by grace through faith in the blood of the Lord Jesus Christ! And the blood of Jesus Christ, His son, cleanseth us from all sin and it keeps on cleansing.

Revelation 1-.5 says, "Unto him that loved us, and washed us from our sins in his own blood" and we'll sing His praises in Heaven. John saw a multitude, a great multitude, and said "what are these." He was given this answer, "these are they that have come out of great tribulation. They've washed their robes and made them white in the blood of the Lamb. Therefore, because they've washed their robes and made them white in the blood of the Lamb, there, before the throne, and the Lamb which is in the midst shall feed them and shall lead them unto the founts of the living waters. And God shall wipe away all tears."

Third, The Bride

Jesus said, "Upon this rock I'll build my church. The gates of Hell shall not prevail against it." In Acts 2:47 after the outpouring of the Holy Ghost at Pentecost, the Lord added to the church daily, such as being saved or those that were being saved.

Acts 20:28, Paul wrote or said to the elders, "Take heed therefore unto yourselves, and to all the flock, over the which the Holy Ghost hath made you overseers, to feed the church of God, which he hath purchased with his own blood."

What a magnificent institution is the Church of the Lord Je-sus Christ. Now there are two aspects of the Church. I don't want to get too technical, but there is a sense in which everybody who's born in the kingdom of God is a part of the Church of Christ, the Church of God, and the Body of Christ.

Then, there's that sense of the church in the local sense, that's represented by the candlesticks in which Jesus was standing in the midst in Revelation 1. This church here is a candlestick. Men and women have been saved and have put their light on the candlestick because men don't light a candle and put it under a bushel. It's been evident here this morning by the testimonies that some of the saints of God put their light on the candlestick and their little light shines. And their still shining today!

I remember the card class teacher. I remember Sister Mc-Donald who hobbled down to Brushy Knob on her cane and called a little group of boys and girls to the back end of the Brushy Knob church on a hot, sunny morning. This is a candlestick. And through the ups and the downs, in the goods and the bad days, Christ is standing in the midst of His churches. I believe the Church will stand. It's a wonder-ful institution.

If you have your Bible and would like to follow this, I want you to look at Ephesians 2-3 and look at some other pas-sages. In the book of Ephesians, the apostle, Paul, gave us that scripture "By grace are you saved through faith, that not of yourselves it is the gift of God, not of works, lest any man should boast." Down in verse 18, chapter 2: "For through him we both have access by one Spirit unto the Father. Now therefore ye are no more strangers and foreigners, but fel-low citizens with the saints, and of the household of God;"

We've got a wonderful relationship. All my ministerial life,] have believed in the local church. I believe in the fellowship of the local church.

> "We share our mutual woes,
> Our mutual burdens bare-,
> And often for each other flows
> The sympathizing tear.
> When we asunder part,
> It gives us inward pain;
> But we shall still be joined in heart,
> And hope to meet again. "

Verses 20-21, "And are built upon the foundation of the apostles and prophets, Jesus Christ himself being the chief corner stone; In whom all the building fitly framed together groweth unto an holy temple in the Lord."

On over in chapter 3, He sneaked in this likeness of the church when He said in verses 14   15 "For this cause I bow my knees unto the Father of our Lord Jesus Christ, Of whom the whole family in heaven and earth is named."

I had the privilege of growing up in a big family. I was one of those 95% that was born at home. My mother had ten ba-bies and I was number nine. On today's market, I wouldn't have much of a chance of getting here. I know what it's like to be part of a family. Last summer, about 90 of the descen-dants of George and Norma Scott got together for a reunion. What a blessed time!

But I have an extended family. Mrs. Scott and I left our par-ents in 1949, moved to St. Louis, and from there to Oklaho-ma and there back to Missouri, and there to Arkansas. And the next move is going to be to Heaven ... I think?

But everywhere we've been we've had mothers and fathers and brothers and sisters. That's exactly what Jesus said if you do the will of God, you will have a lot of kinfolks.

Chapter 4:15-16: He likens the church to the body "But speaking the truth in love, may grow up into him in all things, which is the head, even Christ: From whom the whole body fitly joined together and compacted by that which every joint supplieth," Every member of this church's body has made a substantial contribution and does make a contribution.

The Bride of Christ. Let me give you this passage before I go on. "Husbands, love your wives, even as Christ also loved the church, and gave himself for it; That he might sanctify and cleanse it with the washing of water by the word, That he might present it to himself a glorious church, not having spot, or wrinkle, or any such thing; but that it should be holy and without blemish."

I think of that benediction in Jude 1:24 "Now unto him that is able to keep you from falling, and to present you faultless before the presence of his glory with exceeding joy." Oh, lis-ten to me folks, the best is yet to come!

From St. Louis through North Little Rock, I witnessed and officiated at lot of beautiful church weddings. I think if you'd ask any Pastor what about being a Pastor do not really enjoy? A lot of Pastors would tell you I don't enjoy church weddings. I can tell you why. There's a lot of tenseness. I used stand up there and look out and say marriage is a happy occasion and I'd look over here and here's a mother about to cry and here's a daddy thinking that that man's not good enough for his daughter. So I quit saying marriage is a happy occasion; I just said it's some occasion. You go through rehearsal on Friday night for a Saturday afternoon wedding. Everybody's got an idea and you want everything to go perfect. You go home from the rehearsal wondering how it's going to turn out. Saturday afternoon comes, the preacher leads the bridegroom out and he's followed by the best man and other attendants. You're still standing there wondering how it's going to go. The brides' attendants take their place. But I tell you, there's that one glorious, wonder-ful moment when the organist or pianist starts playing the wedding march. The congregation stands and all eyes are focused backed there on that beautiful, blushing bride attired in white coming down the aisle to meet her bridegroom. And they are going to leave together united.

I stood there lots of times with a lump in my throat and said Forgive me Lord. This one moment is worth it all. The stars dance with anticipation. The trembling clouds know it's time. Musicians are tuning their instruments and the singers are humming: Here comes the Bride!

Somehow, I think its close. I think it's near at hand and you and I friends are going to be a part of that glorious Bride, washed in the blood of Christ presented as the Church in all her glory.

The Blessed Return

Jesus said "I will come again." If that were not anywhere else in the Bible, that's enough, because if Jesus said it, it's true! But it's a New Testament doctrine and an Old Testa-ment doctrine. I don't how it's going to be. I don't know when it's going to be. But I wouldn't argue. I'm just saying it's going to be!

Jesus said I go to prepare a place for you. I believe that. What kind of place must it be? I asked Mrs. Scott the other day. I said If there is another county in Arkansas where once you got inside the boundaries of that county and nobody in that county ever got sick, how many folks you think would like to live in that county? I would. If there was a place where nobody ever gets hurt or nobody gets discouraged or nobody gets despondent. How many would like to live in a place like that? I'm telling you friends, that's the kind of place we're going to! Beautiful place, wonderful place, a place with no sorrow. And Jesus said I'll return and I'll take you with Me.

In the Thessalonian church, some of the people had died. For some reason, some of the folks had been led to believe that they'd all be living when Jesus comes. So, they sent for Paul for clarification. And He tenderly, lovingly said I don't want you to be in the dark: "I'd have you not to be ignorant concerning those who are asleep or those who've died. That you'd sorrow not even as others which have no hope. For, if we believed that Jesus died and rose again, even so them which sleep in Jesus will God bring with Him. For this I say unto you by the Word of the Lord that we which are alive and remain shall not prevent or have an advantage over them. For the Lord Himself shall descend from Heaven with a shout; with a voice of the arch angel; the dead in Christ shall rise first. Then, we which are alive and remain unto His coming, shall be caught up together with them in the clouds to meet the Lord in the air." And He said "Wherefore comfort one another with these words."

I want to say I could stand here a dozen times and try to preach this message. But I'll go home feeling like I come way short. But I declare unto you, if you'll keep your faith in that blessed Book, know your sins are under the Blood, be a part of His church-the Bride, and look for the Blessed Com-ing, you'll make it.

Oh, I want to thank you, thank you so much. It was a privi-lege for many months for Mrs. Scott and me to come up here every Sunday morning. We enjoyed it much. I've been here for revivals. I've enjoyed fellowship with you all for a long time. And we're coming to the end of the trail. I want to see you on the other side.

Sister Geneva asks the other day about an invitation hymn. I thought for a little while. I believe it's on the program "Amazing Grace." I want to sing all four verses and espe-cially as we reflect "through many dangers toils and snares; we have already come. Its grace that brought us safe thus far" and friends, God's grace that will lead us home.

"I Saw Them When They Did It"

From somewhere out of the past, I remember reading book which bore the title, "I Seen Him When He Done It." It was 11 fun-poking look at the crude conduct and lack of common etiquette of some Christians.

The writer satirically scores some points! It is true that many Christians are much lacking in social refinement. Even preachers can be most un-mannerly and inexcusably crude at times.

The purpose of these paragraphs is not to dwell on the crudeness of Christians nor the clumsiness of the clergy. Heaven knows we all could stand some Holy fire Refinement! But what about the consecration and commitment of Christians we've known? Sure, we've had many who were short on education; but they made it up in *dedication!* We've had many preachers who never were permitted to go to college, but they *had* been to Calvary! There are multitudes, in whose debt we stand.

The Preacher's Wife- No group is more deserving of our heart-felt gratitude and praise than this elite collection of special women. We've seen them when they did it! She married a preacher at a young age. Family and friends thought she'd "driven her ducks to a poor market."

She packed, she moved, she cooked, she cried, she entertained, she got discouraged. She was hurt, she was sometimes lonesome and often homesick. Faithfully, she "stayed by the stuff."

Most preachers 'wives are a sacrificial and uncomplaining lot. While they live most of their lives in a parsonage, Lord knows they'd much rather be living in a house they could think of as being their own. God bless those preachers' wives who've ever enjoyed this privilege! I've wondered at times if, in Heaven, the Lord might just let these dedicated women select their own quarters. If Heroes, I think they'd all like a little more closet space, one more bedroom, a bigger kitchen with more cabinets; and I think they'd wish for plumbing that never gets stopped up, or whistles, or snorts, or vibrates enough to register on the Richter.

Those *Moving* experiences . . . I saw her when she did it! Many preachers never move in a *Mayflower.* Some have never enjoyed the luxury of anything more accommodating and elaborate than a U-Rent It, U-Load It, and U-Drive It! And others, bless their hearts, have seen their meager belongings shuffled on a cattle truck, an implement trailer, or a "Bob" with holes in the bed!

Many a preacher's wife has wanted to run and hide when she got to the new destination and saw her living room couch with a new tear, the bedroom suite with a new set of scratches, and some cherished keep-sakes broken.

After a good cry and a little time alone, she came out with composure enough to meet and greet the new church chairman, the Auxiliary ladies, and some neighborhood kids. She rolled her sleeves, held back the tears, put on a smile, and went to work unpacking and re-arranging. The nervous break-down to which she felt entitled would just have to wait. For, in her mind, she knows while she's unloading and unpacking, that. It's only for a while. Her preacher husband's work will be finished. He'll have stayed his time, and will have served his purpose. And once again they '11 pick up the phone to call the U-Name It.

May Heaven help those women! My daddy used to preach a Mother's Day sermon from that Old Testament text spoken by King David, "but as his part is that goeth down to the battle. So shall his part be that tarrieth by the stuff; they shall part alike." U Samuel30:24b) Who can find a virtuous, caring, sharing, patient, loving preacher's wife? Her price is *far* above rubies. She's worth much more than she usually gets!

*   *   *   *   *   *

The Preacher..... I saw him when *he* did it. Names, dates. And places could be given. But I have chosen not to do that. For, while this writer is thinking of those whom he has known personally, *most* of you who read these lines could compile your own list. You also have seen them when they did it.

He was married, had one child, or maybe two. He had just struggled through the greatest battle of his life. For months, even years, he had spent restless nights and wearisome days. "ME a preacher?" Surely the Lord must be playing a joke!

But the Lord wasn't kidding. It was for real. No joke. The conviction became stronger, the struggle more agonizing. And the call more clear. The Lord's will had prevailed. And now a young man stood in his church in a revival service or a Sunday night meeting to "announce" his call to preach.

The pastor commended him: his wife cried. Church members shook his hand and some of the older ones hugged him. The long struggle against God's call was over. He had surrendered! For the moment, at least, he had perfect peace. The tears, the prayers, and the encouragement of the church sure meant a lot. But new battles were just ahead. Doubt raised its ugly head. Fears disturbed his peace. But like Jephthah of the Judges. He had "opened his mouth to the Lord" and he could not ... he would not go back!

I saw him when he did it! He quit his job. His employer thought he was crazy. He sold his house. His possessions left the premises and went in all directions . . . sold at auction.

With the prayers and good wishes of his family and friends. He waved good-bye and headed toward distant city to enroll in Bible College. The lump in his throat lasted 'til he crossed the state line. The tears had stopped after the first county. Some doubted he'd ever get there in that old car that knocked like a thresher, or in that old worn out V-8 that smoked like a locomotive. I've wondered at times, if God hasn't assigned some of his angels to watch over a loose connecting rod or a slapping pistons see that it held together a few more miles. Life at Bible College for many a preacher has been one of testing's, trials, troubles, torments and tears. But, thank God. It usually ends with triumph! A little church 'way off somewhere had called; didn't pay much. Never had a "full· time "pastor before. But they wanted to give it a try, and if the preacher, newly graduated from Bible College was willing...:

He was!

I saw him when he did it! Over and over again I've watched him. He was a married man with a family. He was a High School graduate with a scholarship to a State College, whose High School Counselor thought he was looney for opting to go to a ... BIBLE COLLEGE??

He was a young man, an older man, even a University graduate who changed his major with a Diploma hanging on the wall. The course of his whole life was changed because God had called and he must go. And he DID go. I saw him.

He worked, he wept, and he waited. He laughed with the Young. He groaned with the old. He shared the joy with a family at the birth of a baby. He felt the hurt of a family who lost a loved one by death. He performed marriages, he preached funerals, and the local School Superintendent even asked him to preach a Baccalaureate sermon. He bought a new blue suit and did! He served the people and earned the respect of the community. He was known by many as Preacher, Pastor, and Friend.

He wept with the broken; he knelt with the fallen. He went after the straying and brought some back to the fold. He fed the sheep, and he sheared them. He battled discouragement and emotional depression. He hid his personal hurts, and he never gave in to bitterness. He hid in his heart secrets that he'll take with him to the grave; for no one need know the thoughts, the failures, the blunders, the burdens, and the problems that a member had poured out to him in confidence. He would not break or betray that trust.

I saw him- when he did it. He came to advancing age. Old in body, he remained young in heart. Tired in the flesh, he was renewed in the spirit. Occasional thoughts and dreams of retirement crossed his mind, but hadn't he heard it so often from well-meaners that preachers should never retire? The factory worker, the Government employee, the Military man. And even the farmer might retire; but the Preacher? Didn't he get a lifelong call?

I saw him when he did it! Health failed, he suffered a stroke, or cancer, or a heart attack. And he HAD to quit. Then one day, he came to the end of the trail. God in mercy took him home. And as he crossed the line from time to

Eternity, from the mortal to the realm of immortality, he took a brief look and caught a glimpse of younger men, preacher boys, and ministerial "sons in the faith." Knowing that pulpits still would trumpet the Truth, and God-chosen shepherds still would care for the flock, he wiped a tear, closed his eyes, and was gone.

* * * * * *

The Missionary Family - I saw THEM when THEY did it! The "call" came at an early age. In fact, it was hard to remember a time when the thought of being a missionary was not ever-present.

There were the College years, the courtship and marriage.

And finally, the approval and assignment by the Board. Deputation seemed painfully slow. Feeling so anxious to go. Why were the people so slow to respond and give the needed finances and send? I saw them when they did it. They stayed on the "service" circuit. They overcame weariness of the flesh and discouragement of the spirit. And at last the day of departure came.

Good-byes are never easy; but to know that this one is for years, not months, well, the tears wouldn't hold back and that lump in the throat seemed bigger than a pumpkin. Somehow, to me, missionaries and their families have always symbolized the very essence of commitment and dedication.

One of the few advantages of growing older is the fact that you've lived long enough to have actually seen what many have done with their lives. If you are in the three score bracket. You have lived during the time of our denomination's developing Foreign Missions program; at least, for the greater part.

We've seen them when they did it. They left their home and home-land. They rejected the comfort and security of our country to go to spend their lives in a land of strangeness. Strange people, strange customs, and strangers to the Gospel of God's grace.

We've seen them when they buried their baby. Well. We didn't actually see them, 'cause we couldn't be there. But they did it, and GOD saw them. And the heart of a compassionate Saviour was touched. He saw them when they met with accident, and there seemed to be nobody to help. He saw them in their sicknesses, their sorrows, their loneliness, and He was there.

Yes, we've seen them when they did it! And their dedication and devotion have strengthened and re-enforced our own.

Well, in more than forty years of a preaching, pastoral ministry, and a man would have to be blind not to have seen them when they did it.

A widow gave faithfully from her meager fare. So did a teenager; and a working man and woman. I've seen the musicians, the choir directors, and the trustees, the teachers, the dedicated Deacons and church officers. I've seen them serve! And I've been blessed. I've seen the Woman's Auxiliary Worker, the laymen in the Master's Men. I've seen the promoter, the fund-raiser, the College President, the board member, the professor. I've seen the tireless traveling evangelist. All these, and MANY, MANY more! I've seen them when they did it. I wish I knew how to say THANKS!

* * * * * *

Ole Dick and Red - If ever there was a contrast in personality and disposition, it was demonstrated in my dad's work horses. Now mind you, they both were good men. I mean. Horses. They weren't great big old Clydesdales. They were kin· da little, as work horses go. But when they set their minds to it, they could move some load!

Now ole Dick, he was a sort of a cross between a sorrel land a dapple gray. He was gentle, predictable, intelligent; a steady day-in-and-day-out performer. He would pull! What an inspiration it was to see him pull! He'd dig in, bow his neck, and stretch every nerve, every muscle, and every fiber of his body. When he got down to that kind of business, something just had to move! If local churches took in horses as members, I'd sure like to vote ole Dick in. If there were a "Horse Hall of Fame" ole Dick would merit at least honorable mention.

Ole Red? That's a different story. Now he was a good horse if you handled him just right. He was good, once you got him going. But if there was an unusually heavy load to pull, ole Red would lurch and lunge and often break a tug or tear up a single tree. But once he got the jerks and spasms out of his system, he'd settle down and pull as hard as any horse you ever saw. Really, now that I've thought about it again, maybe ole Red ought to be considered for membership, and maybe get his name in that Fame Hall, too. He was just different; not necessarily bad!

These two old work horses remind me of people I've known: or maybe even a "people" I've been! Preachers, Deacons, musicians, teachers, church workers - most of them, when you get right down to it are pretty good folks. And you hitch them up where they can work, where there's load to lift, and most of 'em will groan and strain, and get down there and grind 'til something gives!

It is very likely that most of the problems in the local church, the State Meeting, or even the National Convention. Can be traced to a difference in temperament and personality.

For the most part, we believe the same Doctrine. We share common hopes and dreams. And we may even be closer in our "standards" than we think. If we ever can learn just to be patient and not peevish with another's impulsive impetuosity; or to be tolerant of a brother's temperament and even sympathetic with another's short-comings; well, there's always hope!

I wonder if ole Dick and Red may not both hav e been represented in that inner circle of Christ's closest fellowship. Ole Dick, era ...John, soft-spoken, gentle, loving, and kind, laid his head on the Master's bosom. Now ole Red, ...Peter, he was O.K., but he'd whack off a feller's ear; or step out of a boat and try to walk on water. And he was known on more than one occasion to put his mouth in gear while his brain was on vacation. Yep, he popped off more than once and had to be reminded by the Lord that he didn't know what he was saying! But now, honestly, were they not both pretty good horses? I mean . . . Men?

*   *   *   *   *   *

Sermonette....Some children in our neighboring state of Oklahoma died after eating poisoned cookies. The cookies were being used by a pest control company and should have been kept locked up and out of reach of children. The man who left the cookies un-attended in his truck seat found himself facing criminal charges. To say that he was negligent is putting it mildly. By all means, he should have been more careful!

It is sad indeed, that children are dead because of another's neglect! But what about spiritual death? Many a parent could be charged with woeful negligence in regard to their own off- spring's Spiritual welfare. Parents, it is YOUR responsibility and mine to see to it that our children are saved! The Devil, with all his forces of evil and sin, is after our children! He leaves HIS poisoned cookies laying around ON PURPOSE to entice our sons and daughters. HOW SAD it will be in the Day of Judgment to face the Judge of all the earth and hear HIM say, "You are guilty of woeful neglect."

* * * * * *

What am I doing here???-Up at Youth Camp one summer, I overheard one of our state's fine laymen as he was talking with another about how he and his wife got started back to church. For too long they had been backslidden on God. The man's testimony went something like this: It was church time one Sunday evening, and there he sat, looking at T.V. trying to find something of interest. Suddenly, the question hit him, "WHATARE YOU DOING HERE?"

It was church time, and there he sat! Somehow, his soul was awakened. His conscience was stirred. His life was changed. And from that evening when a ·voice got through his crusted conscience, he has been a dedicated worker. In his local church he directs the bus ministry, works faithfully in other areas of service, and that summer he had taken a week of vacation time to go to our State Youth Camp to serve as sponsor for a cabin full of young boys.

"WHATAM I DOING HERE?"... A good question: especially if you are not where God wants you to be, doing what God wants you to do!   ·

* * * * * *

Sad Side of Life -While waiting for an elevator in one of our area hospitals, I noticed the Chaplain and a staff nurse. With them was a woman, probably in her sixties, softly sobbing with a faraway look in her eyes. It was apparent that she had just become a widow. In the Chaplain's hand was a small plastic bag which contained the few personal items that a sick man had needed in a hospital room.

The elevator ride was marked with silence. On the lady's finger was a gold wedding band, undoubtedly placed there in happier days by the man who had just died. The Chaplain, the Nurse, and the newly-widowed lady disappeared into a family room.

Outside the hospital, the sky was still a beautiful blue. The hum of traffic revealed that business and other activities go on. Although the birds were singing, it took a while to get that lump out of my throat. I've been around death and the dying all my life, but I don't reckon I'll ever get used to it. I'm sure glad that God has told us about a place where none ever get sick, or disappointed: and where no one ever dies.

* * * * * *

Sermonizin'... While my widowed mother was living, it was always a privilege to spend a few hours, or maybe night in the old home state of Missouri. While in her home on such a visit, I picked up a century old copy of the 4th grade McGuffey's Reader. The following poem entitled, *Lazy Ned,* caught my attention.

"'Tis royal, fun,' cried lazy Ned, to coast upon my fine, new sled, and beat the other boys, · But then, I cannot bear to climb.

The tiresome hill for every time, it more and more annoys.'

So while his class-mates glided by, and gladly tugged up hill to try another merry race, too indolent to share their plays, Ned was compelled to stand and gaze, while shivering in his place. Thus he would never take the pains to seek the prize that labor gains. Until the time had passed; for, all his life, he dreaded still

The silly bugbear of up-hill and died a dunce at last. "

UP-HILL! That's the way it is. It is up hill getting an education. It is up hill getting out of bed to go to work. It is up hill being faithful and consistent in Sunday school and church. It's UP HILL, UP HILL ...rearing family, paying your debts, doing your duty. It's up hill... teaching a class, filling an office, preaching a sermon, bringing an offering. Yep, it's all up hill. But if you've got the Grace and the Grit, it will end in Glory!

* * * * * *

The Sheep-Market Multitude... You've probably heard a radio or T.V. preacher blurt out the come-on, "Something good is about to happen to you!" Well, it may be; then again, it might just be that something BAD is about to happen to you.

There's a verse of Scripture in John 5:14 that

bothersome.

Jesus said to a man who had just received the greatest blessing of his life, "Sin no more, lest a WORSE thing come unto thee." The fellow had just spent thirty-eight years as a helpless, impotent, and paralytic. Could anything worse happen? Surely it could or Jesus would not have said so.

The man had been blessed. He was healed. Where he used to lie helplessly on a pallet, he now walked, carrying his bed. ALL because of what Jesus had done for him! Friend, have you   forgotten what Christ has done for you? Your home was heading for the rocks and He helped get it straightened out.

You needed job and He heard your prayers. You prayed from a hospital room. He heard and helped. You made some promises, like going to church . . . praying ... tithing.

WE may forget our promises, but God doesn't forget that we made them. Could a worse thing be 'bout to happen? Might be!

******

Lost Something??- Some months ago I received in _the mail a book entitled, "Before you lose it all." I thought at first someone was playing a trick on this preacher who has started to get more than slightly bald. It wasn't a trick. It had to do with Government affairs. As a nation, we COULD lose some things that are most precious. As a church, we must always be on guard lest we lose the qualities that are essential to the building of a Scriptural church. In our homes we must be constantly on guard.

There are forces that threaten everything that is good and worthwhile. We must always be on guard! In our own individual lives, there must be a continual vigil. "Look to yourselves that we lose not those things which we have wrought," wrote John.

Christian, don't run the risk of losing what you've got! BEFORE YOU LOSE ITALL ...a good conscience....the right convictions ... a warm church fellowship ...the joy of salvation ... Be sure you don't lose it!

******

Dealing with Discipline.... The Arkansas Razorbacks were playing the University of Texas in a televised Basketball game. It is always interesting when Texas and Arkansas meet in any athletic competition. When game time came, the tip-off found one of our state's most outstanding players sitting on the bench. He stayed there throughout the entire game. Discipline, the coach called it.

Indications were that a star athlete had been late for practice, or had broken a curfew rule: I... something of that order. The team played without him, and won.

DISCIPLINE ...a forgotten word; in the average home, in the church, and to a great extent, in our schools. Lots of church people would not qualify for membership if we went according to the Covenant. Faithful attendance.... Financial support measured by our prosperity ...shunning appearances of evil... How many of our own rules of conduct are frivolously and frequently broken?

No one kicks us off the team; we don't even have to sit out a game. It's been so long since that early church episode of Divine Discipline that modem-day Ananias 'and Sapphire's can sit, preach, pray, teach, or sing in the average Sunday morning congregation and feel comfortable.

I'm glad the R.B.'s won that game. Discipline certainly did not lose any honor that night. You can live about any way that you want to and keep your name on the church roll. But the church roll is not what counts in the day of reckoning. Then. It will be "The Book of Life." (Rev. 20:15) If you want your name to appear in that Book, there are some Divine guidelines. You'll find them in the Book we call the "Holy Bible. "

* * * * * *

Higher Ground ... During a time when we were having so much rain, along with floods, and generally stormy weather. A little note was run on the T.V. screen which read, "Be Prepared to Move to Higher Ground... Conditions got worse. And many, many families had to do just that.

Higher Ground!

Every child of God ought to be continually heading for higher ground. There's no excuse for living in the land of mire and clay. Someday the last trumpet will sound. The

Lord will appear, the judgment will be set. Those who have lived looking for a better world will truly move up higher!

* * * * * *

A Spiritual Report Card - How would it look? Centuries ago, Job declared, "My record is on high. " As parents. We receive a report card periodically from the schools where our children attend. We usually look it over well. Sometimes we're pleased and sometimes we are a little disappointed.

I've often felt that it would be a good thing for many, if God would send His church members quarterly report. That's not the way God works. However, He usually lets us know somehow, if we are not doing too well. He doesn't want us to fail the course! And we need to be reminded often that the day is coming when He will call us collectively and individually to stand before Him in judgment. OUR RECORD will meet us at that appointment.

* * * * * *

The Multitude of the Maimed... "Now there is at Jerusalem by the sheep market a pool; ...in these lay a great multitude of impotent folk, of blind, withered, WAITING ..."

I invite you to go with me to visit one room in University Hospital.

First, there's the 42-year-old wife and mother from North Arkansas. She won't be going home unless a miracle takes place. The Big C. One bed down, there's another lady almost withered- a Southern Baptist preacher's wife. She won't be going home either. Two other ladies in the 4-bed ward are in similar circumstances. Waiting, hoping, praying.

The sick at the sheep market pool were just waiting for an Angel to come down to "trouble" the water. For the children of God, there is no hopeless predicament. Sooner or later an Angel will come down, and if there is no cure for the physical malady, there will be a blessed release from all earthly fetters. Was it not Angels from Heaven that came down and lifted Lazarus the poor beggar out of a diseased body and transported him to Abraham's bosom? Either through a miracle or a move, God's children will be delivered!

* * * * * *

A Remembered Quote: "It's bad to be in bondage: but it's much worse to get adjusted to it." That's what is wrong with lots of church people, they've backslidden on God and have gotten used to it.

Hey, don't you ever, like the prodigal boy, get to remember the good meals, the perfect peace, and the joy that's unspeakable and full of glory? Don't you ever get to wanting to hear the songs of Zion? Don't you ever long for a good sermon?

For God's children, there's something much better than hog feed, loneliness, being friendless, and living in a far country.

Before YOU get any more used to being in the

bondage of backsliddenness, wake up! Shake up!

Everything's still all right ...in my FATHER'S HOUSE!

* * * * * *

Sermonette: In one of our daily newspapers I noticed one morning an ad which read something like this: FOR SALE. .. Antique car, partly restored. Reason for selling, LOST IN- TEREST. Hmmmmm...Lost interest. Children soon lose interest in toys and trinkets. Fads and fashions come and go, because so many lose interest. Lots of WORTHWHILE projects end in defeat because of LOST INTEREST.

With a little imagination, can you not visualize an ad in the classified like this: FOR SALE ... One good Sunday school   class; reason for selling, (you guessed it) LOSTINTEREST. For sale...prayer life...a Bible reading habit ...an ordination certificate ...a voice for singing... LOST INTEREST. For sale ...set of tithing envelopes ...a good church member- ship ...reason for selling. .. LOST INTEREST.

Jesus said, "The love of many shall wax cold...Not only did He say it and predict it, He witnessed it! Take time to read John, chapter six. The chapter begins with a great multitude. It ends with the Son of God asking His Own chosen twelve. "Will ye also go away?" Between the beginning and the ending of the chapter. The multitudes had turned away. They LOST INTEREST. When the free bread ran out and when ·the miracles ceased, the ranks were thinned!

* * * * * *

"Hold your station!"- While parked near Ole Main the other day, I heard these words coming over a loud speaker. The high school band was on the practice field, and the director was giving instructions. I heard him say, "Some of you are not holding your station long enough...

Could it be that some of us in the church, or in the family circle are not holding our station long enough? One of history's greatest battles was won with just 300 men who stood where their commander placed them. STAY AT YOUR POST! Meet your responsibilities! As in a high school marching band. Everything worthwhile requires team-work. If you or I leave our station too soon, some needed notes will be missing, and someone else may get out of step.

** **** **

The Preacher's Ponderings . . . Who bears the brunt in our Denomination's Missionary program? Of course, the missionaries themselves bear the greatest share of the burdens, sacrifice, and deprivation. Beyond the missionary, it must be that the missionary's family, especially the parents, bear the real weight of the load. Over the years, it has been the privilege of my wife and me to have been associated very closely with some of our missionary' families. They have been, and still remain, an uncomplaining group. But who can fully know the hurt and the weight of loneliness that rests upon a mother, or upon a father whose son or daughter must be gone for years at a time?

As a church and denomination, we stand in debt to these brave and courageous souls who give of their own flesh and blood. Their example in giving unselfishly should inspire many of us to be more conscientious and loyal in our own devotion to Christ and His Church.

* * * * * *

Paradise Landing. .. It's up on Lake Conway. That would make a good sermon title. We don't hear a lot of real Scriptural preaching nowadays about Heaven. It's sort of strange. If there were a country on earth whereon one ever got sick, or hurt, or disappointed, I think most people would want to live in that country!

If there were a country on earth where no one ever died, or moved away, or had a sorrow, and everyone was always happy. Wouldn't multitudes be interested in getting into that country?

Makes you wonder why more people don't make preparation to go to Heaven when they die. In Heaven there is no pain, no sorrow, no death, no disappointment; no separation. Those who land in that country will truly have found a PARADISE LANDING!

* * * * * *

Sermonette . . . When a cook bakes a cake, she usually

goes by the recipe in the cook book. When a builder erects a building, he goes by the blue-prints. When a mechanic overhauls a motor, he goes by the manual.

So why is it then that we should rebel at going by God's Rule Book when it comes to such things as establishing a home, living a life, building a church? There's an expression going 'roundin our day which is indicative of today's rebellious society: "Doing your own thing!" We cannot live our lives our own way and please God! Our ways are wrong! If your life is going to measure up, it's got to be lived by the rules. If your home is going to stand, it's got to be built according to God's directions, and not man's.

Joshua spoke an eternal truth when he said, "This book of the law shall not depart out of thy mouth: but thou shalt meditate therein day and night, that thou mayest observe to do according to all that is written therein: for THEN shalt thou make thy way prosperous, and then thou shalt have good success. "(Joshua 1:8)

Why is it that we expect a football team to go by the rules, but in the game of life most folks want to make their own rules? You can say what you want to, but there are still some "do's" and some "don'ts" in God's book of law! Jesus said, "Not everyone that saith unto Me, Lord, Lord, but he that DOETH ..."And, "Blessed are they that DO His commandments that they may have right to the tree of life, and may enter in through the gates into the city."

*   *   *   *   *   *

He *"bottled"* to the BOTTOM. .. He used to be sober; and he USED to be active and regular in attendance at a Free Will Baptist church. He USED to have a good business; and he USED to be in good health. But that's all in the days of used-to-be.

Now, he's in a place where they try to retrieve and rehabilitate the folks they call alcoholics. Now, he's a confessed backslider who would like to get back right with God. Now, he's under a doctor's care, trying desperately to regain some degree of normal health. And he's just past the point in life that we call middle age.

HOW did it all happen? According to this man's own testimony, his life of drunkenness started with BEER. His backslidden condition started by missing just a Sunday or two at a time 'til he completely lost interest in church.

No one can really know for sure just what his health might now be, but it is evident that alcohol has contributes to present physical condition. This man is not an imaginary figment of this preacher's imagination. He is real, and there are multitudes like him. That's why I am afraid of beer! And that's why I get an uneasy feeling about church members who start missing a little here and there for no real reason. I'm aware that not everyone who takes the first beer will wind up being a drunkard. I know that some can put on the brakes. But how many there are who cannot! And, my boy, or yours may be the one who cannot stop once he has started.

And I don't think God will send a soul to hell for

missing a Sunday morning Sunday Schooler worship service. But there is REAL DANGER! That's the way backsliding starts! More people lose contact with God from a slow leak than from a big   blow-out! More houses are destroyed by tiny termites than from forked lightning! May Heaven help us to see the danger in "Little Things?"

• • • • • •

It gets better on ahead ...Christians are not weaklings Struggling against overwhelming odds, finally to be defeated in a lost cause. Daniel looked through the prophetic telescope and saw the end. After the conflict has ceased, the smoke of battle has cleared, and the final chapter has been completed, that elderly statesman of prophets gave us a glimpse of this picture: "But the saints of the Most High shall take the Kingdom and possess the Kingdom forever, even for ever and ever." Hang in there, Christian! The END is better than the beginning!

• • • • • •

Remembered Quote: "It's a poor frog that won't praise his own pond." With that hill-country, home-spun philosophy, I AGREE! If you've got a good church, say something about it to OTHERS. If you've got a good wife, give her a compliment or an occasional corsage! If you work for a good employer, say some nice things about the company you work for! The Bible says, "It is a good thing to give praise!"

• • • • • •

Mockingbirds, Milk Cows Mortals - This preacher watched a Mockingbird our state bird) give chase to a black cat the other day. It seems that this cat had gotten too close to the tree in which the Mockingbird had built its nest. You should have seen that Mockingbird go after that cat! I don't know if the young birds have hatched yet, but that Mockingbird was instinctively protecting her helpless and defenseless offspring.

When I was growing up on a country hillside farm in Missouri, my dad had one ole milk-cow, Ole Darling that had a very bad disposition. Why she had been named DARLING, I never could quite figure out. Her disposition was a lot worse when she had a young calf. You dare not get too close to that little calf, or here would come that mother right at you! I've seen her put more than one kid right over the fence.

It's a part of nature that a mother will protect her young.

That is, birds will; cows will; other animals will. But what about us MORTALS? How concerned do we become about protecting OUR offspring? Oh, we protect them in a physical sense, but what about the things that have to do with moral and Spiritual issues?

In the spring of '75 a survey was taken of the junior class in one of our area High Schools pertaining to the drinking problem. The junior class members gave the following answers to these questions. Incidentally, the questionnaire was filled out in secret, so there is no reason to doubt that the students answered honestly.

Question 1. How would you describe your drinking habits? Light, 159; Medium, 65; Heavy, 8; None, 91. Question 2. Who purchases your liquor for you? Parents, 26; older friends, 168: Strangers, 5; self, 39. Question 3. Do your parents know? Yes, 102; No, 133. Question 4. Do they approve? Disapprove, 33; DON'T CARE, 156. Question5. What do you usually drink?

Beer, 137; Wine, 38; Hard Liquor, 52. Question 6. Do you know any teen-age alcoholics? Yes, 114; No, 128. There were other questions asked. It was revealed in the survey that 97 reportedly began to drink while in the 13-15 year age bracket. There were 98 who said they knew of liquor being brought on campus this past schoolyear. There were 93 who said they had used Marijuana.

If that Mockingbird could preach sermon, I wonder what it would preach about to us poor, mixed-up mortals. I don't know: but I do know what one of the Old Testament Prophets had to say. Joel said, "And they have cast lots for my people: and have given a boy for a harlot, and sold a girl for wine, that they might drink. ··

* * * * * *

Important Decisions- Having once heard the Word of God, every person who reaches the age of accountability then becomes responsible for his own soul. What a terrible thing it would be if a person lost his soul and was consigned to eternal hell because of a jury's decision. But how much more terrible will be the pangs of hell for the soul that is lost, knowing that he is lost BECAUSE OF HIS OWN CHOICE!

The evening train was coming through a town in N.E. Arkansas. Two men and a teenage girl sat in a tavern drinking. they left the tavern, someone remarked that the "six o'clock special" was coming through. In the distance, the rumble of the fast freight train could be heard. The driver of the pick-up truck remarked, "I believe we can beat it." And with their six pack of beer, the two men and the teenager drove off thinking they could beat the fast train.

Their LAST decision in life was to try to beat the train. It was a fatal mistake. They were hit broad-side. Their mangled bodies were picked up by the ambulance crew.

It Isa terrible thing to make a wrong decision! Especially, if it turns out to be your last! TODAY will be someone's final day on earth: the LAST CHANCE to decide for Christ! The fast-freight, the locomotive of God's judgments coming down the track! There's only one way to escape, and that is to be in Jesus! When God's judgment comes, be SURE you're in Christ!

* * * * * *

Just thinking . .. It would be great if all God's children could be insulated against the bitter experiences of life: but such is not the case. Becoming Christian does not guarantee that we won't face hard and trying experiences. In fact, a verse in the Bible declares: "Many are the afflictions of the righteous." But the verse goes ahead to say, "But the Lord delivereeth him from them all." (Ps. 34:19)

* * * * * *

Blighted Beauty ... October, 1980: It's good to see it here! But the beauty of the hills and valleys is BLIGHTED this year as a result of the searing summer heat and the pro-longed drought. The rain that came last week-end has already revived the grass and weeds. However, the country-side will bear scars from the drought for a long time. Some very old. Rugged, and beautiful trees are dead. Some of them will stand for years to come as reminders of this past summer's heat and devastating dryness. SPIRITUAL DROUGHT is much worse than physical drought. All over our country there are signs of deadness and moral blight. Revival showers could help, but for many who are already beyond recall, the showers will come too late!

* * * * * *

Just Rambling. .. "If you want to grow a squash you can do it in three months. If you want to grow an oak. It takes much longer." The churches in the business of growing trees. Not mush-rooms, or squash. To grow something worthwhile requires WAITING, WEEPING, and WATERING.

* * * * * *

Human Reasoning or Holy Writ? I was talking with a lady, not a member of this church, last Monday morning. She said, "I went fishing Sunday. It's the only day I have. And I believe I can be just as good a Christian out fishing on Sunday as anywhere else."

If you take that case to the court of HUMAN REASONING, maybe so. If you take it to the court of HOLY WRIT (the Bible) it won't stand a chance! In sports, in school, in business. And in other matters we don't mind conforming and going by the rules laid down in the rule book. But when it comes to religion, we want to HAVE IT OUR WAY, prescribe our own medicine, and set up our own standards.

The Bible says, "Christ also loved THE CHURCH and gave Himself for it." And the RULE BOOK also says, "Not forsaking the ASSEMBLING of ourselves together, as the manner of some is; and so much the more as ye see the day approaching." The church in our day suffers and often struggles just to survive. So many have" reasoned "away all personal responsibility! To those who did so in Christ's days upon earth, the Lord never said to any, "You're excused... In fact, "EXCUSED" is a word He never spoke.

* * * * * *

Co-Incidence??? .. . You can nearly always bank on the weather's being upset during the week before Easter. It's true. Nature seems to show her other side, as if to punctuate the crucifixion scene.

Of course, some folks who worship nature are like some who think only of one part of God's nature. God IS love: He IS good! But He also is SEVERE! Nature is devastating when her fury is turned loose. That babbling brook can become sweeping, overwhelming flood. That gentle breeze can be turned into a furious, frightening hurricane or tornado. Somewhere, some day in Divine Judgment, God's love will   give place to justice and wrath!

* * * * * *

*The Mayor's Mistake...*All people make "em: but this one was a dandy! A family in our church had just brought home from the hospital their first baby. They received a card from the Mayor's office which undoubtedly was meant to be a congratulatory card. Instead, it was a sympathy card expressing "sorrow at your recent bereavement. "Makes you wonder if some family who had recently lost a loved one might have received a card expressing "CONGRATULATIONS! We share with you the joy of this blessed event! "

* * * * * *

Thanksgiving Day: The Psalmist wrote, "The lines are fallen unto me in pleasant places; yea, I have a goodly heritage." It's hard to think of THANKSGIVING without thinking of COUNTRY, HOME AND THE CHURCH.

Thanksgiving Day is traditionally a family day. Many of us can bring up so many fond memories of other days when we were carefree children, growing up in a home where love abounded!

If you had a happy childhood, you should consider yourself wonderfully blest! And, as a parent, we should pass it on. OUR children deserve a happy childhood. The same thing is true. Of course, pertaining to the church and to the nation. As we have received, so should we give? Let us pray most earnestly that the rising generation will know the blessings of a good home. Church, and country that we have had the privilege of knowing.

* * * * * *

Sunday School Attendance ... How important is it'? It's MIGHTY Important! If no one attended, there would be no Sunday Schools! I heard some time ago of a very fine Chris- tian man who would say to his family on Sunday mornings. "All that's planning on going to Sunday school. Start getting ready; and all that's NOT planning to go, you start getting ready, too!"

I like that! In my opinion (unless there is sickness) there ought NEVER to be any dilly-dallying around on Sundays over the matter of going to church and Sunday school. It IS the Lord's Day, isn't it? A lot of church people ought to settle the matter once and for all time to come: and it should remain an established pattern for life!

* * * * * *

Just Rambling... The favorite month of this preacher

is October. I do not know what seasons there will be in Heaven. But I hope they have a lot of October! Someone asks ever:-· once in a while, what are we will be in Heaven. I don't know. But I think if they'll let a feller be about thirty-five and make it October all the time. That would be pretty Heavenly.

* * * * * *

More Rambling. .. Bumper stickers furnish some interesting reading. They also afford a commentary on the state of humanity. Personally, one that I least appreciate, is the one that says, "I'd rather be ...." It may be flying, fishing. Hunting, golfing, or any number of other things. Makes you wonder sometimes, doesn't anybody like and really enjoy what he is doing?

* * * * * *

There's fire and there's Wild fire! - Some radio preachers can really get far gone. I heard one recently who takes the cake! This feller claims he has had 15 ordinary tooth fillings miraculously turned to GOLD fillings in his mouth. Says he's got a hundred people in his congregation who have had similar results. Man, that's wild! And, yep, I'm from Missouri; and you know what that means.

* * * * * *

Sense   Nonsense. .. I read in the paper a few days ago that a school district in Virginia had started using the old McGuffey Reader as a REMEDIAL reading tool. It worked so   well that they were at least considering using it as a text for teaching in reading classes.

Well, that won't get very far: it makes too much sense! Then. Too the McGuffey Reader has more Scripture in it, and more practical lessons for life than lots of Sunday School Quarterlies and Sunday sermon shave in some churches and pulpits.   It might be noted, though, that our country got along pretty well when our youngsters learned to read from a book that had some SUBSTANCE to it.

* * * * * *

The Difference between Faith   Sight . . . Right now, in mid-January, sight looks out at a garden spot and sees ice, snow, barrenness. But FAITH looks at the same spot and sees a coming day. Faith can look beyond the cold barrenness of winter and see the coming of spring, the budding of flowers. The growing of a beautiful and fruitful garden.

Likewise, Faith can look right on through the dark coldness of a grave and see a resurrection, life, immortality!

Maybe that's why the Bible says, "We walk by FAITH, not sight. " Ice, cold, and snow may stymie our sight: but they can· not make a failure of our faith!

* * * * * *

Missing Men From Meroz . .. Most folks wouldn't KILL

the church; but a lot would just let her die! Most of her members would never vote to close her doors, but more than we realize would let her just fade away.

There's a verse in Judges 5:23which reads: "Curse ye Meroz, said the angel of the Lord; curse ye bitterly the inhabitants thereof; because they came not to the help of the Lord, to the help of the Lord against the mighty. " A tyrant, was running rough-shod through the land. And the citizens of Meroz, just sat there! They never lifted a finger to protest the evils that were rampaging. The CHURCH of Jesus Christ is always beset by many foes. The war is raging! Don't just sit there, do something! Get up early next Sunday; get the family ready and go together to the house of the Lord. The Church needs YOU and YOU need the church!

* * * * * *

Leap Year Day. .. February29, 1984. .. Since it won't come again for another four years, we might as well give a little thought to the subject of LEAPING. In the midst of troublesome, trying times, Isaiah foresaw a better day ahead. He wrote, "Then shall the eyes of the blind be opened, and the ears of the deaf shall be unstopped. Then shall the LAME man LEAP as a hart, and the tongue of the dumb shall sing. For in the wilderness shall waters break out, and streams in the desert. And the ransomed of the Lord shall return, and come to Zion with songs and everlasting joy upon their heads: they shall obtain joy and gladness, and sorrow and sighing shall flee away." There's one thing for sure, for BEAUTY and BLESs- ING you cannot beat the Holy Bible!

One more verse: "For by Thee I have run through a troop: by my God have I LEAPED over a wall." (II Sam. 22:29; Ps. 18:29) It just might be that someone who reads these lines may be about to give in to the pressures and problems of life. Take heart! You CAN run through a TROOP, and you CAN leap over a wall, no matter how high!

* * * * * *

Christ Children. .. Jesus said, "Take heed that ye despise not (think lightly of, neglect, or cause to be lost) one of these LITTLE ONES; for Isai unto you, that in Heaven, their angels do always behold the face of My Father Which is in Heaven." (Matt. 18:10) If there is any group of persons in this world that needs a special awakening, it is the PARENTS in our day. CHILDREN are a gift of God. God loves them, Heaven is interested in them, and angels are assigned to them. But God, Heaven, and angels cannot do it all! Parents have their responsibilities, too! And, daddy, mom, you and I are going Tobe held responsible! "If the lambs are lost, what a terrible cost some sheep will have to pay!"

• • • • •

Some of the Preacher's Predictions . . . That the Susan B. Anthony dollar would never become popular. Seen one lately? And, that the much publicized *Reader's Digest Condensed* version of the Bible would fizzle. Somehow, some of us just could not believe that a Bible shortened forty percent by a Publisher's Pen-knife would ever make it.

AND ONE MORE. ..This preacher predicted some years ago that the time-honored, Bible Name of FATHER when referring to God would be replaced by some present-day modernists and liberals. Sure enough, the prediction has come to pass. The literature committee of a MAJOR denomination met in Nashville, Tennessee in February, 1982, and came up with the recommendation that all references to God and Christ in the male gender be changed.

Somehow, I just don't believe that one will ever catch on. Either! It's just too much to expects ole country preachers to open our prayers with "Our Mother, (or Parent) which art in Heaven." It might be noted in passing, that the earthly parents of Jesus took the Baby (Whom they thought to be a Boy) up to the temple to do after the custom of the law. Yep, they believed they had a baby Boy! How long do you reckon the Almighty will put up with such religious nonsense as is be- in displayed in our day?

*   *   *   *   *   *

From This Preacher's Heart. .. There's a verse in Proverbs 23:22 which says in part, "Despise not thy mother when she is old." Of course, that should be interpreted literally. None of us should neglect, forsake, or fail to properly care for our mothers. She gave us ·life and she cared for us when we needed attention the most. Personally, I also feel a sense of obligation and loyalty to the DENOMINATION which gave me Spiritual birth and life.

She's showing signs of old age; and sometimes she seems a little clumsy and tottery.   But however many times she stumbles, I cannot forget that she held this boy in her arms as a young Christian and later as an infant preacher. She gave nourishment, opportunity, and much tender care. While some are swayed, swept, and swallowed by the passing parade of attractive movements, I '11 remember the Spiritual cradle in which I was rocked. That tired old Denominational mother will have my love and loyalty. She has not forsaken me. I'm not going to despise her when she is old!

* * * * * *

Silliness of some scientists ... On an evening news cast a group of scientists had met and were shown with their collection of human skulls and bones. After lining them up in perfect order, they joyfully proclaimed that they had at last presented undeniable evidence that man came into being by the process of evolution. They called it, IRREFUTABLE PROOF!

To me, a FUNDAMENTALIST, BIBLE-BELIEVING, GOD-FEARING, Ozark hillbilly, country-boy preacher, the whole ordeal looked perfectly silly! The scientists spend their time contemplating where man came from. The saints spend our time anticipating where we are going! For Christians, the answer to both questions (where we came from as well as where we are going) is found in that blessed old Book!

* * * * * *

That Subtle Serpent... The Devil's a smart old coot! He makes every sin look so pretty and harmless. One of his most recent concoctions is the two percent beer that is on the market. How could beer with half the normal alcohol content   be harmful? I'll tell you why it's harmful. It's just a subtle trick to get young people and others on the stuff. Make it look harmless and nobody's afraid of it, no one's going to oppose it, and chances are a feller will be criticized for attempting to ex· pose it for what it is.

The danger is this: Most people who wind up drinking the hard stuff started out on the so-called harmless stuff. That's true of both alcohol and dope. Most begin on beer, not liquor. They start on Marijuana, not cocaine. The Devil's strategy is to get 'me started. The preacher's problems how to get 'em stopped.

By personal conviction and by church covenant, I'm against alcoholic beverage in any form. While T.V. pretends to show the "finest product" of the brewer's art, preachers, doctors, funeral home directors, law enforcement officers, emergency room attendants, and divorce courts see the FINISHED PRO- DUCT of the brewer's art. I've never known a man yet who was a better husband and daddy because he drank. "Ten gallons of gas and a pint of gin; and all they found was a mess of tin."

• • • • • •

Eruptions... (May21, 1980) In the North West it was Mount St. Helens blowing her top. Volcanic ash covered the state and drifted eastward over ours and other states. It reminds me of the first awful eruption of SIN that began in Eden and has drifted into every continent, every country, every home, and has touched each individual life.

The other eruption was in the South East, the city was Miami. Violence and crime erupted in its ugliest forms. Lives were lost, property was destroyed, and scores were wounded. Bitterness and hatred erupted in violence. Flowing like molten lava, none in the area could feel secure. That's SIN running rampant.

• • • • • •

Mother's Day . . . Industrialized, computerized America doesn't have much of a place any more for that one special per- son multitudes have tenderly spoken of as M O T H E R!!

Something has died in the soul of our country. Much of our moral and Spiritual decay can be traced to the doorsteps of an unhealthy, if not dying, home life. Well has it been said, "An ole timer is one who can remember when a baby-sitter was spelled''M O THE R.''

It may be already too late, but some of us who can remember "Happy days of Childhood, 'round the fireside long ago," can't help but wish for a return to a more simple, sensible, and Scriptural home life for our day.

• • • • • •

Signs of the Times . . . "The earth also was corrupt

before God, and the earth was filled with violence." (Gen. 6:11) Two words from this verse describe perfectly the conditions prevalent in present-day society. . . CORRUPT and VIOLENCE. And the conditions that now exist are identical to conditions before the flood. Jesus said they would be!

Some of our older readers can recall the days of Pretty Boy Floyd, Dillinger, and Ma Barker; all of whom were notorious outlaws in their day. In this present generation, crime and violence have become so commonplace that nameless, in- famous common run-of-the-mill heartless crackpots fill our columns with gory tales of murder, rape, robbery, theft, and other acts of violence. Crime is so common today that you'd have a hard time becoming a notorious criminal.

• • • • • •

God's Grace for The Daily Grind. .. All kinds of remarks are made in regard to religious matters. In the early '50s, I was having a baptismal service in Western Missouri. It was an extremely cold late November day. Looking down at the ice on the water, I mentioned to an old fellow that the water sure looked cold. That old man said, "That kind of faith's not good enough for me; if your heart's right with God, that water won't be cold!"

I've often wished since that day that I had pushed him in! I'd have found out if his heart was right. That water was cold. Any water with ice on it is cold, whether you are a Christian or a sinner.

I think there's a message therefor some of us. In our generation we've got a lot of miss-led folks who are always looking for a miracle or a so-called "gift." Now I could use a few miracles, and I could use a few gifts. But I'll take GRACE any day, 'cause when the gifts play out the GRACE will still be there. The Lord I serve never promised that He'd warm all the cold water or cool all the flames. He did promise that His grace would be sufficient. It has been; it is now; and it always will be!

* * * * * *

Sermonizin'.... "I have seen servants upon horses, and princes walking as servants upon the earth." (Ecclesiastes 10:7) That's the writer's way of saying that things don't always tally out down here. How true!

In our day, a foul-mouthed, beer-guzzling, swaggering sports figure will be paid a million a year, while a school teacher gets less than twenty thousand. A missionary couple or family receive very little glory, and LESS of this world's goods, while an un-principled, immoral, so-called entertainer gets rich.

Nope! Things don't always even out down here. Sometimes princes have to walk while a servant rides the horse. But the Judge of all the earth will one day render to everyone his due! ·

His scales will put everything in proper balance!

* * * * * *

Her Name was Mary . . . I met her in University Hospital. Deserted by her husband, mother of three young children, at age 29 she was dying. Fast-spreading cancer.

Before coming to Little Rock's University Hospital, Mary took her children to an Assembly of God Children's Home and committed them permanently to their care. She never saw her children again. She died a few mornings later at 5:00 o'clock.

I prayed with Mary. And she prayed. I remember her last day before lapsing into a coma. At the close of the prayer she gripped this preacher's hand and muttered the last recognizable words ... "my children ...my children." I guess I never fully appreciated ours and other denominations'

Children's Homes quite as much as I should. May God bless these dedicated souls who so faithfully minister in this area of God's vineyard. There'll always be the "Mary's" who for one reason or another will have to commit their children to the love and care of someone else.

• • • • • •

A Faithful Man's Funeral ... Up in the hills of northern Arkansas attended a funeral of a dedicated Christian menthe old preacher, in paying tribute to the deceased brother, said, "He hoed his row and he hoed it clean. When he came to the end of the row, he laid down his hoe and went home with God." God bless those who faithfully "hoe their row."

* * * * * *

I still remember. .. The little boy who greeted me that morning in the yard with these words: "Preacher, I don't like to go to Sunday school; I'm like my daddy! " And I'm old enough now to have seen the outcome of the kids who were left to go their own chosen way.

Children need guidance! And the best guide is a life that is a worthy example! A little boy's daddy will have more influence on him than a boat load of Baptist preachers! PARENTS, our own off-spring are on the auction block. The devil bids high. How much do YOU care?

* * * * * *

That Old Ship of Zion ... I have always believed in the church, and I always will! The church has given me so much! It is hard for me to understand the nonchalant, take-it-or-leave-it attitude so many have developed in our day toward that sacred, blood-bought institution the Bible calls the Church.

I believe in the sacred institution of marriage. When I got married, I understood that I was to give up some things. I understood that I was to make a contribution to the cause of the home. And I had the understanding that in good days and bad, I was married, whether I felt like it or not, and that my obligations and responsibilities were just the same as when I took the marriage vow.

And so is it in the church. Things have not always gone the way I wanted them to go. The church has not always been on the mountain top. Sometimes she has been way down deep in the valley. But I am a part of the church, and I'll ride that ole Gospel Ship all the way to glory!

Thank God for the Christian church! She has survived the most vicious and the most subtle satanic attacks. She has weathered every storm and her flag is still flying. Someone often asks, "Can a person be a Christian and remain outside the church? "

That's a logical question. It merits an honest answer. Personally, I do not believe that any person can live for the Lords he ought and deliberately refuse to support the church. Of course, there are some who cannot attend and support because of providential reasons. God understands that. But there is aloof difference in a reason and an excuse!

The churches Scriptural! Its purpose and principles are right! Of course, there are counterfeits and hypocrites in the church. Always have been! And there are counterfeit organiza-tions which call themselves a church. However, it's always the counterfeit that is cheap, not the real thing. The church is still the church. The Achans, The Annaniases, the Liberals, the Modernists, the compromisers, and the appeasers will never keep the church from being the church! And one glorious day, with all the wrinkles ironed out and all the spots and blemishes removed, the Lord will present HIS BRIDE, THE CHURCH! That ole Ship of Zion ... she's one ship the stormy waters won't sink!

* * * * * *

Is there a hazard in your house? A daily newspaper carried an article few days ago about a lady in Mississippi who was killed by her dogs. She kept between twenty and thirty dogs, all pets. For some unknown reason, they turned on the lady and left her dead. Strange and unusual, though this happening may be, there might be a lesson there.

Is there something in your house that may someday turn on you or your children and do harm? What about that T.V. that blares out violence, lewdness, and vulgarity? What about that carton of beer in the refrigerator? (May Heaven forbid that any of our church members should have any?) What about those days of sulkiness and sourness in the home? And what about the woeful neglect of church, Sunday school, Bible reading, and prayer? Will there comes a day when these things will rise up and turn on those we love to injure, kill or destroy? Some things can be most hazardous that look so harmless. We might do well to stop and ask, "What have they seen in thy house?" (II Kings20:15)

* * * * * *

Lasting Impressions. .. Early one morning I stopped in for a moment at a place of business. The attendant, an elderly lady, noticed the FWB church sign on the front of my car. She said that she had been brought up in a Free Will

Baptist Church, but had vowed as a child that she'd never join a FWB church 'cause she thought the seats were too hard and the sermons too long.

Well, I suspect from her age that most every other church had hard seats and long sermons during the time she was growing up. I can remember a few long sermons and a few mighty lengthy services. One brother used to come to Brushy Knob once a month and I think he did four Sunday's preaching in one sermon. He could keep Jonah in the whale the longest! This boy like to've got in trouble one Sunday. 'Twas about 12:30 and the preacher didn't show any signs of slowing down. I remember taking out of my watch pocket one of those 89centWestclox or St. Regis watches and holding it up, letting it swing back and forth where the preacher could have seen it. Only trouble was, the wrong persons saw it and the preacher didn't; or if he did, he wasn't intimidated by it.

On the happier side, I'm glad I can remember some MIGHTY GOOD services and sermons, even when I was too young to understand 'em. But I KNEW they were good by the way the people responded. HARD SEATS won't kill you; neither will long sermons! Most of 'em are not half as long as a ball game, nor any harder than a stadium seat!

* * * * * *

Just thinking . . . From time to time read in bulletins and other church publications that a church is setting a goal and "shooting for" a certain number in Sunday school: 350... 175 ...500. I think that honest goals are commendable, and all of us should strive to reach the highest goal possible. There is a danger, though, of getting caught up in a numbers contest for numbers' sake.

How would it be to say, "Let's shoot for good music; for good preaching; for warm fellowship; for generous giving; let's shoot for faithful attendance; for fervent praying." I say, let's set our goals for these things; and if we hit what we're shooting' for, Christ will be glorified, the saints will be built up, sinners will be convicted and converted, and everybody will be blessed. Let's set our sights on these things and keep shootin'!

* * * * * *

Getting Older . . . One thing I've noticed about getting older; you wake up one day and realize that you've got about as many friends on the other side of the rivers you have down here. 'Cording to the record, there's going to be a Glad Reunion Day! We WILL meet again. Since I know that my days are numbered down here, and since I believe that all the Bible says about Heaven is true, (it's true about all other subjects, too) I'd be worse than a fool to live and die having made no preparation to meet God and to go to such a place as Heaven.

* * * * * *

Just Rambling. .. Upon Petit Jean mountain is the estate of the late Gov. Winthrop Rockefeller. It's one of the most beautiful and attractive places you ever would want to see. There are beautiful cattle, sprawling pastures, the meandering river, palatial buildings, the air strip long enough for landing jet planes, and much more. It is as well-kept as when the Governor was living there.

While visiting there with some of our elderly folks, it was remarked by some of our people that when the man died, he took NOTHING with him. That's true. It's still all there. Paul, the Apostle, wrote: "But Godliness with contentment is great gain. For we brought nothing into this world, and it is certain we can carry nothing out." The Lord Jesus Christ declared, "Take heed, and beware of covetousness: for a man's life consisteth not in the abundance of the things which he possesseth." The same Jesus also warned, "Lay not up for yourselves treasures upon earth, where moth and rust doth corrupt, and where thieves breakthrough and steal: But lay up for yourselves treasures in Heaven, where neither moth nor rust doth corrupt, and where thieves do not break through nor steal: For where your treasure is, there will your heart be also."

* * * * * *

Good Advice.... Asa young preacher just starting out to preach. I was given this verse by the Ozark mountain country preacher who was my dad. "Preach the Word, and preach it true; and it will surely take you through." Today, after more than forty years of preaching that Word, I'd like to say, A-men, dad. I still believe in the BOOK, in the BLOOD, and in the BLESSED RETURN!

* * * * * *

Years Ago Jonathan Edwards preached, "Sinners in the hands of an Angry God. " Some time ago, I heard a preacher on the radio who reversed the title and preached on"God in the hands of angry sinners. "If He is, it's only a temporary arrangement!

To some extent, at least, God's been ruled out of the classroom; He's been declared dead. His title has been changed from Father to mother (or parent) and He's been denied as Divine Creator. But I figure God can still handle Himself quite well; and one day in His Own good time, He will rise from His throne and bring an end to the whole shebang. 'Till then, be faithful, and live for Him!

* * * * * *

A Deacon said it.... "If you wait 'til Sunday morning to decide about going to Sunday school, you've waited too long." And the Deacon's right! Settle it, once and for all, that you're going no matter what! If you wait 'til Sunday morning, that bed will feels good; or company will come; or anyone of a hundred other things will keep you from going. SOME THINGS ought to be settled ONCE! And that ought to take care of it for life!

* * * * * *

Who Killed Mr. Barr?
A few days ago a terrible crime was committed not far from here. A 19-year old and a 14-year old boy shot a man in cold blood, then brutally beat two young ladies, killing one and sending the other to the hospital. Also, they'

seriously! Wounded the man's wife with two shots from a shotgun. When the smoke had cleared, this is what remained: two dead, two more in hospitals, critically wounded. Add to this when totaling up the score, two youths, not yet twenty years of age, facing the penalty for murder. An awesome and gory scene!

But who killed Lenny Barr? In an editorial which appeared last week in the *Democrat News,* the writer expressed the opinion of many when he declared that the youths probably would not have done such a thing had they not been under the influence of beer. If Thisbe true, then what about the tavern operator who sold the beer to minors? And what about a society of people who will allow such things to be done without ever raising a voice of protest? Furthermore, consider this: Will alcoholic beverages sold illegally to a nineteen-year-old youth come any nearer causing him to commit crime than the same beverage sold legally to a twenty-one year old? What difference does it make whether it is sold legally or illegally? Or whether it is sold to a young man nineteen or twenty-one?

What kind of a nation are we to legalize such a product knowing full well its possible results?

But it doesn't concern you? That's what hundreds of innocent folk said last year; but when they found themselves at the mercy of a drunken driver or a maniac wielding a gun under the influence of strong drink, it began to concern them greatly. Our highways are stained with the blood of hundreds of folk who said, "It doesn't bother me;

it's everybody's business if he Wants to drink!'' Your blood and mine may be next!

(From the church bulletin July 26, 1959, Fredericktown, MO)

*   *   *   *   *   *

The following lines are taken from a sermon preached at North Little Rock on the CRUCIFIXION of Christ.

Where you and I were guilty and we deserved to die, Christ stepped up and He took our place. He took our cross and died bearing our sins in His Own body on the tree.

As I stand today, nearly two thousand years from that crucifixion experience, I recall that "On a Hill Far Away, stood an Old Rugged Cross," and sacred to the memory of Jesus Christ is that old rugged cross;-HE DIED FOR ME!

I walked through an old cemetery last summer down in Tennessee. I was intrigued by some of the inscriptions on the grave stones. There's one there that especially attracted my interest. Caleb winters. It said on the monument that he came to that community in the 1700's.And it gave a whole list of descendants. In the community, there's Caleb Creek and there's Caleb Cave. Caleb Winters was a preacher. I was interested in that; the antiquity of it was fascinating. I thought about what it must have been like nearly two hundred years ago. What was it like to live in a cave, raise a family, and try to preach?

I walked up the hillside, and I noticed on a head stone, a date. The name slips my memory. The date stated simply: Born, 1931; Died, 1951. He died in service in Korea. You can call it what you want to, friends; but there's something in my patriotic soul that stirs the blood of this preacher. And I stood at the grave of a young man -just twenty years from the time he was born 'til the time he died. And I said aloud, "Young man, I don't know you; I don't know who you were, but I want to thank you for what you did."

He took MY place. He died for me.

Now I want to tell you something. You wonder sometimes why preachers get cranky and a little discouraged and upset. I'll tell you, friend, if fifteen car loads of company come to my house, I had better not forget that Jesus took my place! He did it for me! If the fish are biting' better than they ever bit before, and my fishin' blood is wanting to go, I'd better not forget that Sunday is the LORD'SDAY! And when I couldn't help myself, when I couldn't save myself, Jesus did it for me! He died in MY place.

Somebody says, "What we need today is a greater love for souls." No. You get your love for Christ straightened out, your love for souls will be all right. Somebody says, "We need to educate our people to love the church. " No. You get your love for Christ straightened out and you'll go where Christ is, and Christ is in the church!

* * * * * *

"The Ministry of the Church"

The following lines are excerpts from this sermon preached at the Arkansas State Association, August 17, 1977.

Let's get down to the business of preaching in the local church. I believe in preaching, and I want to give some reasons why. Paul said in Titus 1:3: "But God hath in due time manifest His Word through Preaching." Somebody asks me every once in a while, "What do you think about religious movies?" Well, I'll tell you, I'd rather hear a man of God anointed with the Spirit of God to preach, bring a simple Bible message than to see all the religious movies that have ever been produced. He chose to manifest His Word through Preaching!

Don't put preaching in the closet. Bring it out in the sanctuary. I say to you, the people of this great congregation tonight, you don't build strong churches without strong preaching. I hear someone say once in a while about a preacher, "He's not much of a preacher, but he's a good promoter." If He's a good promoter, couldn't he be a good preacher? Churches that stand the test of time are built on more than promotion. Churches that stand are churches that are built on strong preaching.

* * * * * *

The Apostle Paul wrote, "Whereunto I am ordained preacher and an Apostle." I'm made to believe that somewhere down the line there is a distinction between Apostles and preachers. It's tragic in our day that we've got a lot of so-called preachers going around trying to act like Apostles. An Apostle could get bit by a poison viper and he didn't swell up and die. The average preacher gets bit by a poison viper and he will swell up and die. One did it the other day. The Apostles could heal the sick. The average preacher cannot do that. The Apostles could do other things that preachers today are not commissioned to do. But the Apostle Paul said, "I'm ordained Tobe a preacher." The need for Apostles served its time and wore out. But the need for preaching has not worn out! There's a difference between being a preacher and being an Apostle. Paul was both.

* * * * * *

You know, we've got a lot of crookedness and a lot of corruption going on in the world today. We point a finger at Washington, and we say the politicians are the ruination of our country. But I want to tell you the politicians are not as much to blame for the pitiful condition our country is in as the pulpits of America are to blame. When our nation was great she had strong pulpits! When the church was strong, she had strong preaching. When the church was going like she ought to go, there were preachers who stood and preached like they ought to preach! I think much of the preaching is sort of sickly in our day. May God revive us, and bless us, and give us a generation of preachers. I told the young preachers in our State Ministers' Retreat last February, LEARN TO PREACH! If God's calling you to preach, learn to preach! Get out on a stump somewhere and practice. Driving down the highway, take a text and preach. When you get through preaching, give an altar call. You might get someone saved. There's nothing wrong with that. Practice preaching! Learn to preach! We need preachers who are not afraid to preach!

* * * * * *

The Bible says, "In those days came John the Baptist PREACHING ... PREACHING in the wilderness of Judaea and saying, Repent, for the Kingdom of Heaven is at hand." I've always been impressed with this verse: "then went out to him Jerusalem and all Judea and all the regions round about Jordan and were baptized of Him in Jordan, CONFESSING their sins. 'The right kind of preaching will make you afraid to live in sin! In fact, the right kind of preaching may scare you almost to death. And not only that, it will make you want to go to Heaven! It'll make you want to get right with God. It'll make you want to live right! The right kind of preaching will move your soul to a close relationship with God. A good sermon ought to make a man afraid to sin!

• • • • • •

Let's keep our priorities straight. I don't care how big a church gets. I hope your church gets to be a thousand. I don't care about that. But let me tell you something, friends. Don't put a brand on a ma's work and call him a successor a failure and judge his ministry on the size of the congregation he's got. I suppose every preacher would like to have a multitude. That's what I'd like to have. But I don't know if I could ever get a multitude. I thank God for what I've got. Today we've got all kinds of giveaways. But listen to me, if you've got to give them a hot dog to get them there, sooner or later, you're going to have to give them a steak to keep them. The Lord Jesus said to the crowd in John, chapter six, "Unless you eat My flesh and drink My blood you have no life in you." You know what they said? They said, "This is a hard saying!" And MOST of them went away.

* * * * * *

Let me mention a preacher of another day. He lived in a terribly discouraging day. For something over a hundred years he labored, and he is called in the New Testament "preacher of righteousness." How many days the sun must have set and Noah looked out and saw his neighbors going their sinful way, and he wondered, Lord, will anybody ever believe and will anybody ever be saved? When this boat is finally finished, will anybody come on board with me? There came that glorious day when it was finished, and God said to Noah, "You've been faithful; come aboard; it's going to rain, a flood is coming upon the earth." I imagines Noah was walking down the gang- plank there was still this question going through his mind, "Will anybody get on board?" And he turned to look; and there came Mrs. Noah. And I believe he shouted. He took another look. There came three boys: Shem, Ham, and Japheth. Along with them there came their wives. Ah, listen to me, brother. I'd rather save my family than to save the whole county! And I believe you can see your family saved. I believe we can, and I believe we have a responsibility to do so.

* * * * * *

"Not for filthy lucre." Do you know that when Paul wrote to Timothy, he got more serious about money than anything else? You know what? It's hard to have a lot of money and be honest about it! You just mark it down, friends; it's hard to have much money and be honest about it! Either you didn't get it honestly; or you're selfish with it instead of giving it to God. Even the Lord Jesus talked about this thing. He said it is hard for a man who is rich to enter the kingdom. Paul warned that the love of money will side-track you! It's the root of all evil! Don't be involved in the business of preaching for "filthy lucre's sake." Somebody says something often about our preachers getting paid. I'm thankful that preachers do get paid. But I'll tell you what; you can cut off the preacher's pay check and never pay him another dime, and the God-called preacher will be somewhere next Sunday morning preaching! I believe that! I didn't start preaching for money; and most of you didn't either. But let me warn you, it's hard not to worry sometimes about money. You've got a boy in Bible College, costs are high! You've got a family to feed, car payments to make, insurance premiums, and all kinds of responsibilities to meet. It's hard not to worry some about money. But I can look back down the road tonight and I'm bound to say that God has supplied EVERY need and I thank Him for that!

* * * * * *

There's one more negative here, and I really don't know what to say about it. I really don't. "Neither as being lords over God's heritage. " Now, preacher, you don't OWN the church! And, Deacon, you don't either! The preacher is a SERVANT of Jesus. The Deacon is a servant of Jesus; a servant of the church, if you please! Nobody in the church owns the church. It is Jesus' church! "I'd rather be a door-keeper in the house of my God than to dwell in tents of wickedness." It takes some of us a long time to reach any degree of ministerial maturity. That old fellow whom we think has got to be throwed out of the church or the church is going to die; well, I don't know. He was there when you came and he'll probably be there when you're gone. That's not to say that we ought to tolerate sin. You know what I really believe? I really do believe that the right kind of preaching ought to straighten up the problems in the church. But now let me tell you preachers something; it's a dangerous thing to load your preaching gun for one fellow. You work all week and you've got your sermon just exactly to fit that fellow; and he's not there and you're stuck. Don't be a lord over God's heritage. Be an under shepherd. What you do, do it in love.

*   *   *   *   *   *

Let me say a word about the preacher's commitment. By his commitment, I just simply mean, STICKINGTO IT! Some issues ought to be settled once, and that ought to settle it for life. I got married once. I ought Tobe married as long as I live; or until one of us dies. I don't get up in the morning and say, "Am I going to be married today?" Of course, I'm going to be married; that was settled 'way back in October of 1948. It was a once in a life time commitment. Surrendering to preach ought to be a once in a life time commitment! Nail it down. Beloved! We've seen preachers by the score leave the ministry in recent years. Make a commitment! They tell me that when an airplane starts down the runway, it reaches a certain point where it's committed to take off. As a preacher, you reached that point of commitment. There must be no turning back! The Lord said to one fellow one day, "Come and follow me." The man said, "Lord, I will follow you, but first let me go bury my father." The Lord said, "Lethe dead bury their dead?" Did you ever notice that the fellow who said that was a preacher? He was! The Lord said, "Let the dead bury the dead, but go thou and PREACH!" He was a preacher making excuses. Preachers, turn loose of the plow handles. Turn loose of the cash register. Turn loose! The world is dying. You may not fill the biggest church pulpit, but you can fill a pulpit somewhere and some soul will be saved. If you wait 'til you get the dead all buried it will be too late! "Go thou and preach the Kingdom of God."

Listen, Isaiah, after he had seen that great vision said. "Lord, how long?" "Lord, howling do you want me to be com· mitted to this call?" You know what the Lord said? "Until the cities be wasted without inhabitant, and the houses without man, and the land be utterly desolate." As much as to say, as long as there is a man in the city, a soul that needs to hear, GO PREACH! There's no place to quit! Jeremiah, chapter twenty, verse 9:- Jeremiah had had a bad day. Sunday school was down; the offering was low; some of the teachers were absent. The music was off for some reason. "Then said I, I won't preach anymore! I will not make mention of Him, nor speak any more in His Name. 'Jeremiah said, ''I'll just quit!'' He got up on Monday morning; the sun was shining, the birds were singing; his wife smiled at him. He didn't hand in his resignation. "But His Word was in mine heart as a burning fire shut up in my bones, and I was weary with forbearing, and I could not stay. " Jeremiah had Holy fire burning in his bones and he couldn't quit when he wanted to quit!

Ezekiel, chapter two, verse one: "And He said unto me, Son of man, stand upon thy feet, and I will speak unto thee. " Did you ever look at that and wonder why God said, "Get up, Stand up? "I'll tell you why; as long as a man's sitting down, he's not going to do anything! "Stand up on your feet, Ezekiel! And I will speak unto thee." There's no point in telling a feller to do something as long as he's sitting. There's marching to do; there are battles to be fought, victories to be won! "And he said unto me, Son of man, I send thee to the children of Israel, to a rebellious nation that hath rebelled against me: they and their fathers have transgressed against me, even unto this very day. - And they, whether they will hear, or whether they will forbear, (for they are a rebellious house) yet shall know that there hath been a prophet among them. "Let the people know, friend, whatever their response, that they've been preached to when they go out the service on Sunday morning. If they don't come back on Sunday night, that's their decision and not yours. The Apostle Paul had the determination that every one of us ought to have when he said, "Now behold, I go bound in the Spirit unto Jerusalem, not knowing the things that shall befall me there; save that the Holy Ghost witnessed in every city, saying that bonds and afflictions abide me. But none of these things move me, neither count I my life dear unto myself, so that I might finish my course with joy. "We need that kind of commitment, beloved. No turning back! I heard of someone who settled on the shores of Old Mexico one time. Whence got his belongings off the ships, he gave commandment or his men to bum the ships. They were not going to go back! "How long? " Just as long as you're here; as long as there's a soul that needs to be preached to!

*   *   *   *   *   *

Let me say just a word about the preacher's compensation.

God's got a pay day for His preachers. He's got a pay day for ALL His children. I was driving down Highway 430 the other day and got to thinking about the preacher 'spay day. Got to thinking about some of the old songs our fore parents used to sing. "My father took the bible and's gone home to glory; bright angels a waitin'at the door!" I got to thinking about that and forgot where I was. Looked down at the speedometer and was going almost seventy miles an hour. Andheri came a car with a blue light on it. If you think that won't bring you back to reality! God's preachers are going to have a pay day! Lis n. you remember that verse: "Be not deceived, God is not mocked, for whatsoever a man soweth, that shall he also reap. He that soweth to the flesh shall of the flesh reap corruption: but he that soweth to the Spirit shall of the Spirit reap LIFE EVERLASTING." 'Bout the only way we ever preach that, we talk about that old fellow out there wasting his life in sin, and we say if you don't straighten up, you're going to reap what you sow! And he WILL reap! But Paul went ahead and said, "Let US not be weary in well doing; for in due season WE shall reap if we faint not. 'Yes, the wicked are going to reap: but the RIGHTEOUS are going to reap, too! "We shall reap if we faint not. " You say if there were no Heaven I'd still preach: no, you wouldn't. I don't think you would. You say, if there were no hereafter, I'd still live for God. No, you wouldn't. You say if there were no hereafter, no pay day, you would still go through it all. No, you wouldn't. I don't think you would. Who is the best man, one of the best men in the Old Testament? Moses. You know what made Moses do what he did? The Bible says," Head respect unto the recompense of the reward. ·· He said, "I'm going to get rewarded one of these days." And incidentally, some of you fellows have been working on this reward business; and I've worked on it a little bit, too. I had it straightened out a long time ago and some of you kind of got me tangled up! And I've come back right where I started! You know what God's going to reward you for? For being FAITHFUL! You say that one fellow has done a lot more than another fellow. That may be true. But let me give you what Paul said, "The Spirit beareth witness with our spirit that we are the children of God. AND IF CHILDREN, heirs of God, and JOINT HEIRS with Christ if so be that we suffer with Him." Stay in there! Be faithful! "When Jesus comes to reward His servants, whether it be noon or night; FAITHFUL to Him will He find us watching, with our lamps all trimmed and bright? " A missionary wrote years ago, "In spite of sorrow, loss and pain; our watch-word ONWARD still. We sow on Burma's barren plain; we REAP on Zion's hill! ""He that goeth forth and weepeth, bearing precious seed, shall DOUBTLESS come again with rejoicing, bringing his sheaves with him. "

No More sea

From the sermon, "No More Sea"
Preached at Pocahontas, Arkansas, May, 1964

And so it is with the mystery of life itself. Very little do we really know about life, for life comes from God, a Supernatural power? No man can manufacture life. It cannot be produced in the plants and factories of our land. Life is a gift from God, and life is God's to take or to give. We'll never be able to under- stand the mystery of life.

But if life is a mystery, much more is death a mystery. One Moment you're speaking and breathing, laughing and talking With your loved ones, the next moment, the next day, or the next year -deathly silent. You're sleeping the sleep of the dead. And we pass by and we wonder, Lord, where are they? What are they doing? Will we see them again? Yes, death re- mains a mystery. It has been described in the Bibles being a sleep. It has been described by a writer of old as being a journey from which no traveler returns. It has been described in other symbolic terms. And yet, the most that we can say is, that death remains mystery.

I want to give you this illustration which I think may offer some source of comfort and hope. Nobody will ever know what death is really like, or what it really is, until you take that step and experience it. I remembering other days wondering as I

Would gaze into the skies and see the mighty planes flying overhead, "What's it like to take an airplane ride?" I recall one experience in particular, of taking a preacher friend to Lambert Airport in St. Louis. He bought his ticket, we went up to the observation deck, and we talked 'til it was time for his departure. I helped him carry his baggage down the long hall to gate number such and such; and right there was a sign which read, "Beyond this point only passengers are allowed to go." I was no passenger. I wasn't going anywhere, so I said "Goodbye" and stood back. I watched my friends he walked through the gate, met the ticket man, walked on out to the plane, climbed up the steps, boarded the plane and away he went. And I went back home wondering what it was like to take an airplane ride.

One day I knew. I remember the experience well. Two preacher friends took me to the same airport, Lambert Field. I got a ticket, and we stood around and talked and laughed and joked. After a while it came time to depart. I walked down the very same hall to gate number such and such. This time it was I who went on through the gate. I walked out through the gate to the plane, and left my friends behind. And I found out what it was like to take an airplane ride.

I have stood by the bedside of loved ones who were dying in the faith of God. And though there was not any visible sign, I knew there was a point which said, "Beyond here you can't go. Only those who are taking the trip can go beyond this gate." And I stood there with my arms folded, knowing this is as far as I can go. And I've watched them as they moved out of that body of clay, boarded the Ole Ship of Zion and headed for Heaven's glory. And I've walked out of the room wondering, "What's it like, Lord? What's it like?"

One of these days, I don't know when, I don't know what the circumstances will be, but under normal circumstances someone will stand by my bedside. We'll approach the same gate and the sign will read, "Beyond this point only you can go, because you're a passenger." And I'll walk on and leave my friends behind. And I believe the old Gospel Ship will be there   waiting. When Lazarus came to that point, he didn't know how to get home; he didn't know what it was like. God said to some of His angels that were not doing anything else, "Go down and get Lazarus." They came down and got Lazarus, and they bore him on their pinions home to be with God!

John said that there was no more mystery; no more separation, no more trouble. All of it is over! The cares of life all behind. The realities of Heaven's glory can be yours and mine in that wonderful place. I want to admonish you, friends, this morning, if you don't already have preparation made, you come and get your ticket! And when they finally call your number you can leave this world, board the plane and be taken home to be with God.

The Local Church

From a Sermon on the Local Church
Preached in North Little Rock Church

I want also to say this morning that the responsibility of be- Inga good member in a local church is a tremendous responsibility. I've learned to accept this fact; I've never learned to like it, but I've learned to accept this fact. The church gets from her members just exactly what we want to give - nothing more, nothing less. Nobody gets fired because he doesn't work in the church. Nobody gets a pay cut because he doesn't work at building his class. The preacher, of course, can get shipped out, and he ought to be shipped out if he doesn't work and give a good day's labor for a day's pay. But the members give to your church what you want to; no more and no less. Now a shoe factory couldn't operate on that basis; a grocery store couldn't exist on those terms because there would undoubtedly be days when the employees wouldn't want to go to work. And yet somehow the church has managed to survive, and I believe it will keep on surviving. We ought to love the house of God enough to give it our very all.

The most touching experiences of life that bring us the most deep emotional experiences are involved in the house of God. I don't think of any greater delight than to recall the marriage altar; when you stood before the country preacher and the old country saints of God. In tenderness, and love, and affection two lives became one. And that's still a tender experience.

I don't recall any greater joy, really, than going into the house of God carrying a new-born baby. It's a real thrill to   parents to come to church bringing your own for the very first time. There seems to be a special blessing about bringing that baby to the house of God.

Then there are the days when the songs of Zion sung in the sanctuary have lifted our souls above the cares, the turmoil, and the strife. I'll tell you, friends, if I did not have the privilege sometimes of getting together with the saints of God and singing, "There's a Land that is Fairer than Day, and by Faith we can see it Afar,"- If I couldn't ever hear the saints of God sing "Heaven Will Surely Be Worth It All," - If I couldn't ever get together with the children of God and hear the songs that lift us up above the strife and the noise and confusion of this world in which we live, I think the song would go out of my own soul.

Then perhaps the most heart-touching, emotional experience of all -that day when you come into the sanctuary; and the preacher, be he young or old, stands up to give the last memorial tribute to your companion-your loved one -in the house of God. And you leave that earthly sanctuary feeling like the roof has caved in and the walls have collapsed and the very bottom has dropped out as far as this world is concerned. But you leave looking Heavenward with a song in your soul even though ears are in your eyes.

I honestly confess to you today, that as a man, I have a multitude of faults and shortcomings. But after I am dead and gone, if anyone wants to say one good thing about me, I hope that after have quit the walks of this life, that somebody will honestly say WITH ALL OF HIS SOUL, HE LOVED THE CHURCH! And with all that in me is, I love the house of God! I love the people of God, and I love the Word of God and the work of God.

Tell It Not In Gath

North Little Rock Church, Jan. 24, 1982

Second Samuel, chapter 1, verses 19 and 20- "The beauty of Israel is slain upon thy high places: how are the mighty fallen! Tell it not in Gath, publish it not in the streets of Askelon; lest the daughters of the Philistines rejoice, lest the daughters of the uncircumcised triumph. "

I ran across this text some time ago, a text which I have never preached, nor have I personally heard anyone else preach from it. In verse 20, the text, "Tell it not in Gath." Gath was a city, and I think I know why David did not want the message told in Gath. Incidentally, it was a very sad message. Gath! Where did I ever hear of Gath? Do you remember that story of David, when he was a shepherd lad? He went down to see about his brothers who were supposed to be in battle. The main actor in that drama was a "giant named Goliath, of GATH." Gath was one of the five royal cities of the Philistines. Ashkelon was another.

David was at this time in a very sad state. King Saul had just died in battle, a miserable death. And from the time of his youth, David and Israel had always been confronted by the Philistines. They were arch enemies. David was so hurt at the death of King Saul. He was especially grieved that the Philistines might have cause to gloat over the death of Saul. It was in this line of thinking that David said, "Tell it not in Gath."

There are at least three sad events recorded that involved man of God and the Philistines. From the Book of Judges we read the account of the strong man, Samson. Samson was Strong because he had a covenant with God. He was the strongest man who ever lived; and his special strength came from God. Let's look at some of his exploits. Judges 14:5-6:

"Then went Samson down, and his father and his mother, to Timnath, and came to the vineyards of Timnath: and, behold, a young lion roared against him. And the SPIRIT OF THE LORD came mightily upon him, and he rent him as he would have rent a kid, and he had nothing in his hand." In verse 19 of the same chapter, "And the SPIRIT OF THE LORD came upon him, and he went down to Ashkelon, and slew thirty men of them, and took their spoil, and gave change of garment to them which expounded the riddle." Now Askelon is Philistine territory! God WILL be with His people when we're in this world of sin and un-Godliness if our relationship with Him is right. In verse 4 of chapter15, "Samson went and caught three hundred foxes and took fire brands and turned tail to tail and put a firebrand in the midst between two tails and when he had set the firebrands on fire he let them go into the standing corn of the Philistines and burned up the shocks and also the standing corn with the vineyard and olives. " Now the Philistines wanted to get ahold of Samson; they wanted to put a stop to him; but as long as Samson was in a right relationship with God, Samson had every victory; he came winner in EVERY episode with the Philistines!

Look at chapter 16, verse 3: "And Samson lay till midnight and arose at midnight and took the doors of the gate of the city and the two posts and went away with them, bar and all and put them upon his shoulders and carried them up to the top of a hill that is before Hebron." They thought they had fenced him in, but Samson just walked up and didn't bother to break the lock; he just picked up gates, posts, and all and walked off with them. I want to remind us again, that Samson was in a right relationship with God, and it was the POWER OF GOD that enabled him to do that!

The tragedy begins to unfold in verse 16: "And it came to pass when Delilah pressed him daily with her words and urged Him so that his soul was vexed unto death, that he told her ALL HIS HEART. ""The secret of the Lord belonged unto them that fear Him, "the Bible says. And it was to be kept a secret. But Samson began to flirt with the world and he began to lay his head in the lap of a worldly woman and the Bible says that before it was over,"He told her all his heart. "Now watch. She woke him up and said, "The Philistines be upon thee, Samson. " And he awoke out of his sleep and said, "I will go out as at other times before and shake myself. But he wist not that the Lord was departed from him. "Now, beloved, when the Lord departs from a man his power goes! The text:"Tell it not in Gath! "I'm sorry that the Philistines ever learned this news. I'm sorry that it was ever published in Gath! Or in Ashkelon!

The Philistines took him; they put out his eyes. They brought him down to Gaza. They bound him with fetters of brass and he did grind in the prison house. Now if you want to know what this means, it means that they took Samson, they blinded his eyes; they had an old grinding machine down there kind of like one of these old time sorghum mills like there used Tobe over the country. They take an old mule, tie that thing to a pole that is about thirty feet long, and all day long that animal goes 'round and 'round and 'round turning that thing that grinds the sorghum cane. Samson was doing the work of a mule! And the Philistines were laughing all the time.

Finally, they said, "Let's humiliate him some more:" In verse 25 they said, "Call for Samson, that he may make us sport." They wanted some fun out of it. They called for Sam- son out of the prison house and he made them sport, and they set him between the pillars. This is a sad period in the history of this great man. But I'm not going to leave the story there, for his case is really not that hopeless. "And Samson said unto the lad that held him by the hand, suffer me that I may feel the pillars whereupon the house standeth that I may lean upon them. Now the house was full of men and women; all the Lords of the Philistines were there and there were upon the roof about three thousand men and women who beheld while Sam- son made sport. And Samson called unto the Lord "and if a man ever prayed out of the depth of his soul, this is a prayer of desperation from the heart of a man to the God which once he knew. "And Samson called unto the Lord and said, 0, Lord God remember me I pray Thee only this once, 0 God; that I may be at once avenged of the Philistines for my two eyes. "I think this is the prayer of a backslider getting back in touch with God. I really believe that Samson died in the will of God. I do not believe man can get that earnest and not be heard.

One reason I believe he got back right with God is the fact that God answered his prayer. Samson said, "Let me die with the Philistines; and he bowed himself with his might and the house fell upon the lords and upon all the people that were therein so That the dead which he slew at his death were more than they which he slew in his life." But there's a chapter in the life of Samson which I wish had never been published in Gath!

Turn with me now to another sad chapter in the history of God's people. First Samuel chapter four and also part of chapter five. This has to do with the taking captive of the Ark of God. Now the Ark of God represented God's power and God's presence. You remember when Israel cameo cross over Jordan, there were the priests who stood there bearing the Ark of God. And they went over on dry land as they crossed that last river which I think represents the river of death. But there was another encounter between the Israelites and the Philistines. In verse 10, "And the Philistines fought and Israel was smitten." That's sad. "They fled every man into his tent and there was a very great slaughter for their fellow Israel thirty thousand footmen; AND THE ARK OF GOD WAS TAKEN. And the two sons of Eli, Hopi and Phineas were slain." It was sad news that had to be borne to Eli. He was an old man and here's the way the Bible describes the event. "Now Eli was ninety and eight years old and his eyes were dim that he could not see; and the man said unto Eli, I am he that came out of the army, and I fled today out of the army. And he said, what is there done, my son? And the messenger said, Israel is fled before the Philistines." O tell it not in Gath! He said, "Israel is fled before the Philistines." Shame upon shame! God doesn't want His people ever to be running from their enemies. The reason they were running was that the heart of Israel was not right at this time and the Ark of God had been taken. Now, beloved, if it could happen to Israel of old, it COULD happen to the United States of America today! Tell it not in Gath.

"And the messenger answered and said, Israel is fled before the Philistines; there hath been also a great slaughter among the people. Thy two sons Hopi and Phineas are dead; and the Ark of God is taken. And it came to pass when he made mention of the Ark of God that he fell from off the seat backward by the side of the gate and his neck broke and he died, for he was an old man and he was heavy and he had judged Israel forty years." When Eli heard this news he was so distraught that he fell over backward and broke his neck. Wanton read a few more verses. "And his daughter-in-law, Phinehas's wife, was with child near to be delivered, and when she heard the tidings that the Ark of God was taken and that her husband and father-in-law were dead, she bowed herself and travailed, for her pains came upon her. And about the time of her death the women that stood by her said unto her, Fear not for thou hast borne a son. But she answered not, neither did she regard it; and she named the child Ichabod saying, The Glory is departed from Israel and the Ark of God is taken..."

Now if we could let God speak to our hearts tonight, I think we can see some similar situations in our times that ought to break our hearts and stir up the fountain of tears in our eyes until we cry and weep before God; because some things are happening today that are just as sad as these things that happened in others days.

Let me show you how the Ark of God fared, though. Listen, God can always take care of His own! This is very interesting to me. "The Philistines took the Ark of God and brought it from Ebenezer unto Ashdod. And when the Philistines took the Ark of God they brought it into the house of Dagon and set it by Dagon. "Now Dagon was their idol god. They had to move him around wherever they wanted him to go, 'cause he couldn't walk. They had to hold him up, 'cause when he fell he couldn't get up again. I'm glad my God's not like that. My God can take care of the situation, no matter what it is. "And when they of Ashdod arose early on the morrow, behold, Dagon was fallen upon his face before the Ark of God. " Listen, if my God ever falls down and breaks His neck, I'm gonna change Gods! And the Philistines, if they'd had a lick of sense, they'd have changed gods, too! Someday we're going to be left alone with the God that we serve, and I want to know that I'm serving the God that's got the power to get up again! He's not gonna be down in the first place! "And they took Dagon and set him in his place again and when they arose early on the morrow morning, behold Dagon was fallen upon his face to the ground before the Ark of the Lord and the head of Dagon and both the palms of his hands were cut off upon the threshold; only the stump of Dagon was left. " I imagine God was kinda chuckling a little bit. Dagon, the god of the Philistines, couldn't even stand when he was fastened to the wall in the presence of the Ark of God! And the Philistines showed a little bit of sense. They made an agreement to get the Ark of God out of their territory!

Now go again to the last chapter of the book of First Samuel. This chapter gives us an explanation of what was taking place when I read the words of the text. King Saul was in battle. · "The Philistines followed hard upon Saul and upon his sons, and the Philistines slew Jonathan and Abinadab and Melchishua, Saul's sons. "Saul's three boys fell in battle that day at the hands of the Philistines. Tell it not in Gath! Don't let the Philistines gloat over it. But they were. "And the battle went sore against Saul, and the archers hit him; and he was sore wounded of the archers. Then said Saul unto his armour·bearer, Draw thy sword, and thrust me through therewith; lest these uncircumcised come and thrust me through, and abuse me. But his armor bearer would not, for he was sore afraid. Therefore Saul took a sword and fell upon it. " And I can say with David, "Tell it not in Gath!" "So Saul died, and his three sons, and his armor-bearer, and all his men that same day together."

In chapter one of Second Samuel, a reporter has just come and told David what has happened. The servant said,

"Saul is dead; the Philistines have killed Saul in battle. The sons of Saul are dead. "Let me show you what the Philistines did with King Saul. Listen, the Devil, when he gets what he wants out of you, he'll make a wreck out of your body, out of your spirit and he'll laugh up his sleeve! Because he has made a fool out of a mortal man. The reason David was hurt so deeply was because of what the Philistines did with King Saul. "Bandit cameo pass on the morrow, when the Philistines came to strip the slain, that they found Saul and his three sons fallen in Mount Gilboa. " Now I'm going to say a few things that are on my heart. I think the Philistines had rather have had King Saul than anybody else that was in God's army at that time. I'll tell you something else; I think the Devil had rather get the preacher of this church to sin and do wrong than anybody else in this church! He'll take anybody, but I think he'd rather get the preacher. Let it never be published in Gath that the preacher of God fell! That he sinned and brought shame and reproach upon the name of God.

The Philistines took the body of Saul. They cut off his head. That's sad. They stripped off his armor. They sent into the land of the Philistines round about, to publish it in the house of their idols, and among the people. "It made the headlines! If they had had T.V. and radio, it would have been on every station that broadcast the news:"SAUL IS DEAD. THE CHAMPION OF ISRAEL HAS FALLEN! "The Devil laughs   when he can get anybody to fall and do wrong. And they put his armor in the house of Ashteroth. They fastened his body to the wall of Bethshan.

To their everlasting credit, some nameless men,

inhabitants of Jabesh·Gilead, when they heard of that which the Philistines had done to Saul, all the valiant men arose and went all night. They took the body of Saul and the bodies of his sons from the wall of Bethshan and came to Jabesh, and burnt them there. Listen, friends, there comes a time when there's a cause worth dying for. I think these valiant men must have talked among themselves and said, "We're not going to let these Philistines gloat over having Saul, our leader, our king; we're going to go and get him!"

Now David has just heard this news. It saddens his heart.

He views the situation and he says, "The beauty of Israel is slain upon thy high places: how are the mighty fallen! Tell it Not in Gath, publish it not in the streets of Askelon; lest the Daughters of the Philistines rejoice, lest the daughters of the "uncircumcised triumph. "

Now in the next moments of tonight's message, I'm going to talk with you about what I think are some of the saddest things we ever see... In my opinion, as a preacher who loves God and the cause of righteousness, there is nothing any sadder than a backslidden, lukewarm church. Tell it not in Gath.

The Devil is laughing up his sleeves today! I'm not talking about denominations. I'm talking about the Christian church.

Read about the church in the New Testament Book of Acts. They prayed; and the place was shaken. Their preacher was in prison and a handful of people, the church, if you will, got together and God heard their prayers! The prison bars were burst asunder and Peter was set free by an angel of God because the Church prayed.

The church was a mighty loco-motive going through the land. Every tricycle Volkswagen, and every other machine cleared the tracks! The mention of the church thrust fear in the he arts of the authorities of the day. You know something? The church in that day didn't ask when would be a suitable time to have a revival. They didn't give in to the city council, the PTA, or the Cub Scouts.

Some present-day organizations are all right in their place. But the church in that day was the might y locomotive going through the land; and the other things, the tricycles and the tricycles stopped to let the Church go through.

Beloved, it's a sad day when the church takes the back seat to the world. Tell it not in Gath! What I say, I say with brokenness and sorrow. Brother Payne mentioned this morning, and some of you saw it on the news, that up in Michigan where the super bowl game is being played, some of the so called churches opened up their doors and put in a bar. Of course, they had to get the bingo tables moved before they had room. Now you know what group I am talking about; but here are plenty of other denominations that are capable of doing the very same thing! In our day, lots of so-called churches have obtained license to sell beer.

In Milwaukee a few years ago, the tavern keepers association lodged a complaint with the authorities. They complained that the churches were giving a bottle of whiskey to New Years' Eve party goers. And the tavern keepers said that the churches only had permits to sell beer, not whiskey! Now, folks, if that were not so serious it would be funny. What do you think the Apostle Paul would do if he should be resurrected from the dead and sent to preach up there next Sunday? If his old preaching heart didn't wear out, don't you know they'd hear from him! Stretch your imagination as far as you can, and I ask you, "What relationship can a group like that have with a first-century church that preached righteousness, temperance, and judgment to come?" What relationship can a group like that have with New Testament Christianity? I tell you, it CAN happen in Baptist Churches. Or any group. When we come to the point where we sanction, coddle, and compromise with every worldly trend that comes along, I say may Heaven have mercy upon us! I say with the sadness of David, Tell it not in Gath. Don't let the Philistines laugh. It is too serious for that.

Nothing is any more sad, or sickening, or heart-rending than the Spiritual listlessness, lifelessness, worldliness of the present-day church. I weep over that. And I say to you tonight, let the church be the church! Let the world be the world. But keep the church, the church! Revelation 3:20 was never written to a rank, out and out sinner, "Behold, I stand at the door and knock." The sad truth is, it was written to a lukewarm Laodicea church. And Jesus is standing on the outside of a lukewarm church and saying, "Behold, I stand at the door and knock." It's been so long since Jesus has been in the midst of some church congregations, He'd be a total stranger if He made His appearance. Now let me tell you something, friends, the church is going to get more worldly; and the world is getting more church-y. But tell it not in Gath. Don't let the Philistines laugh.

Not only is a backslidden church as ad sight; a backslidden church member is a sad sight. Solomon mentioned four things of which he said, "They are too wonderful for me to know." In that line of thinking, as a preacher, there are some things that are TOO SAD for me to fully express. A backslidden church member ...the way of a transgressor is hard. There was a time when the service of the Lord was his delight. Like a majestic ship, with all the glory that God can give child of God, that life was transformed and it radiated the beauty of God and the glory of God. And the service of the Lord was his delight. And a backslidden church member doesn't seem to hear because his ears are hard of hearing. He doesn't see because the Devil has blinded his eyes. He doesn't seem to understand because his understanding is dull. You try to get a message through to him and it is almost like pouring water on a duck's back; it runs right square-dab off! That's a backslidden church member. If angels rejoice over a sinner who repents, must they not also weep over a saint that goes wrong? Now, there isn't any outline to what I'm preaching; I'm just telling you what I think are some of the saddest things I have encountered in the years of my ministry.

What is another of the saddest things we've seen in our life- time? The break-down of the home! Of course, not all of it has taken place in your life time and mine; but much of it has. Tell it not in Gath. A lot of it started in World War II; we remember such songs as "Rosie the Riveter." Up until World War II, by far the majority of housewives stayed at home. This change took place in a time of peril. Women by the multiplied thousands took their places in the airplane factories, ammunition arsenals, and defense manufacturing plants. Our nation was at war. The tragedy of it is, that's where they stayed. And say what you want to, it's got to have an effect on the home life of a nation, and no amount of money can compensate for the loss of a mother in the home. Now let me go ahead and say this, which doesn't really make it right; but we've got a situation to· day where "one rooster can't hardly scratch out a living for one hen." But that's the situation we've got. A young feller setting up house-keeping today, if he's not got a whopper of a job and income, it is a hopeless case! So we've worked ourselves into a situation where the family depends on not one, but two, or three pay checks to keep the bills paid, and we have done it to our detriment. Tell it not in Gath. "As goes the home, so goes the nation."

The last thing I'll mention tonight is the degeneration of a generation of young people. Not all young people, by any stretch of the imagination are lost. I thank God for the young people of THIS congregation who love the Lord, who are mannerly, who've got personality, enthusiasm, who can work hard problems, who can do things in their school and I thank the Lord for every young person who is here tonight. But I know you know I speak the truth when I tell you that multitudes of this generation's young people are fallen into the hands of the Philistines. Tell it not in Gath. Because the

Philistines are not good company. I've never been able to understand it that Godless, atheistic, heathen, worldly, entertainers can have the influence that they have. I said it in the early '60s, and I've never backed up, I still believe it, a lot of this started with the "king," the so-called king. He began to do the hip-wiggle, and a generation of young people followed him. He's spoken of tonight as being an "idol." The Bible says an idol is nothing! You had better be sure what you're putting your trust in. Along came the Beatles. And, like the Pied Piper of Hamblen, they began to pipe and a whole generation began to dance to their strange music; both literally and figuratively. And the Beatles who could not understand their own popularity and at one time said, "we seem to be more popular than Jesus," captured with the strange-sounding music, although a lot of it was not very melodious, a generation of youth who followed them. Along with the strange-sounding music and the "Pied Pipers" from Liverpool, there was introduced to America on a much larger scale than we ever had known before, the drug traffic. Say what you want to, but when MANY of us were in High School, nobody smoked marijuana on the school grounds; nobody smoked LMs on the school ground as far as that goes; our principal, Mr. Chevalier, would have beat the tar out of them! And I mean that. They just didn't have it! I drove up to Ridge road the other day and there were some young girls standing 'round smoking. They're burning their lungs up 'way too young! Tell it not in Gath.

Authorities say, Police officers say, School administrators say, that in every school, there is marijuana, other drugs, alcohol, you name it, and it's there! And I say tonight with all the sorrow that David had, Tell it not in Gath. I hope and pray tonight the Lord will get a hold of our hearts. I do not want the Philistines laughing at a lost generation. I do not want the Philistines laughing at King Saul hanging on the wall in their idol god's hall. I do not want the Philistines laughing at a generation of young people that followed the pied pipers of this world to their everlasting destruction. Tell it not in Gath.

If the Lord will lay a burden upon one soul who is here tonight, then I will certainly feel that God has honored His word. If there is another daddy who will get really concerned and burdened and down to business, I'll praise the Lord. If there is a mother who will get more serious about the business of living for God and being what God wants you to be, I'll praise the Lord. By all means, if there is a young person who will resolve in your heart, whether openly or privately, that you're going to stay clean and live for God and never windup in the halls of the Philistines, I'll be glad to thank the Lord that He got through to our hearts. God bless you, every one of us. To the men who serve on the boards of this church, let's resolve to keep this a house of prayer, a place of worship. "Then I'll bid good-bye to the ways of the world." Let the world be the world, but let the church be the church. It may not be the biggest or the most popular in town, but let's be sure that we're in favor with God. God will take care. To the daddy's and moms and the families who are here, God bless YOUR loved ones. And I've resolved that if the Devil ever gets my home, he's going to have to put up a tussle. May it never be told in Gath that our family fell, that our young people were lost, that the church backslid on God. If there is a soul here tonight who needs to pray and repent, and ask God for forgiveness, I hope you will come; and on your knees before God, bare your heart in His presence and commit your life to Him to do His will. Let us pray. "O Lord, there are so many situations in this world today that are sad, but Lord, they're not hopeless. There is the breakdown of the home, the backsliddenness of the church, the waywardness of youth, Kings wind up in Dagon 'shall; but, O God, we still believe the Ark of God is here. We still believe in your power and your promises. Lord helps that we'll discern right from wrong, and always stand forth right. Bless these precious young people, and our beloved aged. And if any need to come to pray, give them the Grace and courage to come; in Christ's Name. Amen.

Peace and Prosperity

Psalms 122:7: "Peace be within thy walls, and prosperity within thy palaces." In the Old Testament days when the Psalmist was writing, and other Bible writers wrote, they often referred to Jerusalem. They spoke of Zion, the city of God. I think every true-blooded Jew who was born looked forward to the day when he personally, could go to that great city that was noted as the city of God. The city of Jerusalem. And there in that city of God walk into the Holy Temple. Every Jew wanted to go to that sacred place and they kept it in their thoughts and in their prayers. It is sad that when Jerusalem became backslidden on God, the whole nation fell apart. And if the church in our day would be what it ought to be, our nation would come a lot nearer being what it ought to be. If the church goes down, the home will go down; and if the church and the home go down, then the nation can do nothing but crumble and fall.

What a joyful experience it was to walk into the temple of the living God! In their prayers and in their songs they sang and they prayed about the joy of the Lord and the blessings of God. The Psalmist wrote about the blessings of going into the sanctuary of God. Now we in this generation are blest to be able to go into the sanctuary of God every Lord's Day, unless providentially hindered.

The Psalmist wrote in Psalms 73 about some things from a personal standpoint that bothered him. There are things that bother you and me. For instance, in Psalm 73:2: "But as for me, my feet were almost gone, my steps were well-nigh slipped. " I said the other day that some of us would have been dead a long time ago if we had not got right with God when we did, and I believe that! We were about to go over! God was gracious to us and if we had not changed our direction and gone to the house of God and got straightened up and begun to live for God, the Lord only knows what would have become of us.

In the same Psalm the writer said that he could not under· stand the prosperity of the wicked, and that it looked like God's children were having a rough time; they were not in trouble as other men. In verse 16 he said, "When I thought to know this, it was too painful for me until I went into the sanctuary of God. Then I understood their end. " He got his picture right in focus. He said, "Surely Thou didst set them in slippery places; Thou casteth them down in destruction." As much as to say, the wicked may prosper for a while, but that is not my worry. Things may not always even out down here, but that must not overthrow our faith because we know that God is in Heaven and in His own time He will reward each one according to the doing of his own ways. The Psalmist said that he could not understand this until he went into the sanctuary of God.   There are some things I want to tell you this morning that this preacher believes with all his heart. In the first place, I   believe that every Christian needs to GO to the house of God. Somebody says, "I believe I can be a Christian and never go to church." There is not one verse of Scripture in the whole Book of God to substantiate that. Unless, of course, you are providentially hindered. Every Christian needs Togo to the house of God for the PREACHING of the Word of God. You say, Brother Scott, I'm not too much impressed with preaching. Well, there've been times when I wasn't either. But when I've gone to the House of God and the preacher leveled his Gospel gun, it seemed he was pickin' on me; but it was God's way of breaking my heart when it needed to be broken. I look back to- day and thank the Lord that even when I was a teenager God had preachers who cared about me.

Every Christian ought to go to church for the comfort that's there. There've been times in my life, and I suspect in yours, too, that you just could not wait for Sunday to come so you could go to the house of God. Maybe you'd had a particularly bad week; things had been bad, and you had experienced disappointment. You knew that the only help for your soul was to get into the house of God, the SANCTUARY of the Lord. Why do you think they call it a SANCTUARY? One of our young men, Tommy Rogers, gave a programing Master's Men this morning. He said that it's not hard to live for God on Sundays and on Wednesday night; and we know what he's talking about. But there's Monday, and Tuesday, and most of the day Wednesday. There's Thursday and Friday and Saturday when you're out there in the world, and the world is not a friend of Grace; and it takes a lot of courage and dedication to live for God. We NEED the fellowship we find in the sanctuary of God. We need to get our Spiritual batteries charged so that waking out and face the frowns of a cold world another week.

We need the strength, the comfort, the preaching, the guiding; we need the music. Listen, everyone's got some music in his soul. Everybody can carry a tune in a bucket; some of us have trouble gettin' the lid off. But everybody's got music in his soul. We NEED the sanctuary of God; and may I hasten to add, the sanctuary needs you and me! Now, God can get along without me, but I can't get along without God. I need the encouragement that comes from being with God's people on God's day, with our thoughts turned toward Heaven and God's Holy Word. And so, with all that in mind, the Psalmist wrote in Psalms 122, "I was glad when they said unto me, let us go into the house of the Lord."

Now down in verse 7 is the text for this messa ge This became impressed on my soul a long time ago, I suppose for various reasons. I want to share some of them with you here this morning. This has become the heart throb of this preacher's soul. It's a prayer, really not a sermon. It's a prayer. The Psalmist was saying, "Lord, when I think of Jerusalem, let peace be there! When I think of Your Holy Temple, let prosperity be there. "My prayer for THIS congregation would be, "Lord, let THIS congregation dwell together in peace, and dwelling together in peace, let this congregation enjoy Spiritual prosperity. "

There is more said in the Bible about the peace of God, than most of us realize. I want to talk to you out of my heart and share some things which really lay heavy on my soul. Everyone who is here this morning, who is an adult, knows of some church congregation at this time that has either come through a rocky turbulent, divisive experience; or you know of a church congregation right now that's in the middle of a church family fuss. We've all known someone whose life has been adversely affected in a spiritual way because of division and discord in a church somewhere that divided and split. I don't intend to try to impose on everybody what I believe; but I do want to base my beliefs on solid Scriptural interpretation. Someone says, "I've known churches that just had to split in order to get along." Well, maybe that's true. Did they split over doctrine? If they did, O.K. if one of them had false doc- trine; but most churches don't split over doctrine. Most churches divide over the color of carpet that's put on the floor, or the color of hymn books that are bought, or whether they bought Stamps-Baxter hymnals for the congregation, or   Whether the choir wears robes, or whether you've got an organ. These are the things that churches divide over; or some person who fills an office. These are the things that churches divide over. Most churches divide over a preacher or a Deacon board, and neither one is worth dividing over, beloved! And I'm a preacher.

The church is bigger than this preacher! Heaven for- bid that the church should ever divide over me. I can ship out and go in peace and let the church move on! If there should ever be a division we can get down on our knees and pray and agonize with God and do some confessin' and some repentin' until the glory of God comes down and the division is removed and then we can part in peace.

There are reasons why I feel as strongly about this matter as I do. I've seen local churches divided; I've seen local associations divided. I've seen families divided. Someone has well said that the worst kinds of trouble are church trouble and family trouble. The tragedy of church troubles that some will live and die and never seek to bring about a reconciliation. I can take you today to community after community where division occurred years ago. Two churches of the same denomination stand in the very same community, often in sight of each other. The names the split selects are interesting. They're often FELLOWSHIP, or NEW HARMONY. They really ought to call them OLD Discord; that's more like what they are.

The first church I ever pastored as a twenty year old preacher was a split from an old established church. It was a good group of country folk, nearly a hundred miles from where I lived. I'd go up on Saturday afternoon and stay 'til after church on Sunday nights. Let me describe our meeting place. To get there, you had to go past the old established landmark Free Will Baptist Church that had stood in the community nearly a hundred years. Our meeting place was a converted dwelling house. Our sanctuary was a nominalize living room. One thing we had was close communion!

Those folks were really good tome, just a kid preacher. But it amazed me that here were those country farm folk who would work together during the week, they'd swap out work to help a neighbor. But on Sunday mornings they'd go to separate churches of the same denomination. They just couldn't worship together, though the churches were within less than a mile of each other. Both groups sang out of the same song books, preached from the same Bible, and talked   about going to the same Heaven. It got ahold of this young preacher's heart and I took it to God in prayer. I couldn't believe it was right; and it wasn't right!

Imlay have disappointed some folks, but I accepted an invitation to preach one Sunday night at the old original church. Still remember the text, First John 3:1. I certainly don't remember every sermon I've tried to preach, but I remember the glory of the Lord that accompanied that one. When the service was over, the folks got together and began to talk. They agreed to have a UNION revival, and we did! What a revival it was! With services both morning and night, as the custom used to be, the Lord had a chance to work. Grown men met in the church aisle, confessed hard feelings, asked forgiveness and embraced as brothers. Women did the same. The meeting closed. Both groups discarded their church books and started anew. The groups united as one, and together they tore the old church building down and built a new one. And it ought to be done over and over in lots of places!

You say, preacher, don't you believe churches sometimes are entitled to divide? Well, I'm looking for chapter and verse. If you ask me what I think, I think a lot of things that I can't find in Scripture. I want to be reasonable with you. When a church splits, one group goes one way; the other group goes the other way. They're gonna stay split, at least in spirit from there on out. And that's the truth unless miracle takes place. They don't hear the same preaching; they don't sit in the same services; they don't have any combined responsibilities; their conscience can become seared. It is a deadly serious thing for the church family to split! That's the reason the Psalmist prayed, "Peace- Peace be within these walls, and prosperity within thy palaces." Psalms119:165: "Great peace have they that lofty law, and nothing shall offend them. "In the first place, church people today ought to be more mature than the First Corinthian church and not get our feelings ruffled over everything that comes along.

Mark 9:50, Jesus said: "Salt is good, but if salt has lost its saltiness wherewith will ye season it? Have salt in yourselves and be at peace one with another." I'm not the first preacher ever to preach peace and I won't be the last. Jesus said, "Get some real saltiness in yourselves and be at peace one with another." John 16:33, Jesus said, "These things I have written unto you that in me ye may have peace. In the world ye shall have tribulation, but be of good cheer; for I have overcome the world. "Hebrews 12:14, the Christian race; the writer said," Follow peace with all men. "Now I've preached this sermon here 'til some of you can almost recite it by heart. But want to tell you, it's a lot easier to preach it up here than it is to actually get out there and live it. You take a bunch of people, if I asked you where you came from, some of you came from down south, some from up north, some from various places, and some of you grew up right here. And none of us grew up alike! My wife and I have three boys, and as far as personality and disposition, we knew the day we brought them home that they were each distinctive and different. And I want to remind us today, that even though we are in the same church family and we're taught to work and pray for peace, we DO have to overcome some actual honest-to-goodness differences.

If I wanted to dwell on the differences, I could do that from now 'til dark. For none of us are alike. Most of you do not part your hair like I do. Some of you are getting toward it, and if you didn't rob from one side and pull it all the way over, you'd be 'bout like I am. I used to pull it over there 'til I ran out of anything to pull. We're not made alike. My wife, I think, is an excellent cook. Her cooking pleases me. Now some of you fellows might be disappointed if you had to eat her cooking all the time. I don't think you would. We don't all like to eat alike. Somethings that some like, others won't even taste! You folks that like collards are welcome to 'em. Eat all you want. I prefer something else. We don't choose the same dentist, the same doctor. The doctor that one fellow uses, another wouldn't take a sick cat to him. We're different! We're different in the cars we drive. Now it doesn't make as much difference to me as it used to. Showmen something that will get 35 miles to the gallon, and I don't care if it looks like a bumblebee; I'll be interested in it.

We're different! A family goes out and finds a house that suits them and they buy it. Not another family in the church would have bought that house. But you did! A fellow gets a day off from work and one fellow will gather up his fishing rod and head for the lake. Another fellow will gather up his golf clubs and head for the golf course. Now if you ask me, "Preacher, do you think it's wrong for a feller to play golf?" Well, I sorta do. It's got to be a sin for a feller to be playing golf when he COULD be a-fishin'. We're different! Just watch it sometime, how people are different. I'm glad we're different. We don't look alike, we don't sound-alike. You know, one of the things that has always amazed me about our Heavenly Creator, is how He can make so many people and give us each so many distinct characteristics from everyone else. There's not another living soul in this world like me, did you know it? And there's not another quite like you. Isn't that amazing? No two of us are alike, except in general terms. And yet, here we are, all different, and the Lord has stuck us here in the same church. He says to us, "lay aside your differences, serve the Lord, get along with each other, and do it in peace and harmony."

I'm conscious of the fact that we're different in our spiritual tastes. When it comes to preaching preference we're different. Some people do not care much for a preacher who ever raises his voice or sweats a little. And others don't feel that they've heard preaching at all unless it was loud. The same thing is true in music. Some like it fast, some like it slow. Some think you haven't sung a song unless it's moved your feet; and others think: you haven't sung if you've moved your feet. I'm not interested in whether it moves your feet or not; it is whether it moves your heart that matters. Some songs ought Tobe sung fast, some ought to be sung slow. Some sermons ought to be preached loud and fast, and some ought to be soaked a little bit. Do you see? I hope you do. Here we are. God said, "Love one another. You're part of the same family. Live at peace!" You read the Epistles in the New Testament. It's a New Testament doctrine. "Let the peace of God rule in your heart. " And I want to take this moment to thank the Lord, and to thank you people that you have been as patient with me as you have been. In the years that I've been here, I've never yet come to a church business meeting with undue worry and pressure and anxiety upon my soul. I've never conducted business meeting in this church that I wouldn't have been glad for the Congress and the Senate, the Governor and his staff - I've never been embarrassed, or would not have been embarrassed to have had the leaders of our denomination to have been here while our people conducted our church business. Thank you for it. With all that makes us different, there is a tie that binds. And it has to be beyond ourselves, 'cause we can- not work it out, we cannot produce it within ourselves. And I want you to join with me in praying daily, "Lord, let your peace be within these walls. "

The last part of the text verse: "And prosperity within Thy palaces." David said, "Lord, let your people prosper." Now I've prayed for our people to prosper financially. And I believe The Lord's heard and answered prayers. I know you've all prayed for it, too. But if prayers are answered we ought to give the Lord the credit for it. We've not had' financial problem and I thank the Lord for it. Now, like most churches, we have some who tithe off and on, and there are some who will and some who won't. But God supplies the means. God has blessed and supplied, and I thank the Lord for that. Prosperity! I'm glad to see you get a promotion. Many deserve it. But I'll be honest and tell you that it makes me feel a little better to see a feller get arise if I'm pretty sure that God's getting His part of it!

Prosperity! May God bless you with physical,

financial, and other kinds of prosperity? But I'm most concerned about your Spiritual prosperity. And if you prosper spiritually, don't worry about the other. Now I cannot control runaway inflation; I cannot control the cost of living, or the interest rates. But to a great extent, I CAN control the spiritual state of my soul, and so can you. Any Christian ought to have sense enough to know when he's gettin' cold and indifferent, and half-way backslidden God. Now when I discover that I'm getting that way, and sometimes I do, I can get in and do something about it and get back right with God. Or I can go on and dry up and never amount to anything for God. The Psalmist prayed, "Let the people prosper."

What are the requirements for Spiritual Prosperity? They're very simple. Psalms 1: "Blessed is the man that walketh not in the counsel of the ungodly, nor standeth in the way of sinners, nor sitteth in the seat of the scornful. But his delight is in the law of the Lord, and in His law doth he meditate day and night. And he shall be like a tree planted by the rivers of water that bringeth forth his fruit in his season. His leaf also shall not wither, and whatsoever he doeth SHALLPROSPER." There's the key to it. The law of the Lord, the Word of God! Hide it in your heart. Let its precepts direct your life. The law of the Lord! That's the only basis on which we can have Spiritual prosperity.

Joshua, the successor of Moses, stood before his people and said, "This Book of the law ..." Listen, you can't prosper spiritually without being in the right relationship \\)iththe Word of God. You can try all the games, the gizmos, the gimmicks, and everything else that you know to try; but Spiritual prosperity only comes from the Word of God. Stand on the ROCK, beloved! Keep this church true to the Word of God. "This book of the law shall not depart out of thy mouth, but thou shalt meditate therein day and night that thou mayest observe to do all that is written therein. For then shalt thou make thy way PROSPEROUS, and then thou shalt have good success." (Joshua1:8)

Now there's one more thing I want to give you, then I am going to close. I don't think we've stayed away from the Word of God; I think we still love the Word of God. I think we still enjoy the Word of God. I think we ARE in danger of fulfilling what Jesus said when He predicted, "Because iniquity shall abound, the love of many shall wax cold." And in light of that, I want to give you II Chronicles, chapter thirty-one, verse twenty-two, "Hezekiah, and in every work that he began in the service of the house of God, and in the law, and in the commandments to seek his God, he did it WITH ALL HIS HEART AND PROSPERED." I don't think a preacher's worth driving to listen to, unless he puts all he's got into his preaching.

I don't think a teacher deserves to see a class grow unless that teacher puts out his best. I don't think a choir is worth the performance if they just go through the motions. Do it with your heart, beloved. I don't think a football game is worth paying the price of admission, just to see a bunch of fellows get out there and go through the routine. PUT YOUR HEART INTO IT! And that's what's wrong with many today. No heart in it. "Hezekiah, in every work that he began in the house of God, in the law, in the commandments, to seek his God, he did it with ALL HIS HEART." O may God helps to be released, as one preacher has put it, from "The Menace of Mediocrity." Just satisfied to exist, while the table is spread. Don't be content just to crawl, when God wants you to stand up and run! This is my prayer today, "Peace be within these walls, and prosperity within Thy palaces." Let's bow our heads while we pray.

For Senior Saints
II Samuel16:1,

"And when David was a little past the top of the hill ..."Today, we honor our Senior Saints. Sixty is not old, but it is the age Paul spoke of in regard to the churches care of widows. IF YOU'RE SIX- TY ...Youkan remember when: One-room school houses were common; an 8th grade education was pretty good. High School qualified you to teach. AUTOMOBILES were still scarce.

Radios were not yet common. Phones were not much in use. Air planes were just coming into existence. IF YOU'RE SIX- TY...you can remember the one-row walking plow, the cream separator, the spring-house or well-house. Electricity was only for cities. T.V. and air-conditioning were unheard of. IF YOU'RE SIXTY ...youkan remember the great depression; you've probably worked for 50 cents a day or less. (But not nearly as many days as you've told your children about it.) You've gone by horse-back or by wagon to church. You kept cool by using funeral home fan. IF

YOU'RE SIXTY ...You can remember home-churned butter and buttermilk. You can remember some all-day meetin's with dinner on the ground. IF YOU'RE SIXTY ...you can remember Hoover, Roosevelt, Lindbergh, Babe Ruth, BILLY SUNDAY! It's not bad, being sixty! Life for most of us has been pretty good! As a Christian, we can testify to the Goodness and Faithfulness of God, Who has always given needed GRACE- A LITTLE PAST THE TOP OF THE HILL...

1. The Perils
Eccl. 12:3: "In the day when the keepers of the house shall tremble, and the strong men bow themselves, and the grinders cease because they are few, and those that look out of the windows be darkened, and he shall rise up at the voice of the bird, also when they shall be afraid of that which is high, and fears shall be in the way - the grasshopper shall be a burden, and desire shall fail because man goeth to his long home, and the mourners go about the streets." Passing the top of the hill may mean -creaking bones, aching joints, baldness, grayness, rootlessness, callouses, corns, bunions: snoring, stumbling, stubbornness. Stubbornness? Aw, not really. Most older people are just an extension in old age of what they've been all their lives.

2.. The Prayers
Psalms 71:9: "Cast me not off in the time of old age; forsake me not when my strength faileth."

v. 18: "Now also when I am old and grey-headed, O God, forsake me not; until I have shewed Thy strength unto this generation, and Thy power to everyone that is to come."

3. *The Promises* - Isa. 46:4:"And even to your old age I am He; and even to hoar hairs will I carry you: I have made,　　and I will bear; even I will carry, and will deliver you. "　　Heb. 13:5:"Let your conversation be without covetousness; and be content with such things aye have: for HE hath said, I will never leave thee, nor forsake thee. So that we may boldly say, The Lord is my Helper, and I will not fear what man shall do unto me. "

"Evendown to old age, all my people shall prove My　　Sovereign, eternal, unchangeable love; And when hoary hairs shall their temples adorn, like lambs they shall still in My bosom be borne."

4. The Provisions
Deut. 33:25: "Thy shoes shall be iron and brass; and as thy days, so shall thy strength be."Vs. 26-27: "There is none like unto the God of Jeshuran, Who rideth upon the Heaven in thy help, and in His Excellency on the sky. The Eternal God is thy Refuge, and underneath are the everlasting arms."

Lam. 3:22: "It is of the Lord's mercies that we are not consumed, because His compassions fail not. They are new every morning. GREAT IS THY FAITHFULNESS. "

5. The Prospects
A. Release - release from this body of clay, with all its imperfections and its limitations. RELEASE from its pains, its sufferings, the separations and heart-aches. "When comes to the weary a blessed release; When upward we pass to His Kingdom of peace; When free from the woes

that on earth we must bear, We'll say 'Good-night' here, but 'Good morning' up there!"

  B. Rest- Rev. 14:13:"Blessed are the dead which die in the Lord from henceforth, yea, saith the Spirit that they may rest from their labors; and their works do follow."

  C. Resurrection and Reunion

  I Thes. 4:13-17: "but I would not have you to be ignorant, brethren, concerning them which are asleep, that ye sorrow not even as others which have no hope. For if we believe that Jesus died and rose again, even so them also which sleep in Jesus will God bring with Him. For this we say unto you by the Word of the Lord, that we which are alive and remain unto the coming of the Lord shall not prevent them which are asleep. For the Lord Himself shall descend from Heaven with a shout, with the voice of the archangel, and with the trump of God: and the dead in Christ shall rise first: Then we which are alive and remain shall be caught up together with them in the clouds, to meet the Lord in the air: and so shall we ever be with the Lord. "

  Conclusion: The infirmities of advancing age can be a real burden. It is sad that so many Godly people spend their last days in pain and loneliness. However, we KNOW that a brighter, better day is coming for ALL God's children. He will not forsake His Own. Rev. 7:16: "They shall hunger no more, neither thirst anymore; neither shall the sun light on them, nor any heat. For the Lamb which is in the midst of the throne shall FEED them, and shall LEAD them unto living fountains of waters: and God shall WIPE AWAY ALL TEARS from their eyes."

Born To Die

The following excerpts are taken from this sermon
preached at FWBBC at the annual Bible Conference,
March 17, 1971.

"And the Word was made flesh ..."When I was a little boy
growing up in the hills of southern Missouri, I remember
coming into possession of a little brown-backed copy of the
Gospel of St. John. Since books were not nearly so common
in those days, I carried that little book of the
Gospel of John in a pocket. I recall that even as a little
child there was something about John 1:14 that fascinated
my mind. "The Word was made flesh."

I didn't understand it then; and neither do I
understand it fully today. But I'll tell you what, though I
don't understand it, I certainly appreciate it!

Some years ago when we were moving from
Pocahontas to Jonesboro, we had a little boy in the family
who really did not care about moving. These moves which

preachers sometimes make can be disturbing to little boys. A family in the church from which we were moving had a litter of pups. They thought they would do us a favor and give our little boy a pup. They did the little boy a favor; they didn't do me any favor at all! To cap it all off, the little pup was half Chihuahua.

This matter of naming a dog is a proposition. We wound up naming the little dog "Buckshot." He grew up to be as ornery as he could be. He was ill-tempered, he was stubborn, he was rebellious, and in general, a trouble-maker. He got hit by cars, he was attacked by larger dogs, and he just wouldn't die!

The only person in the family who loved that little dog at all (the neighbors didn't love him) was that little boy. He loved him. He was really the only friend Buckshot had. One summer afternoon, I remember it distinctly, this little boy was sitting on the front porch and Buckshot was lying at his feet, looking up, licking his lips, and rolling his eyes. The little boy patted him on the head and looked up at me and asked, "Daddy, do you suppose buckshot really knows that we love him?" I was glad that dog couldn't read my mind!

As I sat there, John 1:14 came to my mind. Suppose I DID love that dog, and suppose that I did want to tell him I loved him. I could say, "Buckshot, I love you," but he wouldn't understand. The only way· I could ever make him understand would be if I could be made like him, or come down on his level, speak his language. Then I could feel his hurts.

And when I read in the Gospel of John that the "Word was made flesh and dwelt among us" I recall the Word of the Lord that says, "Thou shalt call His Name Immanuel, which being interpreted means, God with us. "I believe when Jesus Christ came into this world in the form of flesh, human flesh that God was saying through Christ to a sin sick lost, weary world, "Though you have sinned, we still love you, and we want you to know that we do love you."

I've wondered sometimes why Jesus did not come in the form of an angel; but I think I know partly the reason. Simply because angels do not die. Jesus pointed this out when He said that "Ianthe resurrection they neither marry nor are given in marriage, neither can they die any more, but are as the angels." So Jesus could not take the form of an angel because angels don't die. But Jesus Christ was made in the form of human flesh, He took upon Himself our nature, as far as this flesh is concerned, the part that dies. "That He by the Grace of God should taste death for every man."

It is by His death that we are saved! A lot of people say concerning Christ, "He was a good Teacher, or a good Preacher, but that was all." And they put Him in the same category as Buddha, and Confucius, or other mortal men who   main shall be caught up together with them in the clouds, to meet the Lord in the air: and so shall we ever be with the Lord."

Conclusion: The infirmities of advancing age can be a real burden. It is sad that so many Godly people spend their last days in pain and loneliness. However, we KNOW that a brighter, better day is coming for ALL God's children. He will not forsake His Own. Rev. 7:16: "They shall hunger no more, neither thirst anymore; neither shall the sun light on them, nor any heat. For the Lamb which is in the midst of the throne shall FEED them, and shall LEAD them unto living fountains of waters: and God shall WIPE AWAY ALL TEARS from their eyes."

Christ Had To Suffer.
I Peter 3:18:

"For Christ also hath once SUFFERED for sins;" Oh, how He suffered! "The Just forth unjust, that He might bring us to God; being put to death IN THE FLESH."- "The Word was made 'Flesh.'"

The prophet Isaiah said concerning Christ, 'His Visage was marred more than any man; and His form more than the sons of men. "His visage, that's His head. That head was marred more than any other man. His form, that's His body. His body was marred more than the sons of men. Oh, how He suffered!-

The forgotten man in this whole story, I think, is Barabbas. Sitting in prison, condemned to die, Barabbas should have been on the middle cross. I don't know how Barabbas felt when he was informed that he had liberty to go. I think he must not have believed it! That may be what Isaiah had in mind when he wrote, "Who hath believed our report?" It's too good to be true! And Barabbas must have said, "What do you mean, I can go free? I'm condemned, I'm a criminal, and I'm guilty! The mobs crying for my blood." And the jail-keeper said, "But you can go free, because another Man is dying on your cross."

This, my friends, is the GOSPEL TRUTH! And the person who will believe it can walk out of prison a free man!

"And he delivered Jesus to be scourged." You all know what that means. Brutally whipped. His flesh was tom. His body was bloody. His head was beaten. He would have been unrecognizable had you not known who He was. Follow these proceedings as described in Matthew• 27. Verse 27: "Then the soldiers took Jesus into the common hall and gathered unto Him the whole band of soldiers." They're gonna make a big production out of this thing. They wanted all to be in on it who wanted to be. Verse 28, in shame it is written, "They stripped Him." They stripped Him of His garment.

Somebody said in mockery, "This is the King of the Jews." Someone laughed hideous laugh and said, "Who ever saw a king without a robe?" So they put a robe upon Him, a scarlet robe and they said, "If He's a King, we'll make Him look like a king." So they began by putting a scarlet robe on Him. Verse 29, somebody sneered and giggled and jeered and said, "Who ever saw a king without a crown?" He had no crown, so they made a crown of thorns to go with the scarlet robe. And upon His beaten, mutilated, bloody head they pressed down a crown of thorns; and they laughed in their fiendish glee. They said, "He looks more like a King now; He's got a robe; He's got a crown. This must be the King."

Someone said, "Well, who ever saw a King without a sceptre? " The sceptre's the symbol of authority. "If He's King,

He must have some authority. "And so, in utter mockery, they slipped a little willowy, bending, flimsy reed in His hand. They said, "Here's His sceptre. "

Now He has a robe, and He has a crown, and in His hand He has a sceptre.

They said, "If He's really a King, then He must have sub- jects." They said, "We'll be His subjects." They bowed the knee before Him in total mockery and said, "Hail, King of the Jews, "which literally means "Long live the King! "

'Bout that time, they got their fill. Verse 30 says, "They spit upon Him. And they took the reed, and they smote Him on the head; and after that they had mocked Him, they took the robe off from Him and put His Own raiment on Him and led Him away to crucify Him ..."

Look at the last part of verse 35:"They parted my garments among them and upon my vesture did they cast lots. And sitting down, they watched Him there. "

The drama of the ages was being enacted. But this

was no stage production; this was for real!

In mockery they said, "Heaved others; Himself he cannot save! " They said, "He trusted in God. Let's see if God will have Him. "

Now when I get to this point, I'm inclined to speculate a little. I want you to remember the scene, the setting. Jesus, hanging on a cross ...the Son of God! He was with the Father when the worlds were made 'cause "Ianthe beginning was the WORD and the WORD was with God! And the Word WAS God! "Now here come the enemies; the jeering, mocking crowd. They said, "Let's see if God will have Him; surely God will have Him if He is the Son of God."

You know what the next utterance of Christ was? "My God, My God, why hast Thou (even Thou) forsaken me? "From His human side at least, I cannot help but think that Christ turned to the Father and said, "Father, You will have me, won't YOU?" And there was nothing but stony silence!

The blackest moment this world has ever known was that moment when Jesus yielded up the Ghost. The sun refused to shine; rocks rent, graves opened. "Well might the sun refuse to shine and shut his glorying; When Christ, the Mighty Maker, died for man, the creature's sin?"

I read this clipping some time ago. I think this happened in Atlanta, Georgia. 'An all-Negro cast was enacting its own free version of *Green Pastures.* To some, the language seemed careless, and some of the scenes appeared to be almost sacrilegious. But near the last scene of the play, a bolt of Heavenly light broke through. The Lord was sitting on His great white throne, high and lifted up. Before Him marched a blustering angel, up and down the golden balcony of Heaven. In his hands was a silver trumpet with a golden bell. Now and then impatient Gabriel would lean far out over the golden balustrade pleading, "Lawd, let me blow this here trumpet! Look at them poor, mizzable sinners, a fightin' and a killin' - Lawd, they's in an awful shape. Let me blow one toot on this home and windup the whole shebang!"

But the Lord protested, "Haldon, Gabriel; de Lawd am a-thinkin'. Do you reckon all that sufferin'down there might just mean de Lawd Himself gotta get down there and suffer? Too? "In shocked disbelief Gabriel remonstrates,"Lawd, you suffer? Why, Lawd, You ain't no mizzable sinner; you is the   King of the whole creation! "And then it happened. Blinding streaks of lightning flashed and thunder rolled across the scene. Slowly darkness fell over the shuddering earth. Far in the distance, 'the shadow of a cross arose upon a lonely hill.' Above the muffled roaring of a crowd and the whistling of the wind came one piercing woman's cry,"0, Lawdy, look at 'em! Look at 'em! Look at 'em nail Him to dat cross! "

Back to the center of the scene came one light to play upon the face of "de Lawd" upon the throne. Gone was the golden   crown, and in its place crown of thorns! Down the agonized face came the livid streams of His Own blood. His lips moved. "Yes, Gabriel, that's just what it means. It means 'de Lawd' Himself gonna suffer most of all."

"And the Word was made flesh" in order that He might die! I don't ever read Matthew 27 anymore but what I also turn to Revelation 19. I don't want to leave Christ in that pitiful mess!

I don't want to leave Him in the grave. I don't want to leave Him in the hands of His enemies.

Now the scene has changed. Whether the scene in Revelation 19 is figurative, that's beside the point! John said, "And I saw Heaven opened, and behold, a white horse." And this is not any measly donkey like He rode down the streets of OLD Jerusalem. He's riding down the streets of New Jerusalem now on a white horse, a symbol of power and authority. "And He that sat upon him was called FAITHFUL and TRUE and in righteousness He doth judge and make war. His eyes were as a flame of fire and on His head were MANY crowns . . ." And not one of them a crown of thorns! "And Head a Name written that no man knew but He Himself and He was clothed with a vesture dipped in blood." Not the vesture that men gambled for, either! "And His Name is called THE WORD OF GOD!"

The Word that was in the beginning with God, the Word that was God, the Word that had become flesh and had dwelt among us and had gone to the cross and died for us, His Name is called "The Word of God." "And the armies which were in Heaven followed Him upon white horses clothed in fine linen white and clean. And out of His mouth goeth a sharp sword that with it He should smite the nations. And He shall rule them with a rod of iron, and He treadeth the winepress of the fierceness and wrath of Almighty God; and He hath on His vesture and on His thigh a Name written,   KING   OF KINGS ANDLORD OF LORDS!"

The Word was made flesh; and God said, "I love you." And Christ died in OUR Place. "Down from His glory, ever living story; My God and Saviour came, and Jesus was His Name. Born in a manger, to His Own a stranger; A Man of sorrows, tears and agony. Without reluctance, Flesh and blood His substance, He took the form of man, revealed God's hidden plan; 0 glorious mystery, Sacrifice of Calvary; and now I know   Thou art the great I AM!"

The Discipline of Salvation.

Somebody said not long ago, "This is the most un-disciplined generation that ever lived." Maybe that is true. We need to be reminded that Jesus said. "If any man will come after me, let him deny himself and take up his cross and follow me." Paul wrote in Titus, chapter two, "For the Grace of God that bringeth Salvation hath appeared unto all men, teaching us that denying ungodliness and worldly lusts, we should live soberly, righteously, in this present world." That is discipline!

But where is the discipline in our day? Where is the dedication? Where is the cross-bearing? The first-century Christians lived lives that were characterized by discipline and dedication. We desperately need the same in our day!

I grew up under old-fashioned country hill preaching that just scared the day-lights out of me; and I really believe the right kind of preaching ought to scared fellow a little bit. They made me believe that if I didn't shape up and live right, if I died in my sins I stood in great danger of going to hell. And I'm glad they preach edit that way. One of the things they emphasized was that when a fellow got saved he was supposed to act and live like it.

We're living in the generation that says, "I've gotta be me, I did it my way, and don't fence me in."

As a result of this philosophy, we've got churches filled with "Wandering Stars,"

"Trees with no fruit," "Clouds with no water."

We've got too many births with no labor pains of repentance and conviction. We see sports figures and so-called "celebrities" get religion. They get up and give a testimony and, figuratively, if not literally, they hold the Bible in one hand and the "bottle" in the other.

Entertainment personalities get religion, but they go on entertaining in the night club, or wherever they want to. I read the account of one female entertainer not long ago. She said she really had a problem. She had made a profession of faith in   Christ. She had a commitment in Las Vegas. She said, "I wrestled with the decision, didn't really know what to do; I felt like I ought to get out of it." But she said, "I finally came to this conclusion: I'll go ahead and I'll perform, and I'll conclude my program with a religious hymn." And she went ahead to say that it {the singing of a hymn) was the most popular thing.

But where is the cross? Where is the discipline of the cross?

It doesn't make a bit of difference whether it's a sports figure making a million dollars a year, {which is about nine hundred and ninety thousand more than they are worth) or whether it's somebody like you and me who have been called upon to leave the things of the world and follow Christ. There's a cross to bear! Thank God that we still have in our hymn books, the blood and the cross. But we had better have it in more than the lyrics that we sing: we had better have it in the lives that we live!

I've lived in the greatest days of our denomination. I remember in 1952, a young couple, Carlisle and Marie Hanna, took their newly born daughter, Sheila Marie, and went to India. I was pastor of the church in St. Louis where Marie and her parents were members. I'll never forget a few months after they left, a telegram came. Sheila Marie had taken dysentery and suddenly died. Every time ·I see Carlisle and Marie I can- not help thinking how much they and some others as Foreign Missionaries have been called upon to bear.

Are the demands and discipline of Salvation any greater for missionaries than for a church member here in the home-land? I'm speaking to us tonight about things that really matter. I don't have any right to dictate to God where I'll go, or under what conditions I'll serve! But while we send our missionaries to a foreign land for four years at a time, their children can die, their parents can die, conditions can get terrible; and we say to them, "You stay on the mission field for four years." And here in the homeland, we've got multitudes of church members who haven't been in church FOUR SUNDAYS straight.

There's the discipline of FAITHFULNESS. Do you remember that Jesus, the Captain of our Salvation, was made perfect through suffering? Are we, His servants, greater than" our Lord? I admonish you and me, beloved, hang in there! The Captain of our Salvation DIED at His post. I want to die where the Lord wants me to die; and I want to be doing when that moment comes what the Lord wants me to be doing!

John chapter six is an interesting chapter. It begins with Meat, Miracles, and a Multitude. You deal in meat and miracles, and you can get a multitude! But when the chapter ends, the meat's played out; the miracles have ceased, the multitude is dispersed, and the Lord Jesus is saying to a handful of Disciples, "Will ye also go away?"

I read the story the other day of Elisha when he was called to follow Elijah. He was ploughing with twelve yoke of oxen. Elisha was a big farmer. Elijah came by and cast the mantle of the prophet upon him. Elisha said, "Let me go and kiss my father and my mother. And then I'll follow you." And he did. Can you imagine Elisha coming home and he embraced his father and his mother and said, "Mother, I won't be seeing you now for a while? Dad, I'm going and I won't be seeing you any time soon." "Where are you going, son?" "I'm just going wherever the Lord wants me to go. The Lord has called and I must go! "He slew a pair of oxen;

he built an altar. He forsook his profession. He forsook his possessions. He kissed his dad and mom good-bye, and multitudes of people tonight have never kissed anything good-bye! "Must I be carried to the skies on flowery beds of ease, while others fought to win the prize, and sailed through bloody seas?" No!

There is the discipline of DILIGENCE. Free Will Baptist doctrine emphasizes diligence. Peter did, too. He wrote: "Besides this, giving all diligence." He then admonished that we add these Christian graces ... Virtue, knowledge, temperance, Godliness, brotherly kindness, charity... "For if these things be in you and abound they make you that ye shall neither be barren nor unfruitful in the knowledge of the Lord. He that lacked these things is blind and cannot see afar off and has forgotten that he was purged from his old sins. "

Now what's the opposite of diligence? I think its neglect.

And the writer of Hebrews asks this question, "How shall we escape if we neglect so great Salvation? " Sinners REJECT. Christians NEGLECT. Be diligent! How are we going to escape if we neglect?

There's the discipline of SEPARATION. I don't know how separated we can get. I'm sure that none of us are as much separated from this world as we ought to be. I'm not like they used to say about the Puritans. When ice cream came along they said the Puritans wouldn't eat it. They said nothing could taste that good without being sinful!

The Bible does say, "Be not conformed to this world." And again it is written, "Having these promises dearly beloved, let us cleanse ourselves from all filthiness of the flesh and spirit perfecting holiness in the fear of God. "

"The church and the world walked far apart on the changing shores of time; the world was singing a giddy song; the church a hymn sublime.

'Come, give me your hand,' cried the merry world, 'And walk with me this way.'

But the good church hid her snowy hand And s olemnly answered 'Nay.'"

The following verses describe the compromise of the church as she gives in to the allurements and temptations of the world, and the final sad conclusion can be stated like this:

"The sons of the world and the sons of the church, Walked closely, hand and heart; And only the Master who knoweth all, Could tell the two apart. "

I'd like to say last of all a few things about the DESTINY of salvation. God gets kicked around down here. His Name is blasphemed. Jesus Christi's still the Rejected Redeemer. He's ruled out of the class room. He gets a raw deal in the court room by the judge and the jury. Entertainers would be hard- pressed to come up with a line if it were not for "hell" or God. Or some vulgarity.

Sermons, Sayings and Such

Some of you have heard Dr. R.G. Lee's message, "Pay Day Some Day." I listen to it every once in a while. Ahab is going on in his sin. The blood of Naboth has not been avenged, and Jezebel is going her merry way. Justice seems to have been aborted.

I can hear this old preacher as he cries out, "Where is God?

Where is God? Is He deaf that He cannot hear? Is He blind that He cannot see? Is He paralyzed that He cannot move? "

No, God's not blind, or deaf, or paralyzed. We know where God is. He is still where He's always been. One of these days it is going to all be over down here, and God's going to have His way! The LAST chapter is the most interesting and exciting! 'Cause when you read the last chapter you know how it's all going to turn out.

A few years ago during one of our Arkansas State Ministers' Retreats, I was staying in a motel room with some of our state's younger preachers. During this time, Arkansas' Razor- backs were playing Texas A M's basketball team in a very important conference game. The game was shown on a delayed telecast. That means the game was already over when the telecast started, and the score was already determined.

I knew what the score was. I already knew who the winner was. The game had been won by one point, and I knew which team had the victory! So I went to bed and went to sleep!

If I didn't know how this thing was going to turn out, I'd have a nervous breakdown. I know! I've read the last chapter. I'm not alarmed about how it's going to turn out. I know who is going to be on the victory side.

I'd like to talk to Daniel for a moment. He seemed to have a special insight. Daniel? ...He said, "There'll be a time of trouble like there never has been." But he's got more to say than that. How about it, Daniel? Daniel says, "The saints ...the saints of the most High shall take the Kingdom and possess the Kingdom ... forever, even for ever and ever." And I like that!

Jesus said, "Fear not, little flock; it's your Father's good pleasure to give you the Kingdom. "

John, the isle-of-Patmos John? "After this I beheld and lo, a great multitude which no man could number of kindred's and people and tongues stood before the throne and before the Lamb clothed with robes and palms in their hands and cried with a loud voice, SALVATION to our God Which sitteth upon the throne, and unto the Lamb."

What's it like, John? John said, "They shall hunger no more, neither thirst any more, neither shall the sun light on them nor any heat; for the Lamb Which is in the midst of the throne shall feed them and shall lead them unto fountains of living waters and God shall wipe away all tears from their eyes."

Another look, John. "And I saw Heaven opened, and behold a Whitehorse and He that sat upon ·him was called, FAITHFUL and TRUE. And He hath on His vesture and on His thigh Name written, KING OF KINGS AND LORD OF LORDS.

The last chapter of this whole thing turns out well. The   saints take the Kingdom. Christ reigns as King. God is still the Almighty. The prophets have learned about that Salvation of which they enquired. The Master's minority has become a mighty multitude. We lay down the cross and take up the crown. We quit our sighing and start singing. And we proclaim "Worthy is the Lamb."

I close with this benediction: "Unto Him that loved us and washed us from our sins in His Own blood; and hath made us Kings and Priests unto God and His Father, to Him be glory and dominion for ever and ever. A-men. "

How to Know You're Really Saved

(Written for *Contact* magazine and was
published July, 1983)

The importance of this matter cannot be overstated. The subject under consideration brings into focus such serious matters as life and death, Heaven and Hell, time and Eternity. SAVED - a word to rejoice the heart. It's amazing how often the word appears in sacred Scriptures. When it comes right down to the matter of what is important and what is not, the matter of being saved is the ultimate. That's why the Lord Jesus came, to be the Saviour of men. "For the Son of Man is come to seek and to save that which was lost. " (Luke 19:10)

Can a person really know he is saved? Years ago I ran across three words which often surface in any serious discussion dealing with Salvation and assurance - FACT, FAITH and FEELING. From a Biblical viewpoint, the least important of the three is feeling. Unfortunately, the "feeling" often gets the most attention, since we are emotional beings.

It's great to feel good -Spiritually, emotionally, or physically. However, we are not healthy because we feel well; we feel well as a result of being in good health. Likewise, we are not saved because we feel good. We feel good because we're saved. The FACT and the FAITH deserve the greater attention. Someone has written, "For feelings come and feelings go: And feelings are deceiving. My warrant is the Word of God; Naught else is worth believing."

Our final and only reliable authority is the Word of God.

What God says is true. You can depend on it. You can rest the case of your personal Salvation upon God's Word. That's the fact! Any doubts or misgivings that arise must somehow be traced to a flaw in our faith. Let's get the facts straight. Jesus said, "He that believeth and is baptized shall be saved." (Mark16:16 a) Paul agreed, "Believe on the Lord Jesus Christ and thou shalt be saved." (Acts 16:31) Again Paul wrote in that familiar Romans 10:8 passage, but what saith it? The Word is nigh thee, even in thy mouth, and in thy heart: that is, the Word of Faith, which we preach; That if thou shalt confess with thy mouth the Lord Jesus, and shalt believe in thine heart that God hath raised Him from the dead, thou shalt be saved. For with the heart man believeth unto righteousness; and with the mouth confession is made unto Salvation. "

The Word of God is plain, pure, and positive on the formula and fact of salvation. And yet, that old demon, DOUBT, raises his unwelcome head and disturbs our peace time and again. The Devil even tried to work it on the Lord. Following a forty day fast, Satan prefaced his propositions with an IF - "If Thoub the Son of God. " Jesus was hungry. He was alone. He would never be in a more vulnerable position for this particular attack, and the Devil knew it! It offers little comfort, but the Devil knows you and me. He knows where we live, where we go; he knows our weaknesses, and if we have any, our strengths. Against him, it's a mismatch. As much so as David facing Goliath. And unless we know the Word, believe the Word, and use the Word, we're sunk!

The Word says, "But these are written, that ye might believe that Jesus is the Christ, the Son of God; and that believing, ye might have life through His Name. (John 20:31) Our weapon is the Word. Jesus used it when He said, "It is written, Man shall not live by bread alone, but by every word that proceedeth out of the mouth of God. "(Matt. 4:4)

Sooner or later in· dealing with and sealing the matter of assurance, we must come to the book of I John. It is there we can base our closing argument and rest our case. The PRIVILEGE, the POWER, and the PRESENT reality of son· ship and Salvation are declared in chapter three. "Behold, what manner of love the Father hath bestowed upon us, that we should be called the sons of God." (I John 3:1) "Beloved, NOW (a present reality) are we the sons of God, and it doth not yet appear what we shall be: but we know that when He shall appear, we shall be like Him; for we shall see Him as He is." (v.2) the matter of right living must be recognized in dealing with the subject under consideration. Any professed Christian who is living life of waywardness and worldliness will be devoid of any real substantive Biblical assurance. John goes ahead to write in verse three, "And every man that hath this hope in him purifieth himself, even as He is pure." Again, we take note of Me John 2:3-5:"And hereby we do know that we know Him, if we keep His commandments. He that saith, I know Him, and keepeth not His commandments, is a liar, and the truth is not in him. But who so keepeth His word, in him verily is the love of God perfected: hereby know we that we are in Him." Consider I John 5- "He that believeth on the Son of God hath the witnessing himself. " (v. 10)"He that hath the Son hath life. " (v. 12) "These things have I written unto you that believe on the Son of God; that ye may know that ye have eternal life, and that ye may believe on the Name of the Son of God." (v. 13)

Why, then, with all these and many other verses of "Blessed Assurance" should we walk through the valleys where "doubts arise and fears dismay?" The answer: weakness in the Word, feebleness in the faith, or waywardness in our walk. "Christian, stay in the Word. For "Faith cometh by hearing, and hearing by the Word of God. "Little wonder it is written. "Above all, taking the shield of faith, wherewith ye shall be able to quench all the fiery darts of the wicked. And take the helmet of Salvation and the Sword of the Spirit, which is the Word of God. " (Eph.6:16-17) Years ago while living in St. Louis, an elderly lady who was a member of our church found her faith being attacked by one who was peddling poisonwood- trine. The old Christian veteran would not be shaken. In describing her encounter with the man and his error, she simply, but boldly affirmed, "I just put the Scriptures to him. "Shortly before my preacher father died, I asked him in the midst of a long and lonely night," Dad, are you afraid? "Withal voice reflecting triumph borne out of trust he answered, "What have I got to be afraid of? I've just taken God at His Word." And so must we all, if we are to live above the clouds of fear and doubt.

But if we live by the Word and keep our faith strong and growing, we not only can sing, but truly experience the full meaning of "Blessed Assurance, Jesus is mine; Oh, what a foretaste of Glory Divine. Heir of Salvation, purchase of God, Born of His Spirit, washed in His blood." And that can be our "Story and Song, Praising the Saviour all the day long!

I Remember Mama

I remember Mama.   I remember the soothing touch of her hand on my fevered brow in the middle of the night.

I remember her work. Mothers are such busy people! In the summer time, I remember her in the blackberry patch with a well-filled bucket hanging from her arm; she was a good picker, my mom. In late summer I remember her beating a sack of dried beans; that's the way she'd get them out of the hull. I remember her picking the geese. Was there not a house which was full of tired heads needing a pillow, or a featherbed?

A lot of things I remember about Mama: home-made soap, hominy, mullin tea. I remember   her sitting by the old crock churn, rhythmically plunging the dasher up and down, until at last there was the lump of butter, and, of course, the butter milk. I remember her sitting by the dim light of a kerosene lamp, sewing, reading, or patching a pair of overalls. Those knees sure wore out in a hurry, but how can a boy play marbles without getting on his knees?

I remember Mama's prayers. They usually began, "Our Father, Which art in Heaven, Hallowed be Thy Name ..."I remember her words of counsel and wisdom; was it not Mama whom God had chosen to speak to us about becoming Christians?

I remember Mama's songs. She always had a song. Times might be hard; one of the children might be sick, but Mama always had a song. Over the wash-board Mama sang, "Heaven Holds all to me," and "In the Morning of Joy." When Daddy was gone, she sang. When the cows got out, she sang. Mama never lost her song.

I remember Mama's tears. Yes, a mother's heart is often moved to tears. I remember those last precious hours she spent with Father. She would not sleep; didn't she say, "There'll be plenty of time to sleep after he's gone"? She was right. In looking back now, it seems she was always right.

I believe God will remember Mama. Does He not have a prepared place somewhere in His great Heaven for all Godly, Christian mothers? Surely, He does. MOTHER'S DAY is yet to come.

I Remember Papa

"Papa" -quite a man! Had he been a tree, I think he would have been an oak: hard, tall, and with many overhanging branches. Had he been a stone, I think he'd have been granite. As a man he stood straight in stature and solid in character. He was strong, yet gentle; firm, but compassionate. He was often serious. But seldom sour.

He cut no corners and he pulled no shady deals. He was poor, but proud; he accepted the honors that came his way with humility and when he suffered defeat he maintained his dignity. The banker trusted him. Neighbors confided in him and sought his counsel. When he spoke, others listened. Thrust on the sea of life in the midst of many contrary winds, he sailed through life's stormy waters with a fixed course. Resolute determination kept him off the rocky shoals. His eyes were always looking toward a goal higher than the stars. "Distance lends enchantment."

It's been many years since that early morning of March 7, 1957 when the icy finger of death stilled the voice, stopped the heartbeat, and closed the book on the earthly life of the man we called Papa. Memories linger. Influence lingers on. Glad for the privilege of knowing him as my father, it is with humility and gratitude that this son writes, "I Remember Papa."

He was strict, and sober as a parent. His family was his life. He loved "Mama" 'with singularity that was never questioned. He cared for his children and would have fought the most fearsome beast in whatever form to protect those of his household.

I remember him as a man fiercely honest. He met his obligations on time. He never walked across the street to dodge a creditor. He enjoyed a good joke, but was seldom frivolous. He preached with power. Sinners trembled and saints rejoiced. "A Poor Pilgrim of Sorrow, Tossed on this Wide World to roam," he spoke often of a city called Heaven and he determined to make it his home. He never flinched from responsibility. The greater the pressure the better his performance.

I remember Papa; at the supper table with his family, in the field plowing with old Dick and Red. I remember him behind the pulpit stand anointed with power to preach. I remember the comfort of his funeral messages and the conviction of his· revival sermons.

I remember the occasional fishing trips down on Beaver Creek or Gasconade River; the summer trips to places like Jefferson City or Alley Spring. I remember his prayers and I remember his tears. I remember his faith; a faith which, on his death bed gave him the confidence to say, "What have I to be afraid of? I've taken God at His Word."

I remember his stories of boyhood and youth; like traveling to Arkansas in a covered wagon, camping beside the road, picking cotton near Hoxie, or leading a cow down Main Street of Joplin, heading for Oklahoma- Indian Territory. I remember his absences as he went away to preach at week-end appointments or two-week revivals.

As children, we used to go to bed, pull up the covers, and out of the darkness, call out, "Good-night, Papa; Good-night, Mama. " Then we'd drift off to a peaceful sleep. In the morning we'd wake up to begin the activities of a new day. We recall with gladness the multitude of precious memories, and we say, "THANKS." Perhaps soon we shall awake to the dawning of a new, eternal day, and exchange our"Good-nights"for a joyous "Good-morning. "- We remember-"Papa. "

Nickels, Nails, Nuts Bolts

In recent years it seems that almost everybody has gotten into the "Jogging" mania. I've seen some on the jogging trail who looked as if they might be on the verge of collapse.

For this writer, it's not jogging that keeps the blood pumping. No sir! I'm not going to be caught dead from jogging. I've decided to take mine in a slower, more deliberate, and more meditative method ...walking! There are decided advantages in walking. Walking is good for the Spirits well as the physical body. A feller can do lots of thinking, looking, and living while walking.

Mine started some years ago while recovering from heart by· pass surgery. It was very slow at first; and not very far. Before long, however, the pace increased, and so did the distance.

On one of those first slow walks, I found a nickel.

Right there it was in plain sight. Now a nickel's not much, but it's too .much to just pass by. I picked it up and put it in a pocket.

Why, I can remember when a nickel would buy a bottle of "pop." A nickel at one time would buy a "Three Musketeers" candy bar. I mean, one of those that really had *three* separate bars under the same wrapper. A nickel at one time would buy lots of things. I guess it's the fact that I grew up during the "great" depression, but I still pick up all the pennies I find on the ground. And nickels, too, of course.

It's amazing how many nuts and bolts are strewn along the streets. Makes a feller wonder if some worker in Detroit or Yokahama must have missed a turn with a screw driver or a "wrench. I picked up a good size box full.

The nails, that's what gives the soul a lift, 'cause I've always believed that somehow it's the little things we do that really count in life. There just simply are not enough BIG deeds to occupy all of our time. And I seem to recall that the Lord said something about '...giving a cup of cold water in the name of a disciple. "And the reward for that was declared to be "a disciple's reward. "Whatever that is, it must be pretty good! There are lots of nails to pick up. Today I picked up one of those big-head roofing nails, the kind that can easily be stuck into a tire and cause flat. I've picked up 16penny nails, finish nails, big nails, little nails, you name it, and I've picked it up. AND every time I pick up a nail or a similar object, I somehow get the feeling that I may have at least kept someone from having a flat tire. Maybe even my own wife, or son; or maybe a teenage girl or a housewife who doesn't need to be on the city streets trying to fix a flat or change a tire.

Yep, there's inner satisfaction to be found in the "little things" of life. Now I'm like most every other preacher know. I like to preach to a Convention where the crowds are. But since that opportunity comes only occasionally, I'll keep pick in up nails; and nickels, too, if I see any.

Fundamentals of the Faith

And my particular subject is "Salvation. ·· Scripture Reading, Luke 2:25-32.Simeon, an old servant of the Lord, said,"Lord, now lettest Thy servant depart in peace, according to Thy Word: For mine eyes have seen Thy Salvation. "Paul wrote,"From a child thou hast known the Holy Scriptures which are able to make thee wise unto Salvation. "In dealing with this subject there are three points which I'd like to present.

First, the DESIGN; second, the DISCIPLINE: and third, the DESTINY of Salvation. The seriousness of this   subject grips my soul. Peter said concerning Salvation, "The prophets have desired to look into it." Isaiah spoke often of it. Jeremiah wept over it. Furthermore, Peter indicated that even the Angels desire to look into it.

The DESIGN of Salvation. I'm glad that it wasn't left to a committee of men to formulate a plan of Salvation.   I'm especially glad it wasn't committed to a committe e in Washington. If it had come from a bureau in Washington, none of us could understand it, and it would probably take five teen library shelves to hold all the books required to contain it. It was designed, not by man, but by Deity! It is so simple, so plain, that many an eight year old child can understand it and be saved. It is also so simple that many a Ph.D. will stumble over it and die and go to hell.

Remembering that Salvation means deliverance, I think of some Old Testament examples. There was the Ark in Noah's day. It was a matter of life and death; those who were on the in- side were saved; those on the outside perished. On the night of the first Passover in Egypt, it took the form of the slain Lamb, the sprinkled blood on the posts of the door.

As Israel stood on the banks of the Red Sea, it took the form of an East wind as God provided through His power and Grace that the waters should stand back. Moses had said, "Stand still and see the SALVATION (deliverance) of the Lord."

To Rahab the harlot in Jericho, it took the form of a crimson cord; and when Jericho was taken, this woman was spared, along with her household.

To us who are saved, the design of Salvation has been revealed for all time to come in the Person of Jesus Christ, Son of God, Who became Son of Man. He was the Person of promise in prophecy, of whom it was written, "There shall come out of Zion the Deliverer." The Deliverer DID come!

He is the Ark of safety from the flood of God's wrath in judgment. He is the Passover Lamb, the One Who stood as a Lamb slain from the foundation of the world. It is HIS blood that is symbolized by the crimson cord that runs through every Book and every chapter from Genesis through the Revelation.

We speak of the "plan" of Salvation, when in actuality it is more than a plan; it is really a MAN. "There is one God and One Mediator between God and men, the MAN Christ Jesus." The greatest mystery of the ages is that the Creator would become the creature; that God Himself could become one of us. That's exactly what happened. "Thou shalt call His Name Immanuel, which interpreted is GOD WITH US."

At His birth it was declared, "Unto you is born this day in the city of David a Saviour which is Christ the Lord." The Scripture reading from Luke gives the account of an old man, a saint of God, named Simeon. It had been revealed to him by the Holy Spirit that he should not see death until he had seen the Christ child.

There came the blessed day, the day when Joseph and Mary brought Jesus into the temple, an eight-day old baby. I don't know how Simeon must have felt. But as he embraced the Christ Child to his bosom, I think he saw more than a little baby that day.

I think he looked at those little hands: and looking through the years to come, I believe he saw that THESE were the hands that would bless the multitudes. These were the hands that would be reached out beckoning to weary world. "Come unto me, all ye that labor and are heavy laden and I will give you rest." And I believe, looking on a bit further, he saw "the shadow of a cross upon a lonely hill" and he saw these little hands that would be stretched out as a full-grown Man, nailed to a rugged, cruel cross to complete the plan of God's redemption.

I believe he looked at those little baby feet; and he saw the day when they would walk the by-ways and the streets and the lanes of the cities. But he also saw by the Grace of God the day when these feet would walk up a rugged hill called Calvary: and He would stumble under the weight of the cross as He went to complete the will of the Father.

Simeon looked at that little Baby head; and I think he saw the day when that head would be beaten; and upon that head there would he placed a crown of thorns. I think he looked into those eyes and foresaw the day when they would be filled with tears because of a Christ-rejecting world.

Jesus said to Zacchaeus after he had come down from the tree, "Today is SALVATION come to your house."

After Pentecost, Peter, the converted fisherman, said to a group of religious elitists, concerning Christ, "This is the Stone That was set at naught of you builders; Which is become the Head of the corner; neither is there Salvation in any other: for there is none other Name given under Heaven among men whereby we must be saved." And I'll tell you, friend that culls out an awful lot of folks! "None other Name!" It is the ONLY Name by which a sinner is saved and leaves this world to go to the Paradise of God.

The DESIGN of Salvation is Deity. It is not manmade. Consequently, it is a perfect plan of Salvation. It is broad enough to include "Whosoever Will."

When a Church Closes Its Doors
Published in *Contact,* November, 1981

Nobody knows how many there are. Some say that hundreds die each year. Most everyone can think of at least one. Some of us can call to mind the names and locations of several.

The heart beats with a saddened pace. A dead church is a sorrowful sight; especially so, if it is one of our own denomination.

IN RETROSPECT - There she stood, a building of simple design with elegance, beauty and charm. There was the day when men of the community came together to build a house for God. The sounds of hammers, saws, laughter and banter filled the air. From a plot of sacred soil there arose a living monument. A building was completed. It gave silent testimony to all who passed by, a testimony of

God's love for all men and a testimony of some men's love for God. Her doors opened. The people came. Prayers of dedication were offered, sermons delivered. Songs of Zion rang through the rafters of a newly- erected edifice. Saints rejoiced. Women wept. And even grown men sometimes wiped a tear with a red bandana. A community landmark, an old "country church" had its beginning. Revival meetings were conducted. Conviction fell and mourner sprayed at one of the front benches. There were baptizing's in the com- munity creek. Youth meetings (League Rallies, they called them in earlier days) were held. Poems were recited. Plays were presented. Songs -quartets, trios, solos and duets were sung. And as the meeting came to its close, an aged saint endowed with a spirit of exhortation would give a tearful, soul- wrenching admonition - "Children, come on."   And the children went on to become men and women for God.

Sunday after Sunday found the friendly folk meeting for Sunday school. Many a child learned his first Spiritual lesson as a member of the "Card" class. The pictures told the story- "Behold a Sower went forth to sow." Deeper theological sub- jects were discussed and probed by the adults. Young people met, fell in love, courted and were married. Sometimes little girls giggled, little boys talked or fell asleep during the long sermons. And the old church also knew her days of sorrow. A daddy died, and mother. A little boy's funeral moved the whole congregation to deep sorrow. Somehow, Heaven had to be real. No tears- no death- pure waters of life- streets of gold. For tired, weary pilgrims the church provided sanctuary - comfort and strength. When did the glory go? When did the lights and the life go out? And how did "Ichabod" appear - not in letters of Hebrew, Greek, or English-but in peeling paint, broken windows, woodpecker holes, bolted doors? If the erection of a new church building brings thrill of excitement, gladness, joy - then the desertion and forsaking of the church brings a feeling of sorrow, heartache, emptiness. If rising spires, fresh paint, open doors give testimony to God's Grace and glory, then a church that is closed, whose building is in disrepair gives testimony to the power of Satan, to the weaknesses and failures of men. Churches were not built to die. Something must have gone wrong.

POSTMORTEM: -How did it happen? When? Why? The Decline of some congregations can be explained in three words. Spats, Splits, and Splinters. Revival meeting shouts of praise somehow turned into business meeting shouts of anger. Songs of joy and Salvation were replaced with dispositions of jealousy and stubbornness. Some who once embraced as brothers and sisters found themselves merely glancing as rivals: members of the same family, but parties to division and faction. Over such a congregation the Holy Spirit solemnly, sorrowfully writes ICHABOD- the glory is gone.

The decline of others may be explained in less dramatic terms. It is hard to tell when it all started or when it happened. The congregation never decided to disband; it just dwindled. A few of the faithful kept on "keeping on" for a time. Then one Sunday no one came. No songs were sung, no sermon was preached, and no service was conducted. Revival fires that once had flamed no longer even flickered. Church members had become dying embers. A mixture of Old Testament. Israelite backsliding with New Testament Laodicean Luke warmness brought her low. Board her windows; consigner belfry to the bats.

While the demise of some churches may be explained by a population shift, a changing economy, or some other prevailing or passing tide of time, the fact still remains that churches are composed of people. If the people are dead or dying, so is the church. If the people are alive and abounding, the church will be living and thriving. Psalms 40:2-3 tells the thrilling account of a soul being brought from the depths of despair to the heights of Heavenly glory. "He brought me up also out of a horrible pit, out of the miry clay, and set my feet upon a rock, and established my goings. And He hath put a new song in my mouth, even praise, unto our God; many shall see it, and fear, and shall trust in the Lord." That's the account of a dramatic religious experience. As someone has put it, "out of the mire and into the choir." Backsliding, or losing it, is not that dramatic. But if we reverse the sequence, we will see how it happened. Praise is replaced with peevishness. The song goes and is replaced with a sigh. Unsteady, unfaithful feet stray from the Rock, and instead of established goings, there is wandering waywardness. And from the joy of the choir, it is back to the mire.

It happens to individuals; it can happen to preachers, Deacons, teachers and other church workers. Likewise, it happens to entire church congregations. Vision becomes dim. Zeal diminishes. The fires of enthusiasm smolder and another church dies. It didn't intend to do it. It never voted in a business meeting to do it. It just died.

Can these dead church bones live again? Some of them can. But God will have to find a preacher who, like Ezekiel, will "Stand up on your feet." And He will have to find some hardened church member clay that will yield again to the will of the Potter. May the Breath of God- Holy Spirit power- breathe upon every local church congregation so that the church in our day may go forth -"An Exceeding Great Army"!

"If I ever retire from preaching . . ."Which probably won't.

But I've given some thought to. What kind of a church member I would try to be.

First and foremost, I'D ATTEND FAITHFULLY: unless providentially hindered. I'd never allow the matter of whether or not we're going to church to be discussed 'round the breakfast table on Sunday morning. Just as sure as it was the Lord's Day, that sure we'd be going! I'd realize that my dedication was lacking if the matter of going to church had to be discussed and voted on periodically. It would be settled once; and it would stay settled!

As a church member, I would get there EARLY! I would not stir the Superintendent into a stew, or prod the preacher into a nervous wreck. Keeping them wondering if I were going to arrive on time. And since I was there a little early, I'd be right close to the entrance. And if a little boy.

Or a whole family should come in who were strangers and ill at ease, I'd make it my business to relieve the tension, show them where they should be, and try to make them feel at home.

AND when the service was over, I'd stay 'round for a reasonable time and mingle with the flock. I'd especially seek out some who hardly ever get spoken to, and I'd let them know that THEY were also a part of the congregation. And when I did decide to leave, I'd never scoot out a back door. I'd go right out by where the pastor stood. And I'd give him an encouraging word.

As a church member. Sitting in the sanctuary, I'd NEVER use the occasion to trim my nails (either finger or toe!).I'd do my manicuring in a more suitable place than the sanctuary.

And, I'd try to realize that those special provisions on the backs of the pews were BOOK RACKS, not depositories for gum wrappers. Candy wrappers, or dilapidated 81t2xll's that started out as church bulletins, got folded into airplanes of various designs, and after some successful flights and a few crash landings were not fit for flying any more.

As a church member, I'd sing in the choir 'til they throwed me out! I'd bring an offering. I'd say a hearty A-men at least once in a while, even if it broke me out in hives! I'd support the Master's Men! And if I were a lady, the Woman's Auxiliary. I'd study my Sunday school lesson. I'd make every effort to go on visitation. I would try to be the kind of church member that the Lord would be pleased with.

WELL. If you've stayed with me this far on my imaginary itinerary of "ifs" ... bear with me just a little longer.

If I had only one more word to speak... If I knew that I had ONE MORE WORD and that would be my last, know what that one word would be? THANKS! That's what I'd like my last word to be.

First of all, thanks to God Who has been so good! He's kept every promise, supplied every need, and guided every step.He'sbeen right there in every time of need.   He's given Grace beyond measure: and much, much more! Thanks to God the Father. And thanks to Jesus Christ, the Son. His presence. Has been so real, His companionship so close and warm. Thanks. Lord, for allowing this plodding pilgrim to lay his boyish head in YOUR bosom. And thanks to the Holy Spirit who has been everything that was promised He would be; especially, COMFORTER!

I'd like to say thanks to my family; the family into which I was born and the family over which I've had the joyous privilege of presiding as husband and father. Thanks to a wife who has been a true home-maker superb: a companion, a mother, a counselor, a friend. Thanks to three boys who have been a source of indescribable pleasure. And thanks to the girls who became their wives. Precious daughters!

THANKS to PEOPLE for being so kind and tolerant.

THANKS to churches that have called me as pastor or as a visiting revival evangelist. Thanks for the privilege of preaching in your pulpits. THANKS to church people for providing a fellowship that defies description. THANKS to a denomination that found a place in its arms for a clumsy, crude, clod-hopper, stammering, (and almost stuttering) country boy preacher. THANKS. If I knew I had only one more word to speak and then the curtain of death would close the book; just preceding the final period, I'd like to utter THANKS!

Short Snips

A Snow Sermon- First Chronicles 11:22 tells of a man named "Benaiah- the son of a valiant man of Kabzeel-also he went down and slew a lion in a pit on a snowy day." A MENACE ... A lion on the loose; no community can be safe with a lion walking unleashed and unchallenged. No parent could feel secure, knowing his little boy or girl was walking the lanes or by-ways of the community in which A LION WAS ON THE LOOSE! What a menace!

Such is the case in my neighborhood and yours! Drugs, Alcohol, unparalleled violence, murders, robberies, - the lion is on the loose!

THE MAN- Benaiah, which literally means, God's man, orthe man whom God made. We'reshort on that kind in our generation. God's man sees a righteous cause and invests himself in it. God's man cannotbe content to sit and wish. He'll lay his life on the line, and like Benaiah of old, he'll   go down and engage in a life or death struggle wit h an unrighteous enemy. He won't negotiate with a lion; he won't compromise. When the battle'sover, it'll either be God's man or the lion. It is a fight to the finish.

A MEANING... Benaiah slew a lion in a pit on a snowy day. He had no cheering section, no one to go with him to offer encouragement. But he went. Centuries later another Benaiah, God's MAN, the Lord Jesus Christ, went down in a pit ...the pit of death. Alone, forsaken, He went. He met and conquered earth's most dreaded enemy, death. And, thanks be to God, "Up from the Grave He arose With a Mighty Triumph O'er His foes." On Patmos He was seen and was heard to say: "I am He that liveth, and was dead; and, behold, I am alive forevermore, A-men; and have the keys of hell and of death."

*   *   *   *   *   *

Christ HAD to suffer. I Peter 3:18: "For Christ also hath once SUFFERED for sins;" Oh, how He suffered! "The Just forth unjust, that He might bring us to God; being put to death IN THE FLESH."- "The Word was made 'Flesh.'"

The prophet Isaiah said concerning Christ, 'His Visage was   marred more than any man; and His form more than the sons of men. "His visage, that's His head. That head was marred   more than any other man. His form, that's His body. His body   was marred more than the sons of men. Oh, how He suffered!

The forgotten man in this whole story, I think, is Barabbas. Sitting in prison, condemned to die, Barabbas should have been on the middle cross. I don't know how Barabbas felt when he was informed that he had liberty to go. I think he must not have believed it! That may be what Isaiah had in mind when he wrote, "Who hath believed our report?" It's too good to be true! And Barabbas must have said, "What do you mean, I can go free? I'm condemned, I'm a criminal, and I'm guilty! The mobs crying for my blood." And the jail-keeper said, "But you can go free, because another Man is dying on your cross."

This, my friends, is the GOSPEL TRUTH! And the person who will believe it can walk out of prison a free man!

*   *   *   *   *   *

The World is Against Christ. The Scientific world is against Him. Biological Science says that a virgin cannot conceive, having never known a man. But Isaiah proclaimed seven centuries before Jesus was born into this world, "Therefore the Lord Himself shall give you a sign; Behold a virgin shall conceive and bear a Son and shall call His Name Immanuel."

If you're going to take the miraculous and the Supernatural out of the Bible, then I say to you, you might as well replace it with a copy of *Aesop's Fables* or *Grimm's*

Fairy Tales! The Bible is more than a myth! It is the Book of Life! It is the Bread of life. It is the Book that tells you from whence you came and where you are going.

It is said that an atheistic sceptic confronted Mr. Gladstone and said to him, "What would you think if I should tell you that in ten minutes I could produce arguments that would utterly annihilate the Bible?" To which Mr. Gladstone replied,"I'd think about the same as I would think if I saw an ant crawling up Mt. Everest threatening to squash the mighty mountain with its weight."

The Bible lives on! Its critics come and go; kingdoms rise and fall, but the Bible is as real and as relevant today as it ever has been! And the Bible declares that Jesus Christ is God's Son, our ONLY Saviour!

* * * * * *

Last May (1963) our nation's latest Astronaut, Major Gordon Cooper, circled this earth twenty-two times. More than thirty-three hours he spent in outer space. After all those hours in space, he descended within four miles of a waiting ship. Men said, "Pin-point accuracy!"

But I want to take you across the annals of time to a shot that was far more accurate than that. In Galatians chapter four, Paul wrote, "But when the fullness of the time was come, God sent forth His Son, made of a woman, made under the law, to redeem that that were under the law, that we might receive the adoption of son." - Robe adopted as sons!

From before the foundation of the world Christ stood as a Lamb slain. In the Garden of Eden, Christ, the Seed of the woman was promised who would bruise the serpent's head. Althea forces of Hell could not keep Him from coming; and at the fullness of the time He came!

Before this world was ever created, God had a rocket on the launching pad, with its destination marked, "Calvary." The route was marked, "Bethlehem's Manger." The Pilot was the Saviour, the Lord Jesus Christ, at whose birth the Judean hills rang with "Glory to God in the Highest, on earth, peace, good will toward men." A new Star had appeared on the darkness of the earth's horizon; a pure, white Lily had grown on the stalk of humanity; and we believe that He was God in Christ, reconciling the world unto Himself. When it came time for Him to be at Calvary, there He was. When it came time for Him to come forth from the tomb, there He was, nail scars and all! When it came time for Him to go back to Heaven, away He went! And when it comes time for Him to appear the Second time, you had better be ready. He'll be on time!

*   *   *   *   *   *

A Right Relationship with the Holy Spirit ... Men say, "If only I could have lived in the days of Christ, or if only Christ were here upon earth in Person I wouldn't find any difficulty in following Him." But in our day, we don't walk by sight; it is written, "Wewak by FAITH." But even though we cannot see Christ in Person, we are not left in this world as orphans. Jesus promised, "If go away I will pray the Father and We will send you another Comforter which is the Holy Ghost, that Hemet abide with you forever. "

We have almost come to the point where we are afraid to speak of the Holy Ghost. We are afraid somebody will think that we believe in Him! The Holy Ghost is as real as Jesus is real. He lives. He moves. He teaches. He convicts. Yes, I believe the Holy Spirit convicts sinners of their sins. And the same Holy Spirit that convicts a sinner of his sins will also bear witness with our spirit after we are saved to give assurance that we are the children of God!

Yes, the Holy Spirit is REAL! He makes some people act funny. And some people act funny without Him. I've seen people who took the attitude, "If I can jump up and holler and shout, clear two or three benches, men will know I've got the Holy Ghost." Now I don't have anything against shouting. However, I've seen some folks shout who don't tithe! I've seen others shout who had to grab their"Kool's"to keep them from falling out. I haven't got anything against bench-jumping. If you've got to jump a bench, pick out one you think you can handle and jump it. But when your feet hit the ground, be sure you walk and live a Spirit-filled life. That's what the world is going to judge you by!

One of the fruits of the Spirit is LOVE. And one of the characteristics of love is HUMILITY! You remember the disciples sat around talking about who was going to be the greatest in the Kingdom? And while they were doing that, do you remember what the King did? He stooped to wash their feet! We need to remember that the servants not greater than his Lord; and he that is sent is not greater than He that sent him.'

Another characteristic of love is sympathy. There are none   of us, I suppose, who would not like to stand before crowd   and wave the Sword of God as we preached under the power of the Holy Spirit. But some of your best ministry is not behind the pulpit stand. Men may forget the message that you preach and forget the text you used. But you go into a home that is broken and tom with the cares of this-life, shed a sympathizing tear, warm, soft tear ... they won't forget your tears!

*   *   *   *   *   *

*A Proper Attachment t*o this world . . . Or perhaps should say, a .proper detachment from this present world. Someone has well said, "We ought to wear this world like a loose garment," ready to throw it off. With Abraham and the patriarchs of old, we ought to remember that we are pilgrims and strangers down here, and that we are just passing through!

The Bible predicts that "perilous times will come." These are the last times; and these are perilous times. But you try to make men believe these are perilous times! As long as we have PROSPEROUS times, you cannot raita men believe these are perilous times! You go hunt that fellow up who's got two cars in his garage and one of them's got a boat and motor behind it, a big bank account, and more leisure time than he ever had before and say, "Fellow, these are perilous times." He's living better than he ever lived. He doesn't know they're perilous times, because they are prosperous times! OH, how easily we can become too much involved in this world, and too greatly attached to this world.

The last temptation of Christ in the wilderness was a temptation to this world. The Devil showed Him the world and all its kingdoms and offered to give it to Christ if He would fall down and worship him. The Lord said, "Goethe behind Me, Satan!" He also said, "What shall it profit man if he shall gain the whole world and lose his own soul?" Paul wrote sorrowfully of Demas when he said, "Demas hath forsaken me, having loved this present world."

Not only should we guard against too much love for this world. We should guard against becoming too much LIKE this world. Paul wrote, "And be not conformed to this world." I used to think that a worldly-minded man was one who drank and danced and went to every show and did everything immoral. Of course, we all believe that Christian people ought not to indulge in these things. But there's many a worldly-minded man tonight who has not been on the dance hall floor for a long time; but he's worldly minded. He doesn't engage in immorali-ty, but he's worldly minded! All his love and affection are upon this earth. He has no concern for the world to come. He's not interested in Heaven. He's not interested in winning souls to Christ. He's worldly minded!

I don't want to get too well adjusted to this world! Someday we'll hear the sound of the trumpet, the sound of triumphant victory, with which Jesus Christ shall make His second appearing. "For the Lord Himself shall descend from Heaven with a shout, with the voice of the Archangel and with the trump of God. And the dead in Christ shall rise first. Then we which are alive and remain shall be caught up together with them in the clouds, to meet the Lord in the air: and so shall we ever be with the Lord. "

When I hear the trumpet blow, when I hear the announcement, "Time shall be no more," when I see Jesus comingin His glory, I don't want to be weighted down with the cares of this world! I want to bid it fare-you-well and go home to be with the Lord and with those who have goneto be with Him!

*   *   *   *   *   *

The World is Against Christ. The Scientific world is against Him. Biological Science says that a virgin cannot conceive, having never known a man. But Isaiah proclaimed seven centuries before Jesus was born into this world, "Therefore the Lord Himself shall give you a sign; Behold a virgin shall conceive and bear a Son and shall call His Name Immanuel."

If you're going to take the miraculous and the Supernatural out of the Bible, then I say to you, you might as well replace it with a copy of *Aesop's Fables* or *Grimm's Fairy Tales!* The Bible is more than a myth! It is the Book of Life! It is the Bread of life. It is the Book that tells you from whence you came and where you are going.

It is said that an atheistic sceptic confronted Mr. Gladstone and said to him, "What would you think if I should tell you that in ten minutes I could produce arguments that would utterly annihilate the Bible?" To which Mr. Gladstone replied, "I'd think about the same as I would think if I saw an ant crawling up Mt. Everest threatening to squash the mighty mountain with its weight."

The Bible lives on! Its critics come and go; kingdoms rise and fall, but the Bible is as real and as relevant today as it ever has been! And the Bible declares that Jesus Christ is God's Son, our ONLY Saviour!

* * * * * *

Last May (1963) our nation's latest Astronaut, Major Gordon Cooper, circled this earth twenty-two times. More than thirty-three hours he spent in outer space. After all those hours in space, he descended within four miles of a waiting ship. Men said, "Pin-point accuracy!"

But I want to take you across the annals of time to a shot that was far more accurate than that. In Galatians chapter four, Paul wrote, "But when the fullness of the time was come, God sent forth His Son, made of a woman, made under the law, to redeem that that were under the law, that we might receive the adoption of son." - Robe adopted as sons!

From before the foundation of the world Christ stood as a Lamb slain. In the Garden of Eden, Christ, the Seed of the woman was promised who would bruise the serpent's head. Althea forces of Hell could not keep Him from coming; and at the fullness of the time He came!

Before this world was ever created, God had a rocket on the launching pad, with its destination marked, "Calvary." The route was marked, "Bethlehem's Manger." The Pilot was the Saviour, the Lord Jesus Christ, at whose birth the Judean hills rang with "Glory to God in the Highest, on earth, peace, good will toward men." A new Star had appeared on the darkness of the earth's horizon; a pure, white Lily had grown on the stalk of humanity; and we believe that He was God in Christ, reconciling the world unto Himself. When it came time for Him to be at Calvary, there He was. When it came time for Him to come forth from the tomb, there He was, nail scars and all! When it came time for Him to go back to Heaven, away He went! And when it comes time for Him to appear the Second time, you had better be ready. He'll be on time!

*   *   *   *   *   *

A Right Relationship with the Holy Spirit ... Men say, "If only I could have lived in the days of Christ, or if only Christ were here upon earth in Person I wouldn't find any difficulty in following Him." But in our day, we don't walk by sight; it is written, "Wewak by FAITH." But even though we cannot see Christ in Person, we are not left in this world as orphans. Jesus promised, "If go away I will pray the Father and We will send you another Comforter which is the Holy Ghost, that Hemet abide with you forever. "

We have almost come to the point where we are

afraid to speak of the Holy Ghost. We are afraid somebody will think that we believe in Him! The Holy Ghost is as real as Jesus is real. He lives. He moves. He teaches. He convicts. Yes, I believe the Holy Spirit convicts sinners of their sins. And the same Holy Spirit that convicts a sinner of his sins will also bear witness with our spirit after we are saved to give assurance that we are the children of God!

Yes, the Holy Spirit is REAL! He makes some people act funny. And some people act funny without Him. I've seen people who took the attitude, "If I can jump up and holler and shout, clear two or three benches, men will know I've got the Holy Ghost." Now I don't have anything against shouting. However, I've seen some folks shout who don't tithe! I've seen others shout who had to grab their"Kool's"to keep them from falling out. I haven't got anything against bench-jumping. If you've got to jump a bench, pick out one you think you can handle and jump it. But when your feet hit the ground, be sure you walk and live a Spirit-filled life. That's what the world is going to judge you by!

One of the fruits of the Spirit is LOVE. And one of the characteristics of love is HUMILITY! You remember the disciples sat around talking about who was going to be the greatest in the Kingdom? And while they were doing that, do you remember what the King did? He stooped to wash their feet! We need to remember that the servants not greater than his Lord; and he that is sent is not greater than He that sent him.'

Another characteristic of love is sympathy. There are

none of us, I suppose, who would not like to stand before crowd and wave the Sword of God as we preached under the power of the Holy Spirit. But some of your best ministry is not behind the pulpit stand. Men may forget the message that you preach and forget the text you used. But you go into a home that is broken and tom with the cares of this-life, shed a sympathizing tear, warm, soft tear ... they won't forget your tears!

* * * * * *

A Proper Attachment to this world . . . Or perhaps should say, a .proper detachment from this present world. Someone has well said, "We ought to wear this world like a loose garment," ready to throw it off. With Abraham and the patriarchs of old, we ought to remember that we are pilgrims and strangers down here, and that we are just passing through!

The Bible predicts that "perilous times will come." These are the last times; and these are perilous times. But you try to make men believe these are perilous times! As long as we have PROSPEROUS times, you cannot make men believe these are perilous times! You go hunt that fellow up who's got two cars in his garage and one of them's got a boat and motor behind it, a big bank account, and more leisure time than he ever had before and say, "Fellow, these are perilous times." He's living better than he ever lived. He doesn't know they're perilous times, because they are prosperous times! OH, how easily we can become too much involved in this world, and too greatly attached to this world.

The last temptation of Christ in the wilderness was a temptation to this world. The Devil showed Him the world and all its kingdoms and offered to give it to Christ if He would fall down and worship him. The Lord said, "Get thee behind Me, Satan!" He also said, "What shall it profit man if he shall gain the whole world and lose his own soul?" Paul wrote sorrowfully of Demas when he said, "Demas hath forsaken me, having loved this present world."

Not only should we guard against too much love for this world. We should guard against becoming too much LIKE this world. Paul wrote, "And be not conformed to this world." I used to think that a worldly-minded man was one who drank and danced and went to every show and did everything immoral. Of course, we all believe that Christian people ought not to indulge in these things. But there's many a worldly-minded man tonight who has not been on the dance hall floor for a long time; but he's worldly minded. He doesn't engage in immorali-ty, but he's worldly minded! All his love and affection are upon this earth. He has no concern for the world to come. He's not interested in Heaven. He's not interested in winning souls to Christ. He's worldly minded!

I don't want to get too well adjusted to this world! Someday we'll hear the sound of the trumpet, the sound of triumphant victory, with which Jesus Christ shall make His second appearing. "For the Lord Himself shall descend from Heaven with a shout, with the voice of the Archangel and with the trump of God. And the dead in Christ shall rise first. Then we which are alive and remain shall be caught up together with them in the clouds, to meet the Lord in the air: and so shall we ever be with the Lord. "

When I hear the trumpet blow, when I hear the announcement, "Time shall be no more," when I see Jesus coming in His glory, I don't want to be weighted down with the cares of this world! I want to bid it fare-you-well and go home to be with the Lord and with those who have gone to be with Him!

* * * * * *

A Burial near Bethlehem . . . "And as for me, when I came from Padan, Rachel died by me in the land of Canaan in the way, when yet there was but a little way to come to Ephrah: and I buried her there in the way of Ephrah; the same is Bethlehem." (Genesis 48:7)

That's the way Jacob described the burial near Bethlehem. It must be mighty hard to bury your companion whom you love. Especially, when she's just given birth to a baby boy. Just think of the anticipated joy, the hope, the dreams, and the thrill of giving birth. And so near to Bethlehem. But there she died; and there Jacob buried Rachel.

But life DOES go on. It's not easy to leave the place of mourning, gather up the broken pieces, and keep moving. It's just outside Bethlehem where so many lose the victory. Disappointment comes in one form or another. Dreams and hopes crumble. Plans that were laid with so much expectation and excitement suddenly fall apart. And short of realization, they're buried.

The tragedy is, that so many don't have the courage it takes to leave the place of burial and move on. They stay at the place of death, mourning a loss and miss out on the blessings of life. Overhand over again, I've seen it happen. Church members give up on their church and bury all their religious hopes and activities short of Bethlehem. I've seen preachers become bitter over some particular set-backer disappointment, and bury all their ministry outside Bethlehem. I've known of young lovers who lost the love of their life; and all their lives they mourned the burial of a broken love affair, never moving from the place of bitterness and loss.

For some reason, it seems that Rachel, weary with the journey, wanted to make it to Bethlehem. But while still on the journey, the pains of hard labor set in. A baby boy was home but there by the road-side, Rachel died.

Centuries later, another weary mother-to-be walked similar road. She DID make it to Bethlehem. But even in Bethlehem, things were not easy. The birth of her Baby was not in the best of circumstances. HE, who came from Heaven's glory, was born in an ox stall and laid in a manger. But at HIS birth, a new star appeared, a new light began to shine, and a new hope sprang up. It is in HIM we have victory. In HIM we have hope. It sin the fact of HIS resurrection we have promise and prospect of ETERNALLIFE!

Friend, don't bury your hopes and dreams outside

Bethlehem. Anchor your faith firmly in Him who was the Babe of Bethlehem's manager, but who has become the Hope of all the ages, KING OF KINGS AND LORD OF LORDS!

• • • • • •

Don't Miss the Boat! The Arkansas State Highway Department some time ago opened a new bridge on Highway 62, spanning a section of Norfolk Lake. For many years the only means of crossing that part of the Lake was by Ferry Boat. The last time I ever crossed on that Ferry was past midnight after having closed a revival meeting in Fayetteville. The gas station attendant in Mountain Home remarked that the Ferry made only one trip each hour after midnight. It was a quarter 'til twelve.

Well, it was shortly after midnight when this tired traveler pulled down to the shoreline where the Ferry loads and unloads. It was a sickening feeling to see the boat no more than a hundred yards from shore, HEADING FOR THE OTHER SIDE! It would be an hour before it would return for another load. The wait was trying on the patience of a preacher who had been gone from home all week and was homesick.

There WOULD eventually be another boat. And I would get   home, although a little later than desired. But WHAT IF that were the LAST boat to sail toward home? I suspect ·that many a sinner has come close to getting on board. But closes not close enough. The folks we love the most, the family members, the place we call home ...it's all on the other shore! The "Ole Ship of Zion" is sailing for home! There's so much waiting on the other shore! I cannot afford to miss the boat!

*   *   *   *   *   *

Pride Gaeth... Bandit also cometh. Not many preachers would ever seriously admit to having a problem with pride. Most of us, in fact, are right proud of our humility! Of course. We've known a few brothers who seemed to us, at least, to be slightly afflicted with the pride disease. But we've prayed so often, "Lord, keep me humble," that this particular "deadly sin" of the Proverbs seldom, if ever, poses a problem.

HOWEVER, we are always subject to momentary lapses. Our humility sometimes becomes victim of passing puffs of pride.

Now you take compliments, for instance. We all secretly like them, and may even fish for them in a subtle sort of way. Most of them we can take and not get swelled up like a toad. Just once in a while, though, one may hit us in a weak moment and cause us to lose control of the humility we think we so carefully guard.

This preacher remembers a momentary lapse. The occasion was a revival meeting in Flat River, Missouri many years ago. I was the visiting evangelist.

The pastor had a young son, who at the tender age of seven or eight, seemed to be unusually bright. It was late March and early April. After the close of one night's meeting, with folks coming by and giving a good word with their traditional hand- shake, the pastor's little boy came by and blurted out so that many could hear, "Preacher, that was a really good sermon!" Wow! If filler can preach such a sermon that a little boy is so deeply impressed. .. Well, pride took control of the throne room for a moment.

It didn't last long. The little fellow came back with a hearty "Ha, Ha, APRIL FOOL!" Pride made a hasty exit. Humility found its way back through the door. And it dawned on me that the date WAS April 1.

*   *   *   *   *   *

Some "Impossible If's"
Maybe you've never in your life foolishly, frivolously, or childishly considered what you might do "IF" you could be the Lord for a while. Perhaps it's because the "little boy" in t s preacher never has quite yielded to the soberness and sound thinking that characterize fully mature, grown-up men, but I do think of it now and then.

Yep, I've given considerable consideration to some things I'd do IF I could be the Lord. When I mentioned this impossible "IF" tom wife, she said, "You wouldn't make a very good Lord!" that's true. But don't worry. The last I knew, there were not any vacancies in that position.

IF I WERE THE LORD ...I'd look down on Sunday morning, and where I saw Church members (especially Free Will Baptist Church members) still in bed at Sunday school time, I'd summon some angels who were not particularly busy. I would send them down and have them sprinkle the beds with a generous serving of itching powder! The sleeping saints would either get up or go to church where they should be, or I'd keep up the sprinkling with that itching stuff 'till they scratched to death. Laodicean Luke warmness if it's not treated can lead to lousy laziness!

IF I WERE THE LORD ... I'd look down on the Sunday morning congregation. I'd spot that feller who hasn't been honest with God and who has robbed Him of His tithe. While this brother's standing up with the congregation, singing heartily, "OH, How I Love Jesus," I'd have an invisible angel rip the thread from his expensive suit (which was paid for with the Lord's tithe) and as he stood there singing, I'd have both coat sleeves slowly slide off and drop right at his feet.

OR, for that family that drove up in a long, shiny, luxurious automobile which was paid for with the Lord's money, I'd have some angels unscrew a few strategic nuts and bolts and fix it so that both front quarter panels would fall off right in the church parking lot!

The possibilities are unlimited! But I think while I was at it, I'd have some tenacious termites tear away that portion of the house that was paid for with the Lord's tithe. And I'd be sure to get the point across that Christians CAN layup treasures in Heaven; and that it doesn't really matter that much whether we live in a cabin or a castle down here, because this world is not our home, anyway! I'd remind the pilfering pilgrims that they're just sojourners swiftly passing through!

And IF I were the Lord, I wouldn't take it all out on the Church going crowd. I'd deal with the other portion of the population, too. I would choke some of these so-called entertainers and comedians 'til they turned as purple as a turnip! I just wouldn't let them get away with their blasphemy and irreverence. Even in the name of entertainment. That old feller who plays "God" would come in for special treatment! I'd consider making another Saul of Tarsus of him, and get him under conviction right there before the T.V. audience, the Hollywood moguls, and the whole blasphemous crowd. I'd teach the whole bunch that it was not funny to ridicule righteousness, to desecrate Deity, or to poke fun at purity. Well, really, I think the Lord's had some of these suggestions in mind for a long time and has just been holding back. He's a lot more patient than I would be! I do seem to recall, though, that He did one time turn a king into an ox. At least, he got on his all fours and ate grass like an ox. It served a good purpose, too! It sure made a converted believer out of ole King Neb!

* * * * * *

Above the Clouds. .. Things are bound to be different in that world of the celestial that exists somewhere up there. It's not hard for a Christian to believe in Heaven. Nothing brings to life our belief in "The Land That is Fairer than Day" any · more than a funeral for a close friend or family member. It's not hard for us to believe in those moments that the resurrection is a reality.

January 19, 1978 was a cold, snowy, wintry day in

Central Arkansas. I remember it well. The responsibilities for that particular day included the conducting of funeral services for a thirty-nine year old mother who had died after a losing battle with cancer. My job included the task of bringing comfort and hope to a husband and three girls; a husband now without the companionship of a wife. And three girls with no mother.

Since the place for the funeral service was fifty miles or more   away, I found myself way before daylight in the softly falling snow putting on tire chains. What a day for a funeral. My thoughts were with the family and lumps kept coming in the throat as I secured the chains around the rear tires. Something in the distance caught my attention. Over in Little Rock at Adam's Field, a big jet-liner was becoming air- borne. The noise of the powerful jet engines pierced the pre- dawn atmosphere that had been so silent. I thought about the folks who were on that jet-liner. In a matter of minutes, if not seconds, they would break through the clouds. The snow and the cold that covered the earth would be beneath them. Above the clouds, the sun would be brightly shining and earth's snow cover would not be visible.

Maybe that's kinda how it is with our loved ones who died in the Lord. The unseen Gospel Ship with angels serving as officers and crew, momentarily stop to pick up a passenger. And in an instant the cares, the troubles, the daily grind of this earthly life are all shaken off. The body that has fought disease and lost, releases the soul and spirit. The real person takes a flight ABOVE THE CLOUDS to be with the Lord.

Well, really, I guess death is not such a bad thing after all. OH, yes, it leaves our family members and friends with a void and a hurt that only Christ can comfort and only time can heal.

But since Christ Himself came out of the grave and has been seen holding the keys of Hell and of Death, well, death's just not the frightening monster that it once was. It's still tiger, but one without teeth; it's still a beast, but one without claws; it's still a serpent, but one without fangs. ABOVE THE CLOUDS ...things are far different up there!

*   *   *   *   *   *

Nickels, Nails, Nuts, Bolts ... In recent years it seems that almost everybody has gotten into the "Jogging" mania. I've seen some on the jogging trail who looked as if they might be on the verge of collapse.

For this writer, it's not jogging that keeps the blood pumping. No sir! I'm not going to be caught dead from jogging. I've decided to take mine in a slower, more deliberate, and more meditative method ...walking! There are decided advantages in walking. Walking is good for the Spirits well as the physical body. A feller can do lots of thinking, looking, and living while walking.

Mine started some years ago while recovering from heart by· pass surgery. It was very slow at first; and not very far. Before long, however, the pace increased, and so did the distance.

On one of those first slow walks, I found a nickel. Right there it was in plain sight. Now a nickel's not much, but it's too .much to just pass by. I picked it up and put it in a pocket.

Why, I can remember when a nickel would buy a bottle of "pop." A nickel at one time would buy a "Three Musketeers" candy bar. I mean, one of those that really had *three* separate bars under the same wrapper. A nickel at one time would buy lots of things. I guess it's the fact that I grew up during the "great" depression, but I still pick up all the pennies I find on the ground. And nickels, too, of course.

It's amazing how many nuts and bolts are strewn along the streets. Makes a feller wonder if some worker in Detroit or Yokahama must have missed a turn with a screw driver or a wrench. I picked up a good size box full.

The nails, that's what gives the soul a lift, 'cause I've always believed that somehow it's the little things we do that really count in life. There just simply are not enough BIG deeds to occupy all of our time. And I seem to recall that the Lord said something about '...giving a cup of cold water in the name of a disciple. "And the reward for that was declared to be "a disciple's reward. "Whatever that is, it must be pretty good! There are lots of nails to pick up. Today I picked up one of those big-head roofing nails, the kind that can easily be stuck into a tire and cause flat. I've picked up 16penny nails, finish nails, big nails, little nails, you name it, and I've picked it up. AND every time I pick up a nail or a similar object, I somehow get the feeling that I may have at least kept someone from having a flat tire. Maybe even my own wife, or son; or maybe a teenage girl or a housewife who doesn't need to be on the city streets trying to fix a flat or change a tire.

Yep, there's inner satisfaction to be found in the "little things" of life. Now I'm like most every other preacher know. I like to preach to a Convention where the crowds are. But since that opportunity comes only occasionally, I'll keep picking up nails; and nickels, too, if I see any.

* * * * * *

A Burial near Bethlehem . . . "And as for me, when I came from Padan, Rachel died by me in the land of Canaan in the way, when yet there was but a little way to come to Ephrah: and I buried her there in the way of Ephrah; the same is Bethlehem." (Genesis 48:7)

That's the way Jacob described the burial near Bethlehem. It must be mighty hard to bury your companion whom you love. Especially, when she's just given birth to a baby boy. Just think of the anticipated joy, the hope, the dreams, and the thrill of giving birth. And so near to Bethlehem. But there she died; and there Jacob buried Rachel.

But life DOES go on. It's not easy to leave the place of mourning, gather up the broken pieces, and keep moving. It's just outside Bethlehem where so many lose the victory. Disappointment comes in one form or another. Dreams and hopes crumble. Plans that were laid with so much expectation and excitement suddenly fall apart. And short of realization, they're buried.

The tragedy is, that so many don't have the courage it takes to leave the place of burial and move on. They stay at the place of death, mourning a loss and miss out on the blessings of life. Overhand over again, I've seen it happen. Church members give up on their church and bury all their religious hopes and activities short of Bethlehem. I've seen preachers become bitter over some particular set-back or disappointment, and bury all their ministry outside Bethlehem. I've known of young lovers who lost the love of their life; and all their lives they mourned the burial of a broken love affair, never moving from the place of bitterness and loss.

For some reason, it seems that Rachel, weary with the journey, wanted to make it to Bethlehem. But while still on the journey, the pains of hard labor set in. A baby boy was horn, but there by the road-side, Rachel died. Centuries later, another weary mother-to-be walked similar   road. She DID make it to Bethlehem. But even in Bethlehem, things were not easy. The birth of her Baby was not in the best of circumstances. HE, who came from Heaven's glory, was born in an ox stall and laid in a manger. But at HIS birth, a new star appeared, a new light began to shine, and a new hope sprang up. It is in HIM we have victory. In HIM we have hope. It sin the fact of HIS resurrection we have promise and prospect of ETERNALLIFE!

Friend, don't bury your hopes and dreams outside Bethlehem. Anchor your faith firmly in Him who was the Babe of Bethlehem's manager, but who has become the

Hope of all the ages, KING OF KINGS AND LORD OF LORDS!

• • • • • •

Don't Miss the Boat! The Arkansas State Highway Department some time ago opened a new bridge on Highway 62, spanning a section of Norfolk Lake. For many years as a means of crossing that part of the Lake was by Ferry Boat. The last time I ever crossed on that Ferry was past midnight after having closed a revival meeting in Fayetteville. The gas station attendant in Mountain Home remarked that the Ferry made only one trip each hour after midnight. It was a quarter 'til twelve.

Well, it was shortly after midnight when this tired traveler pulled down to the shoreline where the Ferry loads and unloads. It was a sickening feeling to see the boat no more than a hundred yards from shore, HEADING FOR THE OTHER SIDE! It would be an hour before it would return for another load. The wait was trying on the patience of a preacher who had been gone from home all week and was homesick.

There WOULD eventually be another boat. And I would get home, although a little later than desired.

But WHAT IF that were the LAST boat to sail toward home? I suspect ·that many a sinner has come close to getting on board. But closes not close enough. The folks we love the most, the family members, the place we call home ...it's all on the other shore! The "Ole Ship of Zion" is sailing for home! There's so much waiting on the other shore! I cannot afford to miss the boat!

*   *   *   *   *   *

Pride Gaeth . .. Bandit also cometh. Not many preachers would ever seriously admit to having a problem with pride. Most of us, in fact, are right proud of our humility! Of course. We've known a few brothers who seemed to us, at least, to be slightly afflicted with the pride disease. But we've prayed so often, "Lord, keep me humble," that this particular "deadly sin" of the Proverbs seldom, if ever, poses a problem.

HOWEVER, we are always subject to momentary lapses. Our humility sometimes becomes victim of passing puffs of pride.

Now you take compliments, for instance. We all secretly like them, and may even fish for them in a subtle sort of way. Most of them we can take and not get swelled up like a toad. Just once in a while, though, one may hit us in a weak moment and cause us to lose control of the humility we think we so carefully guard.

This preacher remembers a momentary lapse. The occasion was a revival meeting in Flat River, Missouri many years ago. I was the visiting evangelist.

The pastor had a young son, who at the tender age of seven or eight, seemed to be unusually bright. It was late March and early April. After the close of one night's meeting, with folks coming by and giving a good word with their traditional hand- shake, the pastor's little boy came by and blurted out so that many could hear, "Preacher, that was a really good sermon!" Wow! If filler can preach such a sermon that a little boy is so deeply impressed. .. Well, pride took control of the throne room for a moment.

It didn't last long. The little fellow came back with a hearty "Ha, Ha, APRIL FOOL!" Pride made a hasty exit. Humility found its way back through the door. And it dawned on me that the date WAS April 1.

From The Threescore-Twelve and More

"THREE SCORE TWELVE" is a collection of writings that cover a considerable time period. Several of the articles are from the Mid-week News, which was a publication while pastoring North Little Rock's First Freewill Baptist Church. In retrospect, what a privilege to have pastored that church. And what pleasant memories!

Mrs. Scott, the boys, and I rolled into North Little Rock the last week of February, 1972. Little did we realize this would be our last pastorate and that it would cover a time period just two months short of 24 years.

There are no perfect churches, including North Little Rock. But I could wish for every pastor at least some of the blessings and benefits this good congregation afforded my family and me. There are so many good qualities incorporated in the structure of that church. I will always be indebted, but humbly thankful for the privilege of serving as pastor. That church has made substantial contribution to the cause of Christ and to our denomination. From a purely personal standpoint, it was a great decision and a great day when the church called a young college graduate, Mark Stripling, to serve as Director of Youth and Music. He and his family were a special blessing to this aging preacher and helped extend my pastoral tenure.

Having mentioned North Little Rock, I want also to say, as I retrace the pastoral trail, our family holds precious memories and cherish lasting friendships from Jonesboro, Pocahontas, Fredericktown, Mo. Oilton, Oklahoma, Third church, St. Louis, and all the way back to Mtn. Valley, that century old church nestled in the hills of Wright County, Missouri. We hold so many warm and cherished memories. And in retirement, it's a pleasure to enjoy the warm fellowship of Sutton church, where our membership is now.

During the few years of retirement from pastoral service, it has been a privilege to preach in a good number of churches. Some, in revivals, others as a pulpit supplying absence of the pastor. The closest I've come to pastoring again was a multi-month tenure as interim pastor at Myrtle, Missouri. Until health conditions dictated differently, it was a joyous privilege for Mrs. Scott and me to make the 28-mile trip from Pocahontas to Myrtle each Sunday morning. The faithful folks of that historic church have my utmost respect.

I'd like to express my deepest and most sincere appreciation to Quenelle, who has been a superb pastor's wife. To Randy and Debbie, son No. I, who now has the unenviable task of being my pastor. To son No.2, Fred and Terry servings pastor in Garner, N. Carolina; and to son No.3, Len and Aimee, serving as pastoring Clarksville, Tennessee. To grandchildren and their spouses, Jason and Melinda, David and Amy Carson, to Bethany, Kailey, Kaitlen, Benjamin, and Claiborne. As a family, we have had some down days. But through the years and some tears, we sure have laughed lot!

Thanks to the good Lord who has guided, given grace, and blessed beyond my fondest expectations. Thanks to the churches that have given me the privilege of preaching in your pulpit, either as pastor or as a visiting revival evangelist or pulpit supply. It has been an interesting, exciting, and wonderful trip. And the BEST is yet to come!!

"THE ENDOF THE TRAIL"...The pastoral trail that is. January, 1996...Having just recently retired from more than half a century of pastoral ministry, I find myself answering a lot of questions. Most are from others. Some are my own.

One of the questions asked most often..."What are you going to do?" Well, first of all, I'm going to review the financial figures once more. Will Social Security, a little retirement fund, and some other limited income spread far and wide enough to cover house payment, utilities, health insurance, groceries, gas, a few drug bills, and leave a little for fish bait and a few shot gun shells? Tack the tithe right up there at the top of that expense list. If the "Fixed income" doesn't balance with "accounts payable" it's too bad. Look out, boys. Here we come!

Not really. Not yet, anyway. The Lord, Who has so graciously met every need during the long ministerial trail has made provision for the rest of the journey, so let's return to the previous question. Like most retiring pastors, I give the stock answer. I hope to preach some revivals as the Lord directs, do some pulpit supply for pastors who need an occasional fill-in, and do a little writing. In addition to that, I'd really like to go fishing a few times without the pressure of getting back for a meeting of some sort. And twice a year, mid-April and mid-October, I'd love to roam the turkey trails up on Possum Creek for more than the standard two or three days.

And, not exactly in the order listed, it'd be nice to see the kids and Grandkids between Christmases. And I honestly confess that the thought of just acting "retired" has crossed my mind a time or two. However, the old fire keeps burning and the passion for preaching keeps prodding. So, as these lines are being penned, there are a few preaching appointments marked in the pocket calendar. Genelle and I are making plans to see the kids. And, it should be obvious if you're reading these lines that I've pecked on the typewriter to tum out a few paragraphs.

"THE END OF THE TRAIL"...Wups, I've already used that line, but here 'tis again. For many years little framed print has hung on a wall of this pastor's study. It's that image of an Indian warrior or hunter with a long spear, a pony, and a mountain peak. The warrior appears to be very tired. The horse seems to be road-weary. The mountain peak is the highest one in sight. The original painting is properly title, "The end of the Trail." For this preacher, that painting has provided a lot to ponder. Since there's latitude for personal interpretation, I have pondered.

The centerpiece of the painting is the weary warrior. With a little imagination, youkan almost hearth words of another soldier from another day, as he surveys his battles and says, "I have fought to good fight ..." Then there's the pony. A feller could get pretty attached to a good faithful horse, especially one that carried him around wherever he needed to go.

Another picture I've had in an office desk drawer is that of my father. Ordained to preach in 1918, he rode "Ole Ode" to his preaching appointments before buying his first Model T. I've heard mom tell of listening late at night for the return of her preacher husband. From quite a distance on a still night in those Ozark hills, she could catch the sound of approaching horse hoofs. Watching and waiting 'til they came in view, she could catch a glimpse of a spark from a horseshoe striking the stones in the rocky road .Me thinks the spirit and dedication of those early circuit riders struck a spark of revival fire in the hearts of those hill country folks.

A rider...a horse ...a mountain peak. The end of the trail. Someone has pointed out that the most beautiful hours of any day are Sunrise and sunset. Now that I'm well past the proverbial three score and ten, I'm beginning to recognize a lot of beauty that I never noticed before in the sunsets.

Now, for some more lines about "The rest of story."

THREE SCORE AND TWELVE!! Wow! Ancient by some people's thoughts. Compared to a few Octogenarians we've known, not so old.

Birthdays have never been as big a deal in our family as some seem to make it. We don't re-finance the house for an expensive gift, and very rarely do we have a family gathering just to observe that one of us has changed his age one year. Not that those things are un-important. It just hasn't been our privilege over the years to observe birthdays that way. BUT WHO can be nonchalant when he steps out of bed one morning and faces the reality that I'M SEVENTY-TWO! I suppose it's because of Psalms 90: I 0 that anything beyond seventy seems to be borrowed time. It's sorta sobering. Such a milestone calls for REFLECTION, RESIGNATION, and ANTICIPATION.

REFLECTION... Try as we may, those of us who've been blessed to achieve this milestone cannot keep from drifting down memory's lane. We rehearse and rehash the experiences of other days. And we come to the inevitable conclusion that things are just not what they used to be. If it's any consolation to our kids who've heard that verse of the song so often, your day will come!

The journey from 1924 to 1996 and beyond (only the Lord knows just how much beyond) has witnessed many changes. Probably no comparable priod in all recorded history has seen so many drastic changes. At age seventy-two, I'm sitting here at this Brother Word Processor (WP-75) pecking out these lines. The keyboard is silent. Sorta like these modern cash registers. Now there's a change. I catch myself listening for the familiar clang of a REAL cash register. This boy learned to type on an Underwood manual typewriter in the early forty's at Mtn. Grove High School. That's one course I've always been grateful that took. Typing is little like riding bicycle. Once you've got the hang of it, you'll always have it. Although I have worn out an electric typewriter or two, and now I'm working on this thing whose keyboard resembles that of a Computer, this is as far as I plan to go. Computers are for a different generation. I've never knowingly as much as turned one on. I may have once or twice turned one off.

TRANSPORTATION and COMMUNICATION are two of the areas of life that have changed so much. When I was born, my country preacher father rode to his church appointments on horseback. At times, he rode considerable distance; twenty miles or more. As stated before, I recall mother tell of listening late at night for the sound of approaching hoof beats as dad came home from a weekend of preaching services.

DAD'S FIRSTCAR was a model T Ford. By today's standards, not much of a car! Talk about "basics," that's about it. There was an engine, not a very powerful one, it might be noted. There were four wheels, plus a steering wheel. It wasn't even "closed in."When winter came, we installed those glass curtains. The model A which came along in '28 or '29 was quite an improvement. Glasses that rolled up or down ...a gearshift sticking up from the floorboard. A revved up engine that could pull you over most any hill. It's been an interesting experience, watching the evolvement of the auto. WOW! That first automatic transmission in 1941, Air-conditioning in the early fifties, plus all the countless (and somewhat expensive) gadgets and gismos. And I'll just skip the modern jet planes and rocket ships.

COMMUNICATION has sure taken on a new look. It's an amazing thing that we can punch a few numbers on the telephone dial and talk with someone on any continent. A far cry from the old crank wall phones and the party lines to which they were connected. Those on the same party line could ring each other by turning the crank in a designated way. My wife's folks were on party line 32F. Their number was 32F03. That meant no long rings, just three short ones. It was pretty interesting! All who were on the same party line knew whose phone was ringing and it wasn't unusual to hear a number of "clicks" when you made a party line call. Is'specta good number of folks down the Mtn. Valley road listened in as the future Mrs. Scott and I discussed our plans for an evening date. Of course, not many of the good folks would ever admit to eavesdropping, but believe me, it did take place!

IN THIS DECADE, I see drivers talking on their car phones, trying to negotiate heavy traffic. Take a walk through the mall and you'll probably see folks with a small cellular phone talking to someone at some distant place. And I've not even mentioned computers or E-mail. Since this country boy has never gotten involved in that world of computerdom, I think I'll just let that go.

THREE SCORE AND TWELVE ...Life certainly has

remained interesting! Take a stroll through a modern super market. As I type these lines, it's the dead of winter, mid-January. You know what? If I should develop a craving for watermelon, it's available. Or a cantaloupe, or a tomato. Ole-timers reading this will remember when certain food items were seasonal. Remember how scrumptious that first mess of lettuce tasted in early summer? Of course, we hadn't tasted lettuce, even in a salad, since late last summer. It would make your mouth water if should mention that pone of corn bread, baked in an oven heated by hickory or oak split stove wood. And that bacon grease, poured with vinegar, mixed with fresh onions and radishes. If mom were not making a pot of chicken dumplings for lunch this cold January day, I think I'd get in my "closed-in" truck, equipped with a "self-starter," shift my automatic transmission into drive, turn my power steering toward Kroger's and go buy a head of lettuce. But who knows? By the time I strolled through the produce section and then the deli, no telling what these taste buds would be calling for. Since the aroma of that slowly boiling chicken is seeping into the make-shift office of this retired pastor, think I'll just settle for some of Genelle's special flavored chicken dumplings. Best I can tell, they're 'bout like our mothers used to make. And that's pretty good!

TRUTH IS, this whole business of being three score and twelve is not too bad. If I get sick, there are excellent, state-of-the art medical facilities available. And since Medicare is not yet totally bankrupt, it's no big deal going through the emergency room, getting X-raysor ultra sound and going into that special room for Lithotripsy. That sure beats the way my dad dealt with HIS kidney stones! And the improvement that's been made in surgery. Remember the smell of Ether? Sickening! And recovery time for the most basic surgery was pretty extensive. Nowadays you can have your gall bladder removed and go home the same day; without any scar. Well, not much of one. And they can stop your heart, by-pass your clogged arteries with new plumbing, and get you out of the hospital and home in less than a week. And you don't smell like ether!

AND YET ...we still die. Folks still hurt. Maybe we've not made as much progress, at least in some areas, awe think we have. 'Twould sure be nice if more children knew the love and security of having BOTH parents at home. And wouldn't it be neat if a young family could live on ONE paycheck if they so choose, allowing any young mother who wanted to, to stay home and take care of the children? Looks like society has just about "progressed "itself to death. I feel a spell of nostalgia coming on. Maybe that mess of chicken   dumplings is about ready. That most likely will help some. It's worth a try!

REFLECTION, RESIGNATION, ANTICIPATION ...Since most of what's been written deals with reflection, let's give few lines to RESIGNATION   ANTICIPATION.

Some folks just can't cope with the idea or thought of getting old. As for this feller, I've resolved not to fight it, but to enjoy it! Sure, getting old has its drawbacks. Arthritis, clumsiness, memory lapses, and various aches and pains. But being old is not too bad. At least, it's not bad so long as you can maintain your own home, your companion's still by your side, your physical and mental facilities are still operational.

AND if the worst comes, we might as well resign to whatever fate or condition that comes our way. We knew all along that we didn't come here to stay, didn't we? And haven't we had more than our share of good days?

ANTICIPATION may be the greatest of the three. It beats reflection.

We can't dwell on the past. I've often declared that for a child of God, THE BEST IS YET TO COME! And I believe that! What will it be like to have a NEW BODY? A body free from all imperfection. No sickness. No pain. And, thank God, no more dying. And what about that NEW HOME? At the very best, we cannot possibly comprehend all that our Lord has in store for us. "INMY FATHER'S HOUSE," is not an idle phrase. Our Father DOES have a house. And in that house there's a dwelling place for all God's children. And what about our relationships in that Heavenly Home?

Of this I feel sure...Heaven will be BIGGER than we have thought. It will be PRETTIER than we've ever thought. It will be more wonderful than anything our finite minds can possibly imagine. Someone has penned these words about Heaven...

"There' ll be no sorrow there, and not one hint of sin;
And the sting of death will never be felt again.
And another thing that will make Heaven so fair...
Momma and daddy will both be there,

And look in' so young and fair I see; Not old and

wrinkled Like they used to be. I'll kiss mom, and she'll whisper in my ear, 'We've been waiting for you, son; and we're so glad   you're here' and dad will say, 'Why there's no more need to fear; 'And we' ll sit down and talk for maybe a hundred years ..."ANTICIPATION! What I don't know about Heaven, I WILL know tomorrow. If not tomorrow, before long. That kind of prospect gets pretty exciting. WOW!

GROWING UP ...at BRUSHY KNOB ...Someone asked once if there really was a place called "Brushy Knob. "Yes, there was and still is a rural community by that name. As a matter of fact, there were two such communities bearing that distinguished name; one southeast omen. Grove, and one about five to seven miles northeast of Mtn. Grove. Never knew how the community got its name, but I do know that it lived up (or down) to it. It was brushy, rocky, and I suppose if you looked hard enough you could find something resembling a knob.

THE SCHOOL was a one room, typical, nineteenth century rural American school. One teacher taught all grades from grade one through grade eight. Equipment included a chart from which the beginners learned to read. On two sides of the building there were blackboards on which sentences were diagrammed, arithmetic problems were solved, and the weekly ciphering matches took place. There a were few pull down maps and a globe of the. World. For music, there was a phonograph, with a few records. It was customary at the opening of school each day that we would sing the first and last verses of "America." As we sang the last verse we were always instructed to bow our heads, since the words to that verses seem to be a prayer. There was a small library, which held a set of World Book Encyclopedia, a few other reference books, and some Wild West shoot'em up cowboys and Indian books. The first thing I ever saw remotely resembling a movie was a short film brought to the schoolboy the county Superintendent. He operated the film with a "click" of the thumb. When his thumb got tired, Felix, the cat got a rest.

DISCIPLINE ...With as many as 40 students in one room, how could one teacher maintain any kind of order? Well, strange as it may seem in this day of little or no discipline that posed no problem. My first teacher, Mrs. Nora Parker, was a strong and gifted woman. In her desk, she kept an ENFORCER. It was a long leather belt; probably 45 inches long and an inch wide. We had some BIG boys; girls, too. When things began to get a little out of hand, the whole school could predict with a good degree of accuracy what was about to happen. The neck veins in Mrs. Parker started to show, and her whole face would seem slightly flushed. A sure sign that corporal punishment was about to be administered! Was it ever! A few well-directed licks administered to the seat of learning not only shaped up the poor soul who had been caught in violation of school rules. It put the fear in every kid in the school. And it lasted for several days.

To her credit, Mrs. Parker was one teacher who showed no perceptible partiality. She had no discernible pets. As this72-year-old boy draws from memory's bank, I feel a renewed sense of respect for that first school teacher. What a job she did!

THE PLAYGROUND at Brush Knob...It consisted of a small tract of land, probably about three quarters of an acre. No basketball goals or tennis courts. We did at one time have a volley ball net, but most of the time, no volleyball! Noons and the recess periods, tho, were filled with noise of kids at play. Games consisted of Dare Base, Black man, (it had nothing to do with skin color) hide and go seek, hop scotch, marbles, and a few other games. During the warm seasons we had a pretty good softball team. We even played a two-team tournament with a neighboring school, Fowler. On the west side of the playground was a little stream. Lf nothing else was enticing on a particular day, a boy could always dabble in the water, chase crawdad, or try to snatch a minnow.

OF SPECIAL ENJOYMENT was the old "hoop paddle" thing. The hoop was a metal ring, which had come from the hub of an abandoned wagon wheel. The paddle was a slender piece of board with a crosspiece nailed across at one end. Some of us developed great skills in maneuvering that hoop through hard places. The object was to keep it rolling. Another homemade tool of enjoyment was that of "Stilts." These were usually made of a 2 X 2 about six feet in length. Attached about two feet from one end was a stirrup. With a little practice, a five-foot feller could become seven feet tall! Get out of the way, Goliath!

NOTORIOUS NOVEMBER ...DELIGHTFUL DECEMBER JUBILANT JANUARY...Some of my nieces have asked at times, that I write about the thrills of rabbit trapping. Wow! What enjoyment that brought. It also brought little spending money. A cotton tail rabbit would bring a dime on the market, beginning about mid-November and lasting into January. Usually by January, the price would go down to a Nickel.

I'VE ALWAYS LOVED THE FALL! I think trapping rabbits contributed to that love. The trap was a box trap, made of six-inch boards. The older the board, the better. Or, it could be made from a hollow log. Going to the traps on a cold, frosty morning carries with it certain sights, smells, and sensations that few other experiences can match! The light was a kerosene lantern. Very few flashlights were in use. The batteries cost too much, and then, they didn't last very long. To set that old lantern down in front of the trap, look in and see that little bunny humped up...well, you just had to experience it to understand. To any animal rights activists who may ever read these lines, don't think me cruel or hard-hearted. I am neither cruel nor hard-hearted. In the first place, rabbits were abundant. They served a good purposes a food supply. I was always told that they were shipped "down" to New Orleans or Memphis and sold for a quarter. Don't you know ...some of those good ole southern mommas could fix them up and made a feller' smooth water! Really! And if it hadn't been for rabbits there were families that would have gone meatless.

PERSONAL NOTES...This 72-year-old boys DOES love animals, wildlife of every sort. The love for the woods, the streams, the rocks rills...it still sends thrills of rapture through my very being. Indult life, I've had the privilege of hunting deer and wild turkey. In childhood, these species had become extinct because of overkill and lack of enforced seasons for hunting. Since there were no deer or turkey in the woods of my childhood, I'll never live long enough to get over the pure excitement and thrill of just seeing one of these wild creatures. I'll always be grateful for various states 'Game and Fish Commissions, which have done a tremendous job in bringing back the deer, turkey, bear, and other species. I wilt say, tho, that nothing I've ever experienced in my adult life as an outdoorsman can surpass the thrill of those pre-dawn trips to those rabbit traps. I guess if the Lord would lay all of history out and allow me to choose the period in which my life was to be lived, I'd have to choose that time from 1924 to 1996...or later. Preferably, quite a bit later!

HOME LIFE at Brushy Knob was an experience which affords lots of wonderful memories. What pure enjoyment! During that period of childhood, our family lived at three different places, all in the same community. The one I remember most, tho, was that sixty-acre place just a quarter mile from. The community church and about half a mile from the schoolhouse. Dad was a country preacher, who tried to farm the best he could to supply needs of a large family. For a short period, after the birth of my baby sister, and before the marriage of my oldest sister, there were eight children to be fed, plus dad and mom. Ten hungry mouths gathered around the table three times a day! And, to the everlasting credit of a hard- working, conservative-living dad and mom, none ever went away hungry. We grew our vegetables ...mainly beans and potatoes for the winter months. And we butchered five or six "fattening hogs" for meat. Mom saw to it that we had an ample supply of blackberries, which were available for the picking. With a hunk of cornbread, or homemade biscuits, berry cobbler, buttermilk, and some other stuff, like "thicknin' gravy"we never went hungry.

PEANUT BUTTER SLICED BREAD ...These were rarities in lunch buckets of kids at Brushy Knob School. There were two or three families whose kids did regularly bring that for lunch. When my family did on occasion have those delightful delicacies, a feller made sure that other saw what he was eating. It was somewhat of a status symbol. While my folks were poor, we were not the poorest in the community. There were a few families that were REALLY poor. How they survived, I'll never know. "DADDY SANG BASS"...not really; he was more of a tenor. It was big brother who sang bass. Some of the girls sang alto, soprano, and played the piano. Somehow, dad had struck up a trade for an old upright piano which must have weighed half a ton. Whatever he traded for that piano, it was worth it! We all DID, as Johnny Cash sang, join right in there: and singing did "help our troubled souls!" Barney Chandler was a jolly soul!

A little on the roly-poly side physically, he had a cheerful disposition and was a welcome guest. He came by annually to tune that old piano.

THE RAWLEIGH MAN was another who was highly regarded by the kids; especially this one. He came by periodically, on his selling route for Rawleigh products. He will always be remembered by this kid, not for what he sold, but by what he GAVE. He never came by without giving us kids some of those peppennint lifesavers. What treat! In retrospect, the folks who have impressed the most are those who were GIVERS. Someone has said, "There are givers and there are takers. The takers eat better; the givers sleep better and will be remembered the longest."

BRUSHY KNOB...the COMMUNITY CHURCH ...At least, that's   what it was during my childhood. Originally, it had been established by a Denomination, but for some reason, it had become an inter-denominational, community church. The folks all got along well. I don't recall any elections, or votes on anything; maybe there were some. Somehow, it just seemed natural for a certain young lady to play the pump organ .I believe her last name was Canada. Old Brother Chambers served as superintendent of Sunday school. He lived at least three miles away and always walked, sometimes wading Beaver Creek to get there. As a footnote, Bro. Chambers in later life did get a car and it was the death of him. He hit a pole on N. Main Street ofMtn. Grove. The car he had was one of those early Ford VI 8's with the doors opening at the front. Strange that a feller would remember that, but cars were pretty important stuff in earlier days. Sister McDonald didn't have a car. She had a cane. She was Card Class teacher. She hobbled down the road about a mile to teach her class. Marion Halliburton led the singing. A favorite song in those days was "Stepping in the Light." Under Bro. Halliburton's leadership, we stepped right in.

THE SUMMER REVIVALS...We nearly always had one, and it was a   pretty important event. Don't know just how much deep Theology was expounded. I do know that the pulpit got POUNDED! Somehow, the front pew had been given the name, "Mourner's Bench." It was there the repenting sinners came, mourning over their lost condition. And whether the deep Theological truths were thoroughly comprehended or not, a lot of lives were changed for the better. It might be noted that our country would be a better place if we would collectively or individually do some sincere weeping and repenting over our sins!

FANS FIGHTS ...The funeral homes furnished the fans. Some ornery boys provoked the fights. Air-conditioning was not even heard of. The windows had no screens. When the size of the crowds dictated, some of the fellows perched themselves in the windows for the long revival pennons. That way, they could be as much involved in what was taking place on the outside as they were with what was happening on the inside. What happened on the inside probably had more lasting results, but what was taking place on the outside was pretty interesting, to say the least!

THE FEEBLE-MINDED ...] guess the Lord knew they would always   be among us, so proper instruction was given in Holy Writ in regard to their care and treatment. Unfortunately, those admonitions were not, and even yet, are not heeded. Brushy Knob had two single men who fit the description of "Feeble-mined." They were lovable souls; harmless, easy- going...UNTIL some of the fellows who should be ashamed of themselves, provoked a fight. They'd make up all kinds of stories and relate them to each of the two F.M. fellows. They'd stay at it until the two would get into an actual fistfight. That was pretty much a regular happening during summer revival.

ON THE OUTSIDE lots of other mischief took place. Rowdy fellow   or two would usually wind up being arrested for disorderly conduct. One in particular, would usually get drunk and make a fool of himself. Fortunately, the deputy sheriff for the county lived not too far away. His services were in demand at least a time or two during revival.

ON THE INSIDE lots of good things happened. One of those things   was this boy's own Salvation experience. That took place at age eleven. Yep, it was during one of those mid-summer, hot-as-it-can-be revivals. After more than six decades, the conversion experience is still very vivid. Although the Bible calls for some standard requirements that each penitent sinner must adhere to, I am of the persuasion that some experiences are unique and peculiar to the individual. Did any other sinner ever have Paul's Damascus Road experience? Hardly! Not only in the Salvation experience, but in other circumstances and periods of our lives, God may (but is not obligated) give us some tailor-made, unique, personal experiences. If He does, we are entitled to relish and rejoice in them. However, they should never be forced or imposed upon others.

MEMORIAL TRIBUTES...Two brothers were also saved during one of those summer revivals. Both died too young. One of them, Vernal Halliburton, fell out of a walnut tree down the creek a half mile or so from the house. It was supposed that he had climbed the tree to shake walnuts loose. It was the fall of the year, and kids could make a little money picking up black walnuts. The fall caused the eleven year-old's death. He most likely broke his neck.

The older of the two, Ardell Halliburton, was a care-free, enjoy-life-to-the fullest sort of a fellow. Good natured, of good character, ambitious. He was married and the father of a little girl, probably age 3 or so. World War Two was in full swing and Ardell was called to Military service. He took basic training, came home for a short furlough, and was shipped off to faraway battlefield. A sniper's bullet-Battle of the Bulge pierced his   head. Ardell undoubtedly never knew what a hit him. He loved life; he loved his family. It was said that on the morning of his departure, his cries could be heard blocks away as he was parted from his wife and little girl. Such is the terribly high price some have paid for our freedom.

THE WAR WAS OVER...bodies were being shipped back to the states. I'll never forget that Saturday morning when the train pulled up at the Frisco Station. A casket was taken from the train and to the funeral home. At the request of family members, my father and I viewed the remains for positive identification. It was Ardell's remains. Unique physical characteristics made that certain. It also made this boy certain that FREEDOM and LIBERTY come at a high price. I've seen a pretty sizable number of classmates and personal acquaintances go off to war and come back in a coffin. For that, and for other reasons, I would not want to see some unpatriotic libertine desecrate the U.S.Flag. I have the utmost respect for ALL who paid such a high price; but somehow, even yet, when I hear or sing the Star Spangled Banner, Ardell Halliburton comes to mind; and a little girl, and a woman who became a widow 'way too soon.

GOD BLESS AMERICA!

ANOTHER BOY DIED YOUNG ...He was about eight or nine, I suppose. At the time of his death, my family had moved to Mtn. Grove. This little fellow died from inhaling gasoline fumes. Evidently, there was something about the smell of gasoline that appealed to him. He removed the gas cap from his father 'scar and inhaled so many fumes that he died.

These are some of the reflections on a childhood lived and loved to the fullest at BRUSHY KNOB. The home, the school, the community, and church life all combined to provide a good and solid foundation on which to build an abundant life. "Precious memories flood my soul!"

MEMORABLE MOMENT from 1992...The heart surgeon had   experienced a long, grueling day. The by-pass operation, along with a valve replacement had taken many tedious hours. The patient was ·not doing well. Before the incision was closed, it had become necessary to go back in to stop some bleeding.   It was a tired doctor who came into the family waiting room about 6:30 that evening. After explaining the patient's critical condition to the family, he said, '·I'm not going to leave the hospital tonight. In case I'm needed, I'll be here. "About 4 o'clock next morning he was needed. He was there.

My personal esteem for Dr. Fiser rose a little that evening, although he already had my respect. Three years earlier, he had surgically repaired   and re-routed some of my own faulty plumbing. But I thought about another

Physician, the One Whom we refer to as "The GREAT Physician." He left His followers with tremendous task. But He gave them His solemn word, "Lo, I am with you always, even unto the end of the world." Many of us have trusted Him, we've tried Him, and we've found His promises to be true. When we've needed Him, He's always there.

He'll be there when your health fails. He'll be there when your finances are low. When you are forsaken by others, He'll be there. He'll be there when your baby's sick. And when the hearse rolls up to your door, HE'LL BE THERE!

When I memorized the 121st Psalm as part of an assignment as a student at Brushy Knob grade school, I didn't understand much about it. Today, almost three score years removed from that assignment, I think I understand some of it in part, at least. "He that keepeth thee will not slumber. Behold, He that kept Israel shall neither slumber nor sleep."

Footnote: That patient who received such competent, conscientious care is alive and well at the time of this writing. That surgeon is the son of a retired Methodist Minister.

* * * * * *

THIS PREACHER was the recipient of an unusual Christmas gift, a century-old copy of McGuffey's Fifth Reader. In those old Readers, you'll find lots of Scriptures and many down to earth instructions for successful living. That old Reader closes with a poem about the Bible. The last verse goes: "Thou truest friend man ever knew, Thy constancy I've tried. When all were false, I found thee true, my counsellor and guide. The mines of earth no treasures give, that could this volume buy; In teaching me the way to live, It taught me how to die."

* * * * * *

"WE'RE COMING TO GET YOU, MICHAEL!" The MICHAEL was a U.S. helicopter pilot, Michael Durant. His helicopter was shot down over a faraway place called Mogadishu. He suffered bruises and broken bones, but he was alive. Outside his room of confinement, the body of another U.S.Airman was being rudely dragged up and down the street. We cannot imagine the fear and loneliness that must have gripped Michael Durant.

This story was told ·bay California Congressman. He related how the comrades of Michael Durant kept sending messages that the captive soldier could receive through a small radio he was allowed to keep. The group selected as spokesman the one whose voice the captive soldier would most likely recognize. For seventeen days the message kept coming through ..."Hang in there, Michael...We've not forgotten you. We're coming after you ..."And they kept their word. Michael Durant was rescued and lived to appear on National T.V.

THE CAPTAIN OF OUR SALVATION left His followers a promise. "I will come again and receive you unto myself..."Our Captain always keeps His word. He will come again. And while we wait His coming, we must always remember that this world is not our home. We are just pilgrims passing through this unfriendly world. THANK GOD for the word of our wonderful Lord ..."I will come again and receive you ..."Tune your heart's receiver toward Heaven's station. It's wonderful, the things you may hear!

* * * * * *

SERMONETTE: In the parable of the Sower and the seed as recorded in Matthew13, Jesus told of one who received the seed into stony places. He heard the word with JOY. But the sad commentary goes like this: "Yet hath he not root in himself." He just couldn't stand when problems arose, or discouragement, or persecution. He had no root IN HIMSELF.

How can you get a feller rooted who has not root? It wasn't anyone else's fault. Not the church, not the preacher, not the board. He just didn't have any root in himself. Maybe that's what John had in mind when he wrote, "Look to YOURSELVES that we lose not those things which we have wrought ..."

If you have not root, you can bear no fruit! If you have no root, you are apt to be carried about with every wind that blows. In the HOME and in the Church there is a real need for some Scriptural depth. We each would do well to seriously examine our own selves and see if we have the root depth that's necessary for Christian growth. It's mighty important! "Therefore ...be ye steadfast, unmovable, and always abounding in the work of the Lord; forasmuch as ye know that your labor is not in vain in the Lord.

_* * * * * *

CHIPPIN' AWAY ...CHIPPIN' AWAY ...Siowly, slowly, chippin' away. Like the old love song, "I can feel it SLIPPIN'away," we are seeing lots of time-honored values and standards being slowly chipped away. Today's paper gave the account of a court ruling which forbids the GIDEON'S from distributing Bibles to a class of students in Indiana. No surprise. We have witnessed the abolishment of the Ten Commandments from classrooms. The Pledge of Allegiance to the American Flag has taken a beating. Public prayers as a part of graduating activities are no longer permitted in Jots of schools. Slowly, slowly, CHIPPINGAWAY ...The sanctity of life, Reverence for Deity, Respect for authority...parental as well as Police. We are suffering the consequences of moral and Spiritual erosion .America, as someone has said before, is becoming "The Land of the Spree, and the home of the Rave." May Heaven have mercy!

* * * * * *

BEAUTIFUL SIMPLE...SIMPLY BEAUTIFUL. ..John Jasper was a black man, born a slave. He was converted, began preaching, at first mostly funerals for other slaves. His eloquence became such that the entire Stellate Legislature of Virginia once adjourned to go hear him.

DURING A FUNERAL ADDRESS, Jasper bent over, cupped his hand to his mouth, and called down to the monarch of the lower regions. "Grave! Grave! Oh Grave! Where is your victory? I hear you got a mighty banner down there, and you terrorize everybody who comes along that way. Bring out your armies and furl forth your banners of victory. Show your hand an' let 'em see what you can do. "Then he made the grave reply: "Ain't got no victory down here now; had victory, but King Jesus passed through this country an' tore my banners down. He says His people won't be troubled no more, an' He told me to open the gates an' let 'em pass on their way to Glory."

"Oh, my brethren," Jasper exclaimed, "did you hear that? My Jesus jerked the sting from death, broke the scepter of the king of terrors, and He went into the grave and robbed it of its victorious banners. He fixed a way nice and smooth for His people to pass through. More than that He has written a song, a shoutin' anthem for us to sing when we go out there, pass in' suns and stars, and singin'that song, 'Thanks be unto God, Who gives us the victory through the Lord Jesus Christ.'"

* * * * * *

Copied: "Here lies the body of Benjamin Gray; He died defending his right-o-way.

He was right; dead right as he sped along;
But he's just as dead as if he had been dead wrong! "

* * * * * *

THE HOLY GLOW of HUMILITY ...In Exodus 34:29it is written of Moses ..."And it came to pass when Mosescame down fromMount Sinai with the two tables oftestimony ...that Moseswist not that the skin ofhis face shone...

The Bible speaks of Moses as ing the meekest of all the earth. How do you describe true greatness? And how do you define true humility?It is no surprise that the face of Moses shone. After all, he had been in the mount alone with God for forty days. It's likely that many us would have a more holy halo if we spent a lot more time with God.

But the thing about this experience that has alwaysimpressed me...Everyone knew Moses' face shone...except Moses! It ispossible, I think, that a man could be a good, great man of God. But ifthat man ever comes to the realization that he is a good, great man of God, some of the glow disappears. True humility is a qualitya man cannot keep if he knows he's got it! Bob Feller, one of baseball's all-time greatest pitchers, reportedly said to his manager as a rookie ..."This cap is too big for my head." Replied his manager, "See that it stays that way!"

* * * * * *

Copied: A timid man said to his wife, "We're not going out tonight and that's semi-final!"

* * * * * *

RAMBLING ...While Mrs. Scott was cleaning out some drawers and closets she ran across some old notes and papers we had brought home after the death of my mother some years ago. Among the papers were some hand-written pennon notes from my dad, who died in 1957. One of them was especially appealing with the subject: "The

Lord will take care of His Own." The Text: Genesis 7:16..."And the Lord shut him in."

I don't know what all that ole-time south Missouri preacher said. I wish I did. But I'm sure he must have talked about Noah and his family and the safety they enjoyed in the ark while the outside world perished. The Lord DOES take care of His Own. He calls His sheep BY NAME and leads them out. Christ often appears in the darkest hour of a stormy night WALKING ON THE SEA. His "Peace, be still" has calmed many a troubled soul when it looked like hope was gone. I don't think there's ever been a time when the waves were dashing higher, adverse winds were fiercer, when days were darker, or times were more turbulent. But I do know without doubt that the Lord will take care of His Own. To any troubled soul who may read these lines, Get in the boat (the old Gospel Ship) and sail with Him whose voice calms stony waters and whose peace over rules the stone. He's never lost a battle yet! GO WITH GOD!

* * * * * *

POLISHED GEMS..."Thy shoes shall be iron and brass; and as thy days, so salty strength be. "(Deuteronomy 33:25)

The ETERNAL GOD is thy Refuge, and underneath are the everlasting arms..." (Deuteronomy 33:27)

CHILDHOOD MEMORIES...On rare occasions my dad would take time out to go to a private swimming hole down on Beaver Creek. He'd take this kid out to deep water, give a few instructions on how to swim, and then conclude by making a solemn promise, "I won't let you sink!" And he never did. Midst all the struggling, splashing, spewing, and spitting, there was always underneath, the strong supporting arm of an earthly father. He wasn't about to let his boy drown.

This boy never learned how to swim very well, but he DID learn to trust his father. He never broke a promise. Now, much older, and hopefully little wiser, that same kid is still learning that a loving, caring HEAVENLY FATHER always keeps HIS word! His promises never come up short. His strong arm is always there. And, "What a fellowship, what a joy Divine ...leaning on the EVERLASTING ARMS!"

* * * * * *

SHOW UP for the SHOWDOWN! A few weeks ago, a local sports writer was giving a report on the football teams composing the Southwest Conference. The coach at Texas Tech (I believe his name was Dykes) talked about the weaknesses of his team, but concluded by saying, "We've got some who will show up for the show down." This country preacher interprets that to mean ...win, lose, or tie, they will be there. THE CHURCH needs more members who will show up for the show down! The battles hot. The foes are real. And it's not a game we're playing. We're dealing with ETERNAL matters.   ELIJAH showed up on Mt. Carmel and he called for a show-down. Surrounded and grossly out-numbered by the enemy, he stood there and put the worshippers of Baal to silence and shame. Wonder where the rest of the Israelites were? Somehow, they just didn't show up. Incidentally, following that memorable show-down, it came a SHOWER. Well, more than a shower. It came downpour! The way I figure it, the church of this generation would have a lot more "showers of blessings" if more of God's people would show up more often for a genuine showdown.

* * * * * *

The Bible says it: "But the path of the just is as the shining light that shineth more and more unto the perfect day." (Prov. 4:18)' AND, "For I reckon that the sufferings of this present time are not worthy to be compared with the glory which shall be revealed in us." (Romans8:18)

"There's just one Book!" cried the dying sage;
"Read me the old, old story."

And the winged words that can never age Wafted him home to glory. There's just one Book!

There's just one Book for life's gladness, One Book for the toilsome days;

One Book that can cure life's madness; One Book that can voice life's praise. There's just one Book!

THE BIBLE: "Within that awful volume lies the mystery of mysteries.

Happiest they of the human race to whom their God has given grace to read, to fear, to hope, to pray, to lift the latch, and force the way; And better had they ne'erbeen born who read to doubt, or read to scorn." (Walter Scott)

* * * * * *

MEMORIES of an old-fashioned MOTHER ...The

memories I have of an old-fashioned mother are certainly not the memories youth or child of this generation will carry. That's not to say that my memories are better; they're just different. Much different! Which of our young folks have helped their mother pick geese and then slept on a feather pillow or a feather bed from those feathers? In reflection, I sort of feel sorry for those geese. I do recall that they let out a squawk as their plum mage was plucked. Not many, if any our young folks ever tried to compete with a black- berry-picking mother. Why, she could fill that 8 qt. Milk bucket while I was trying to make sure there weren't any snakes close by.

Which of our church's children have ever heard the rhythmic sound of the dasher in a crock churn? Or helped pitch hay in a barn loft on a hot July afternoon? And none of today's generation had the privilege of hearing a mother softly sing, "Heaven Holds all to me," as she rubbed bib overalls on a washboard.

I HOPE and PRAY that MANY of today's children will hold fond memories of a mother's sweet voice as she sang a sleepy-time lullaby or held that little one close to kiss away some hurt. I hope that many teenage daughters will always be able to recall some private sessions with a mother who still remembered what it was like to be a teenage girl.

TODAY'S GENERATION of mothers are not called on to pick geese, or blackberries, or to rub clothes on a washboard. But mothers of this, and every generation, can and must do the things that are such special responsibilities of the MOTHER. God bless our dear mothers!

* * * * * *

FOR HISTORICAL PURPOSES ...January 4, 1984...The Arkansas River is frozen completely over from bank to bank. That doesn't happen very often. According to reports, the recent spell of extreme winter weather has been responsible for more than 30 deaths in our state. One poor mortal whose car stalled, walked off with an abundant supply of wine and was found frozen to death.

Pastor's note: As this is being written, January 20, 1996, we're in the throes of another cold spell, but nothing like that of January, 1984. We have a tendency to remember the extremes. Undoubtedly, the Arkansas River WILL freeze over again. But it won't happen EVERY winter. Never hope so, when it doesn't, we'll just keep saying, "We don't have winters like we used to have.

* * * * * *

PESTICIDES, PENICILLIN, PREACHING...

A headline on the business page of the Arkansas Dem Gaz caught my attention. It read, "COTTON BUGS GROW RESIST ANT TO PESTICIDE." I think that means that what killed bugs in other days may not even make 'em sick this year. It's that way with Penicillin and other so-called miracle drugs. Somehow, we seem to build up resistance to that with which we become familiar.

Pesticides and Penicillin are not the only things to which we become resistant. Having been a preacher nearly all my adult life, I naturally turn my thoughts to preaching and to the reaction it receives. That which once would really stir us becomes so common that it hardly affects us at all.

It's that way with moral and social conditions. Pray tell, what would it take to shock us these days? We're so accustomed to hearing daily reports of murders, rapes, robberies, and crimes of every other sort that nothing really shocks us. Unless, it's our wife or daughter who got attacked we shrug and say, "That's bad," and we go our way. If the shooting didn't take place on our end of the block, we scarcely blink an eye.

It's the same with sin. That which used to look really bad and black and ugly somehow takes on a softer, lighter hue.

Regarding the moral and Spiritual aspects of life, there are some Scriptural admonitions which come to mind. Like, "Blow the trumpet in Zion. Sound an alarm in my holy mountain. "Or, Take heed, brethren...lest any of you should become hardened through the deceitfulness of sin. " And didn't Paul have some things to say about a"Seared Conscience? "

In the last Book, Jesus is standing outside the church, saying, "Behold, I stand at the door and knock" ... Sadly, most folks don't listen. Do 'YOU suppose it will take the final trumpet sound to really wake us up. That Might be what it takes. 'Til then, Cotton farmers will battle the bugs the best they can. Physicians will practice the healing art with the best medicines available; and preachers will pound and expound in an effort to get folks to hear and heed God's Holy Word.

* * * * * *

"BIG 'POSSUMS WALK JUST BEFORE DAYLIGHT ..."

If you've ever been around preacher Lawnie Coffman very much you've probably heard him use that expression. After hearing him run it by for 'bout the thirteenth time, I asked him just what it meant. According to his explanation, it's true! If you go 'possum huntin' you can catch the little ones in the early part of the night. But if you want to catch the big ones you've got to stay with it! The big ones, he declares, walk just before daylight.

I guess that means that if you want to be successful, you've got to keep after it! The big prize requires patience and persistence. Maybe there are some of us who need to get up and go little farther, work a little harder, pray little more sincerely, give more liberally, work more cheerfully. DON'T GIVE UP, CHRISTIAN! A glorious sunrises about to break!

* * * * * *

FOOD FOR THOUGHT ...A Christian gets a lot of blessings while living here on this earth. However, we are always mindful that there is much more that waits beyond the curtain of death for the child of God. We are given enough of a preview into the glories of the world to come that our interest an anticipation should always be keen.

In our mid-week adult Bible study we considered this verse from Luke 20:36 "Neither can they die any more: for they are equal unto the angels; and are the children of God, being the children of the Resurrection." John wrote: "Beloved, now are we the sons of God, and it doth not yet appear what we shall be: but we know that when He shall appear, we shall be like Him; for we shall see Him as He is."And Paul added, "The Spirit Himself bearish witness with our spirit, that we are the children of God: And if children, then heirs; heirs of God, and joint-heirs with Christ; if so be that we suffer with Him, that we may be also glorified together." Yes, a Christian has a lot of promises upon which he can stand; a lot of joys to anticipate; a lot of glory which will be revealed when Jesus comes. BE SURE you don't miss all the wonderful blessings that are yet to come!

* * * * * *

DAY DREAMING ...With a new winter storm in the forecasts, this country boy preacher can sit here in this warm study and day dream. I can close these eyes and see...Robert   Granny Counts in the middle of the prettiest garden and flower beds in Pocahontas...A turkey gobbler down on Possum Creek in the gun sights of the ole 12 gauge...the hills up at Camp Beaver fork running over with youngsters from all across the state. It doesn't cost anything to dream! On cold day, it warms the heart.

* * * * * *

FROM THE PASTOR'S STUDY...During last Spring's p olitical campaign one candidate's t.v. commercial concluded with the expression, "He knows big wood from kindlin'.I think that was meant to imply the fewer had some good judgment when it came to values. Supposedly, he knew what was important and what was not worth squabbling over.

IF that's the proper interpretation of this down-to-earth expression, there ought to be a Spiritual application. Esau didn't have much good sense when it came to values. He didn't "know big wood from kindlin'" and he sold his birthright for a mess of pottage. Lot wasn't overly brilliant when he "pitched his tent toward Sodom." He gave up daughters for dollars; he lost his wife for wealth. Now, Joseph knew big wood from kindlin'. He got out of Potiphar's house in a hurry. He lost his coat but he kept his character! The list is long. Achan, Gehazi, Judas Iscariot, Demas, and most likely a whole lot of folks whom we've known.

Some pretty good people have played with matchsticks while the big timbers for building went un-touched, un-used. Churches, I suspect, have argued and even split over kinlin' sticks. Our own Denomination, I fear, has at times lost sight of the bigger wood and bickered over trivialities; at least when compared with Eternity and Eternal values. Of course, some were right and others were wrong. But I wonder. ..were the right really that right? And were the wrong really that wrong? What do you suppose might happen if we'd all forget the kindlin' for a while and concentrate on cordwood!

* * * * * *

SIGHTS, SOUNDS, SMELLS of summer...Gorgeous sunsets in a hazy sky; mockingbirds doing what they do best. Wonder if some of their tunes might be Gospel tunes? Smells? How 'bout pickle-making day in Granny's kitchen?

Those mixed-together spices sure do put out an aroma!

* * * * * *

I'VE NEVERFIGURED THIS ONE OUT...The accounts given or referred to in more than one of the Gospels. Luke records it like this: "And there was also a strife among them, which of them should be accounted the greatest." In this case "them"refers to the twelve Apostles. In Luke 22: 19Christ had taken bread, broken it, and said, "This is My body which is given for you ..."Verse 20, "Likewise the cup after supper, saying, This cup is the New Testament in My blood, which is shed for you." And three verse later the whole tone of conversation among the Disciples is a shallow, childish, and immature, "Which of us should be acknowledged as the greatest?" Such frivolous, worldly questions as that ought to be relegated to swaggering sports figures, or screen actors, or politicians.

Do you reckon god has a rating system? I hardly think so. While His Disciples argued and reached for the top, Jesus quietly and humbly reached for the towel and washed their feet. It was our Lord and Master Who said, "And whosoever will be chief among you, let him be your servant: Even as the Son of man came not to be ministered unto, but to minister, and to give His life a Ransom for many." Seems like that ought to deflate our ego, take the starch out of our collar, rid us of foolish pride, and pretty well set us in our place of service.

* * * * * *

Quote: "You've reached middle age when all you exercise is caution."

* * * * * *

THE FOLLOWING LINES were written more than a hundred years ago. They might still be worthy of some consideration.

"The harder you're thrown, the higher you bounce; be proud of your blackened eye!

It isn't the fact that you're licked that counts; its how did you fight and why?

Death comes with a crawl, or comes with a pounce; And whether he's slow or spry, It isn't the fact that you're dead that counts, But only, how did you die? "

* * * * * *

PRAYERS ...I've heard lots of preaching and lots of praying in my time. Some of it I remember; some is soon forgotten. A part of one dear lady's prayer I think I will long remember. She and her husband were hard-working, tough, down to earth country folks. In their home that morning in westerns. Louis County with their pastor, she read a passage from Isaiah and then led in prayer. A part of that prayers truck a note and grabbed this preacher's attention. She said: "O Lord, You know that me and my man's a-getting' old. But Lord, we think thoughts that it ain't fittin' to think; and Lord, You know we ought to be down at that altar praying' up a storm!" It's hard to argue with that kind ofTheology.I s'spect that our biggest battle-ground as Christians is our thought process. I've heard it said: "You can't keep the birds from flying over your head, but you don't have to let them build a nest in your hair."

Likewise, we may not be able to keep bad thoughts from momentarily flashing across the screen of our mind. But we don't have to pull up a chair and let them make themselves at home!

* * * * * *

Copied: They say garbage could be converted into gasoline if we so chose.

Not surprising; it already has been made into books and films and shows!

* * * * * *

FROM THE MID-WEEK NEWS, March 13, 1991...Last fall, shortly after the Baghdad butcher sent his troops to Kuwait, the president of the
U.S. was meeting with other national leaders about the situation. In the group was former British Prime Minister, Margaret Thatcher. Reportedly she spoke up during the discussion and said, "George (Bush) this is no time to get wobbly!" I wonder how many Christians get a little wobbly when the going starts getting hard.

* * * * * *

Remembered quote: "You don't have to be much of a musician to toot your own horn. "

Personal Observations ...From the time of the fall of manin Eden, much of the Old Testament is a repetition account of Backsliding, Sin, Sordidness, Captivity, Bondage, followed by Repentance, Forgiveness, Deliverance ...and then the whole process is repeated .

BUT THE LAST CHAPTER!!That makes it all worthwhile. In our day, God gets kicked around down here. His Name is blasphemed. Jesus Christ is still the rejected Redeemer. He gets a raw deal in the courtroom by the judge and the jury. BUT IN THE LAST CHAPTER, The saints take the Kingdom, Christ reigns as King. God is still the Almighty. The Master's minority have become mighty multitude. We lay down the cross and take up the crown. We quit sighing and start singing. And we join with countless numbers in proclaiming, "WORTHY ISTHE LAMB!" Hang in there, Christian. The BEST is yet to be.

"DIDN'T YOU KNOWI WAS LOST?" A six-year-old boy wandered away from a deer camp and couldn't find his way back. He spent the night alone in the woods, with the temperature dropping to 28 degrees. Of course an intensive search was made, and after 23 hours the boy was found. He Was alert and apparently, in pretty good condition. His first words to those who found him were, "Didn't you know I was lost?"

When something is lost that we care about, it becomes top priority. The church's businesses first of all, to seek the lost. Wonder if anybody might someday tum toward us and say, "Didn't you know I was lost?" We must continue to "Rescue the Perishing; Duty demands it!"

* * * * * *

WELL, I heard an expression the other day I don't recall hearing before.

An elderly gentleman from north of town said, "I was born lazy and have just had a relapse." I know he was putting me on a little, for he seemed to be a most energetic fellow. I wonder, tho, if there might not be some truth in the expression he used. We were all born in sin, and we've all suffered relapses. Some may have been born poor and suffered a relapse. And the old fellow may have been right about some, when he said he was born lazy and had suffered a relapse. NO MATIER WHAT malady we were born with ...sin, poverty, or even laziness, it's not how we were born that matters, but how we LIVE! That's what really counts!

* * * * * *

ABOUT PREACHING..."A good sermon is not a work of art, but of heart." And, "A preacher can't function without unction!"

* * * * * *

Quote: "The lowest ebb is the turn of the tide."

* * * * * *

MOTHER'S DAY ...There were more than a few hard-to-swallow lumps in throats last Sunday, as we tried to honor our mothers. Our TX's efforts seem to come so pitifully short. Precious Memories. We thank God for them. "Around the old home place, her patient, smiling face, was always spreading comfort, hope, and cheer. And when she used to sing of her Eternal King...It was the song the angels loved to hear."

* * * * * *

A TALE OF TULIPS THINGS...Last Spring, Alice Martin

gave me some of the most beautiful tulips this preacher ever has seen. They were gorgeous! Well, since Alice saw that was impressed with their beauty, she gave me some tulip bulbs a few days ago so I can raise my own. Now there's nothing pretty about a tulip bulb. No color, no glamour. They're just plain onion-ee looking things. Following instruction, I planted them last week. They are now out sight where they will wait 'til next spring! Out of those attractive, unsightly bulbs will come forth some of the most brilliant shades of red and yellow. Just wait!

So is it with the Resurrection. We've all seen some beautiful lives that came to an unsightly end by death. We've planted the body (only the bulb) in a burying place and now we wait for the call of God, the trumpet sound. And on that day there will come forth a perfect, beautiful, glorified body, like unto that of the Lord Himself Remember that little baby that death took from its cradle? Or that precious older saint? Paul describes the Christian's resurrection like this: "It (the body) is sown in corruption; it is raised in incorruption; it is sown in dishonor; it is raised in glory. It is sown in weakness; it is raised in power. It is sown a natural body; it is raised a Spiritual body." He further declared, "And as we have borne the image of the earthy, we shall also bear the image of the Heavenly." Christian, cheer up! The best is yet to come! "

* * * * * *

CHRISTMAS THOUGHTS....! Like Christmas Season. I like the memories of childhood. I like the sight of decorated trees, colored lights, and wrapped packages. I like the radiance of a little child's eyes. I like the church Christmas programs, the singing of carols, and the reading of the

Biblical account of Christ's birth. I like the moments spent with family and friends. The Spirit of the season is GIVING. But it is also a season for receiving. The tragedy of the ages is, that Christ has been rejected rather than being received by so many. What a different world this would be if Christ were not crowded out. There was no room for Him in the inn; but we can, we should, and we MUST make room for Him in our hearts if we are to be saved and have Heaven for our home.

* * * * * *

IT TAKES WILL POWER...
To have power and not abuse it.
To have a smart kid and not brag.
To itch and not scratch.
To be tempted and not yield.
To forgive and forget.
To have a horn and not toot it.

* * * * * *

BROKEN BARRICADES ...What would it be like to be driving down a straight highway and suddenly discover that you had taken a fatal, final plunge into the clear, cold, fast-flowing waters of a river? During the early sixties, the State Highway Department built a new bridge over Current River on highway67 in N .E. Arkansas. A temporary wooden structure was built adjacent to the old bridge that was being replaced. When the temporary wooden bridge was operational, the old, narrow bridge was tom away. The old approach was still there, but no bridge.

All that was necessary for a driver was just simply to

slow down, make a slight jag, follow the signs, and cross the temporary structure. Back up the road a way, signs were set up, flashing lights were installed, and appropriate warning were displayed. All went well 'til one night just past mid-night a tired traveler ignored the warnings, failed to slow properly, and plunged into the river. The driver and four passengers perished.

WHAT HAPPENED? Was the driver asleep? Too sluggish to have been driving? Blurred vision? No one knows. The evidence showed that all signs were un-heeded, all warnings were ignored. Skid marks indicated the driver realized at the final moment his tragic mistake. It was too late!

I never cross that bridge without recalling that incident. It still sends shivers up my spine. THERE IS ANOTHERPLUNGE that's worse, much worse than that. It happens every day! Men, women, young people ...folks who are most sensible in regard to business, education, and other matters, completely ignore all the warnings and road signs placed along the highway of life by a loving caring Heavenly Father.

THE BIBLE SAYS, "He, that being often reproved hardeneth his neck, shall SUDDENLY be destroyed, and that without remedy. " Every preacher, including this one, could compile long list of people he's known personally who broke through the barricades and took the plunge from time into an endless Eternity. If anyone reads these lines who is not saved, young or old, won't you please put on the brakes and get right with God?

IT'S NOT HARD TO GO TO HELL. But on the road in that direction, there are some barricades. Like, the LOVE of God...PRAYERS of parents or other loved ones...the PLEADING of friends who care. "He that being ...often reproved ...hardeneth his neck ...suddenly destroyed ...without remedy." An airplane crash, an automobile accident, a heart attack, and it's all over! Except...ETERNITY.

* * * * * *

MASTER' MEN ...Be a leader in your home. I heard some time ago of a very fine Christian man who lived up in the hills of Central Arkansas. He and his wife had ten children. They often had company. On Sunday mornings this man would say, "All that's planning on going to Sunday School and church, start getting ready; and all that's NOT planning to go, you start getting ready, too!"

I like that. In my opinion, unless there's a providential reason, there ought to never to be any dilly-dallying around on Sundays over the matter of going to church and Sunday school. After all, it IS the Lord's Day, isn't it? A lot of men ought to take the lead and set the pattern for your household. Some matters should be settled once, and having been settled, should form an established pattern for life. Joshua put it well when he said: "But as for me and my house we will serve the Lord."

* * * * * *

Quote: "When my father found me on the wrong track, he always provided switching facilities." And ..."The accent may be on youth, but the stress is still on the parents."

* * * * * *

A SERMONETTE ..."I have seen servants upon horses, and princes walking as servants upon the earth." (Ecclesiastes 10:7) That's the writer's way of saying that things don't always tally out down here. How true!

In our day, a foul-mouthed, beer-guzzling, swaggering sports figure will be paid millions year, while a schoolteacher may get a few thousand. A missionary couple or family receive very little glory, and LESS of the world's goods, while an immoral, un-principled, so-called entertainer gets rich.

NOPE! Things don't always even out down here. Sometimes the prince has to walk while a servant rides the horse. But the Judge of all the earth will one day render to everyone his due. HIS scales will put everything in proper balance.

* * * * * *

FOR WHAT IT'S WORTH ..."And God gave Solomon wisdom and understanding exceeding much, and largeness of heart, even as the sand that is on the sea shore." Of Solomon it is said, "And his spake three thousand proverbs; and his songs were a thousand and five."..."And he spake of TREES ...he spake also of BEASTS, and of FOWL, and of CREEPING THINGS, and of FISHES." Do you suppose that even Solomon was a country boy at heart? At least he had a good degree of common sense to go along with his unusual amount of wisdom. With all his greatness he maintained "the common touch."

THE WISEST MAN looked one day at a colony of ants, and he pronounced them "EXCEEDING WISE." The reason, "They prepare their meat in the summer." That's better's a lot of humans do, who live and die and go into Eternity without having made preparation! "Go to the ant," the wise man said, "Consider her ways and be wise."

* * * * * *

SOUND ADVICE ...For years I've heard and used the expression, "Keep your powder dry. " The expression was originally given by a General Cromwell, who said to his men,"TRUST GOD, AND KEEP YOUR POWDER DRY. "There's another expression I've considered often ..."Pray for a good harvest, but keep on hoeing. "Some of today's religious zealots would have us believe that all we need do is simply trust God. Well, I DO trust God. He's NEVER come up short! And He always gives a good harvest.

HOWEVER, there are some things God wants US to do. I agree with the man who said, "God is not obligated to send the wind to drive our ship if we don't have the faith to raise the sails." In the warfare that rages, it's sometimes necessary that we fire our guns! That's the reason we need to keep our powder dry! Wet powder won't fire. God DOES give a good harvest, but He's under no obligation to do so IF WE QUIT HOEING! For whatever it's worth, the same principle applies to healing, having food on the table, and lots of other things. If we don't do what we can, is God obligated to do what we want Him to do?

* * * * * *

DECEMBER 13, 1994...Man...Never saw him before; most likely won't see him again. It was just one of those chance encounters. The place, an outer waiting room at a Juvenile court. His eyes were red and moist. There are times when a feller just has to cry, tho he was trying mighty hard to keep from it.

HE LOOKED as "All-American" as any lad could look. Any dad should be mighty pleased to have him as a partnering a fishing boat. Most likely he could swing a bat or snag a spiraling football. He looked like he'd fit in our church's youth group   Discovery program. Sure wish Bro. Mark could work with him. He might even have a voice for singing. Over-heard someone, probably a lawyer, say he could visit his Grandparents once a 'month.

The way it 'peared to this preacher, a home was at the final stages of disintegration. For that family, rigor mortis was ready to set in. The one who was hurting most was the kid caught between the care-free innocence of childhood and the stark reality of a cruel cold world. A world in which too many adults inflict too much pain on too many kids. I don't even know his name, or adolescent facility he'll be going to. All know is, I saw his tears and felt his fear and witnessed his hurt as he let go of a man and woman who just didn't make it as a dad and mom.

THE RIDE HOME was pretty quiet. I couldn't think of much to say. Mark (Director of Youth Music) couldn't either.

We both swallowed hard. I know I did! It'll take more than a while to put that boy out of my mind. Little wonder our blessed Saviour wept and was moved with compassion when He saw the multitudes. Multitudes that in today's society include too many kids who'll never sit in the other end of a fishing boat and bring in a big bream or a wiggling catfish. Or throw a ball with a little curve and hear a doting dad say, "Good stuff, and son!" The bone-chilling coldness of that December day was not as cold as the heart-wrenching coldness of that brief courthouse encounter. Wherever you are, God Bless you, little buddy!

* * * * * *

Quote: "The soul would have no rainbows if there were no tears."

* * * * * *

THANKSGIVING SEASON...It's such a sentimental time. If we've got an ounce of National pride and Patriotism, it reminds us of the sacrifice and hardship that went into the establishing of this country. If we've got any love for family and friends, it stirs so many fond memories. And, if we care for the church, it stirs within us a sense of Worship, Reverence, and Devotion toward the Almighty from Whose bountiful hand we've received SO MANY good blessings. It's mighty hard to be casual about Thanksgiving Season.

* * * * * *

HOW 'BOUT THAT? A man in Utah said he put a rattlesnake over the shoulder of a 21-month old girl to show her it would not hurt her. The child died from the snakebite and the 24-year old man was convicted on charges of manslaughter. He had pleaded innocent by reason of insanity.

NOW WHO'D DO A DUMB, STUPID, IDIOTIC, SILLY THING LIKE THAT? Well, I'm fixin' to tell you. THIS WHOLE NATJON. That's who. The Bible says, concerning intoxicating drink..."At the last BITETH LIKE A SERPENT, and stingeth like an adder." (Proverbs 23:32) A twenty-one month old baby girl is dead. She died from a serpent's bite, the result of a cruel, thoughtless, crazy deed. Across our country, THOUSANDS die every year (many of them young people) because of beverage alcohol. FIFTY YEARS ago a president's wife said to this nation: "The average girl of today faces the problem of learning, very young, how much she can drink of such things as whiskey and gin, and sticking to the proper quantity."

I wonder how many lives have been taken, how many homes have been broken, how many jobs have been lost, how many childrer: have cried themselves to sleep. Or how many health problems have been caused by the awful, deadly sting of alcohol. I'm a parent and a Grandpa. If I had seen someone putting a rattlesnake on one of my children...or Grandchildren I'd pounce on him like a tiger! I've taught my young folks to stay away from serpents that bite ...and from drink that destroys. isn't it kinda strange that we kill the rattlesnake and license the liquor? "What fools we mortals be!"

* * * * * *

"GIT A ROPE!" ONE OF MY FAVORITE T.V. commercials is that one where the Chuck wagon chef, Cookie, tried to pass off an inferior brand of picante sauce. When it's revealed that the inferior stuff is made in New York City, not San Antonio, the trail boss says firmly and with   conviction, "Gita   rope."   Looks   like   "Cookie"   has   ha d it! RECKON THERE'S A LESSON THERE? What about some of us preachers who give less than our best to a Sunday morning or evening congregation? "Get a rope!" Or a teacher, officer, or any church worker who takes the easy way out and substitutes anything less than the BEST. What about a high school student or a college student who goofs off and flunks the course. "Git a rope." Or what about church members who miss when they could get up and attend? If we want the BEST we've got to get up and work for it. If we're willing to settle for less than the best ...Well, maybe they ought to just go ahead and "git a rope."

* * * * * *

"Great it is to believe the dream
When we stand in youth by the starry stream; But a greater thing is to fight life through and say at the end, THE DREAM IS TRUE! "
* * * * * *

ONE FISH TO ANOTHER: "After you have eaten the worm off the hook, give the line a little tug. He will pull it up and put on a fresh worm."
* * * * * *

WATER BOTTLES   WAY-SIDEWELLS ...Gen.21 tells the story of a mother and her son who were sent into a wilderness with no provisions except some bread and a bottle of water. The bread was gone and the water bottle had become empty. The mother, in deep agony, walked away a good distance to avoid seeing the slow, starving death of her son. In her deep sorrow she lifted up her voice and wept. Evidently, the lad prayed too...for the Bible says, "And Godhead the voice of the lad ..." It is also written that "God opened her eyes, and she saw a WELL of water: and she went, and filled the bottle with water, and gave the lad drink." The lad lived; so did the mother.

IT MAY BE that someone who reads these lines is going through hard, trying times. Your small bottle may be about empty and you can't see any ray of hope. Don't sit down to die! Not yet. You may be nearer to a springing well of water than you ever have been before. God DOES hear the cries of His children and He has all the resources necessary to meet your needs. Don't despair. Take your case to God in prayer. Help may be a lot nearer than you realize.

* * * * * *

This pastor preached sermon from Titus 2, 3 on the importance of GOOD WORKS by Christians. Good works will never produce Salvation, but will always be a product of Salvation. We don't work in order to be saved, but we work because we are saved. You might want to check these verses: Titus 2: 14; 3: l; 3:8; and 3:14.

One of our DISCOVERY young fellows (8 or 9 years old) wrote the following summation on that sermon: "Good works will be remembered. God will remember your work and labor of love. Dorcas was full of a lot of good works.

God will bless those who will work. We all need to be good for something. The only thing you can do, you have to do it in your generation.

Don't you even think about lying down in that coffin with your name on it wishing you had done it? Do it!

* * * * * *

Quote: "God doesn't call the fit; he fits the called."

* * * * * *

'CAUSE MOMMA DID ...That's why! Making salmon cakes around our house usually develops into an interesting project. After she opens the canoe salmon, Mrs. Scott makes it a point to give me a good size bite of that uniquely flavored Alaska pink salmon. Since childhood I've loved the taste of good salmon; especially that first bite.

WITH THAT PART OVER, she mixes in some crackers, an egg, or two, and I can't remember if anything else makes it in the mixture. Then she carefully pats out the round cakes, places them just so in the skillet until they're all very neatly arranged. Then she completes the process by sprinkling just a tidge of finely ground corn meal on each patty. I asked her the last time, "Why do you sprinkle meal on each cake?" Her answer was simply, "Cause that's the way momma always did it."That's good enough reason for me. Her mom did most things right! And you sure can't argue with goodness.

I'M MIGHTY GLAD that my wife and lots of other good ladies still do some things the way they do just because "that's the way momma did it!" The Apostle Paul encouraged older women to teach the young women "to be sober, to love their husbands, to love their children, to be discreet, chaste, keepers at home, good, etc." The writer of Proverbs listed some virtues of Godly women, such as faithfulness to her husband, care for her children, kindness to whomever, and others.

LAST TIME we had salmon, Mrs. Scott made a loaf instead of patties. And she didn't sprinkle any meal on it. I wonder why. Probably just' cause her momma didn't!

* * * * * *

ANOTHER SERMON SUMMARY ...by one of the "little ones"..."Don't give up. Rebellions a sin. Have you counted the cost of disobedience? Take up your cross. You can't get your soul back no matter what you give or do. You don't have to do nothing for the Lord but it is best if you do. "

* * * * * *

Quote: "You can come nearer sneaking daylight past a rooster than you can to sneaking sin past God. "

* * * * * *

HIGH SCHOOL REUNION ...Mrs. Scott and I enjoyed a most unique experience this summer.(1993) We attended the 50lh anniversary reunion of my High School graduating class ...1943...Mangrove, Missouri High School. WHAT AN EXPERIENCE! On graduation night we were a bunch of 18-year-oids. It was almost as if someone had punched a magic button and there we were ...68-69 year old Grandpas and Grandmas. Of the 95 in the graduating class, 18 have died;

5 or 6 can't be located. About 50 were present for the reunion activities .To any of the classmates who may read these lines, you all are in my thoughts and prayers often. May God bless you in your retirement years with health, happiness, and contentment?

We are rounding the bend and headin' home! Note: Since it was remembered that this boy dabbled in poetry while in High School, I was asked to write reunion poem for the class scrapbook. Heretic!

OUR FIFTIETH ANNIVERSARY REUNION CLASS OF '43
Our class-mates all scattered on graduation night; we chose the directions we thought to be right. Some went east and others went west,

Each seeking the life he felt was best. FIFTY YEARS, Haifa century; how time has flown! As we meet in reunion, will we even be known? We're not teenagers, we're Gramps and Grandmas. Our hair looks much different; we sag 'round the jaws.

We've got corns and callouses, ailments galore; Arthritis, heart trouble, and whole lot more.

We're fat and we're flabby; we shake when we walk. We forget what we're saying as we start to talk.

We've got bi-focal, bulges, dentures, and bridges; and around the middle, some un-wanted ridges. But this I can say, with a half-toothless grin, we're a good looking bunch for the shape we're all in!

And, Oh, what a joy it is, just to be here; Most of us haven't met for many a year.

A hug, a "Hoare you" And, "What about your folks?"
A laugh, a tear; "Got any new jokes?"

OUR FIFTIETH REUNION ...We're having a lark! I hope that our lives have left a good mark.
It's been a great journey, made sweeter, I guess
By having been part of MGHS!!

* * * * * *

JUST RAMBLIN' ...1guess most of us have a place in our memory for the home of our childhood. Mine is that old sixty-acre farm place out from Mtn. Grove, Missouri in the Brushy Knob community. Driving slowly by the other day brought back lots of memories. Many of them revolved around the home. Mom, dad, brother, sisters...six of 'em! What enjoyment we had. The old country school's gone. The community church house burned many years ago and now the churchyard is pasture.

Since it's so close to Mother's Day, I could close my boyish eyes and envision mom with an egg bucket on her arm;·or working in the garden with a bonnet blocking the sun. She was a good blackberry picker; and she gave the geese fits as she ripped away those soft downy feathers. Great pillows they made. And have you ever settled down for a night's sleep on a cold winter night all wrapped up in a nice feather bed? Mom had a few favorite songs which she sang sorta softly. Really, she was more of a "hummer." She had a real knack for nudging us kids toward the way of work, study, honest ...truth. She patched my overalls and made the girls some dresses on that old treadle sewing machine. She "opened her mouth with kindness ..."In memory of my mom, and to ALL Godly mothers and good ladies, we "rise up and call you blessed."

* * * * * *

YOUNG LOVE and young lovers claim most of the attention in song and in story. Perhaps that's the way it should be. If the FAMILY, the CHURCH, and ultimately, the COUNTRY are to survive, we simply have to have relationships built on the right kind of love. Nothing less will do.

If YOUNG loves beautiful ...and it is...then what about OLD love?

That is also inspiring and heart-warming. There's something special about love that has lasted! When I see an older couple who have celebrated their Golden wedding anniversary or more, I can't help being blessed. There's a union that has withstood all the pressures that cause so many to cave in. In my mind I'm thinking even now of lots and lots of older folks whose lives have meant so much. They remind me of an old building ...and old farmhouse or barn. Weather-beaten, storm-tested, and out-lasting most of its generation, it stands as a testimony to the solid foundation, the good materials, and the fine workmanship that have made it last. It's sad to see either of these pass from the scene...either a marriage union, or an old building. But if they have served their generation and have fulfilled their purpose, let them tear the old buildings down and let the older souls pass on to their Eternal rest. But please Lord, help us to preserve the memory and the meaning of both.

* * * * * *

A SOBERING EXPERIENCE ...These lines are being written a few days prior to our annual observance of Memorial Day. For the second time this week, I've walked across the parking lot and into Little Rock's Veteran's Hospital. Always a sobering experience, it seems a little more so these days. Maybe it's all the talk about the50th anniversary observance of D-Day.

Lingering in the lobby can sure conjure up a lot of questions in a feller's mind. Like, why is that person having such a struggle breathing, and will he always have to carry his own oxygen? That lady looks like she's been through a lot of anxious moment's .Wonder how many days and nights she spent waiting for a letter or word regarding her husband's status. Couldn't help noticing that ex-POW license plate in the parking lot. Some D.V.'s too. And those men sitting outside on the bench. Wonder where they served and how come some of their limbs are missing?

Spending a few minutes by the bed of a veteran, holding his hand, offering a prayer of thanks, and asking God for his recovery ...It all makes a feller swallow hard and it makes him want to salute the first American Flag he sees.

FROM THIS PREACHER'S HEART ...I have had the

privilege of serving as pastor to lots of Veterans and present-day Military men and women. I can tell you this, I will always feel a sense of love and respect for those who have offered and given so much.

"God of our fathers, known of old, Lord of our far-flung battle line; Beneath Whose awful hand we hold Dominion over palm and pine ...Lord God of hosts, be with us yet,
Lest we forget...LEST WE FORGET! "

* * * * * *

From the MWN May 17, 1989...EVERY MONTH is distinguished by its own personality. MAY is especially so. In climate, it's sandwiched between April and June and seems to have trouble deciding whether to hold on to spring or let go and run with summer. Some mornings we need heat. Some evenings we need A.C.

SENTIMENTALLY, it tugs at our heartstrings. Who can sing with the choir (or hear it sung) "Sweetest Mother," and not get misty-eyed and half-choked? What parent or Grandparent can sit through graduation program and not swallow hard a few times? And who among us can approach MEMORIAL DAY without feeling longing for the sound of familiar footsteps or a voice no longer heard?

THANKS, MAY ...for your beautiful flowers; especially the red roses that seem to be so plentiful. And THANKS for the gift of MEMORY that helps keep alive the blessedness of relationships severed by death or separated by distance. And thanks for the HOPE that's renewed as we watch a graduate walk across the stage or witness a beautiful wedding and hear the exchange of vows ..."Until death shall separate us." MOTHER'S DAY ...The MARVEL of Motherhoods that they're mortals! 0, I know ...it seems that Godly mothers must at least be part angel. But they're not. And this makes a saintly mother all the more marvelous! It's simply amazing that so many Godly qualities can be demonstrated in one mere mortal human being! In retrospect, this preacher bows his head and gives thanks to God for the mother whom God chose to give this boy life, And for all good mothers whose examples have been so inspiring. I don't see how God can put so much energy, good sense, patience, sympathy, understanding, and multitudes of other good qualities in Godly women. Peter Marshall referred to mothers as being "KEEPERS OF THE SPRINGS." To all good women, whether wife or a mother or still single...GOD BLESS YOU!!!

* * * * * *

Remember quote: "Every sermon should have a train of thought, but it should also have a terminal!

* * * * * *

WATCH OUT...The Devil promises GOLD, but pays off in Fool's gold. He promises Diamonds but pays off in dirt. He promises Pleasure but pays off in pain. He promises a life of ease and comfort, but if you believe him you' ll wind up doing the work of a mule, grinding like Samson. The Devil. ..You can't believe word he says! Someone has said: "The bad Devil will try to cripple you and then laugh at you for limping."

* * * * * *

A WINDOWSTICKER in a nearly new car caught this preacher's attention. It said simply, "if this car was a horse I'd have to shoot it! "Now there's an owner who's not happy with his shiny new auto.

* * * * * *

MAN TALK ...MAN TO MAN ...While driving my wife's car the other day, I couldn't help noticing a high-pitched whine. It was sorta like an irritating squeal. 'Would't go away; except when I put my foot to the brake. Following up on the clue that it somehow was related to the brakes I headed for the BRAKE and WHEEL shop. Describing the persistent whine to the feller who knows about stuff Eike that, he proceeded to pull a front wheel and point to a little metal thing he called a "censor." That's the manufacturer's way of warning the driver that it's time to get a brake job.

Don't know if it's true or not, but the mechanic said that if that whine of a warning was ignored long enough, it eventually would go away. BUT...you'd wind up destroying some vital parts and paying dearly for it!

Well ...OUR Manufacturer fixed us up with a censor. It's called CONSCIENCE. And it works pretty well, too. Unless we ignore it and abuse it. Remember that day, as a grown man, when you lied a little? At least you border-lined it. Or that deal in which you cut some corners, or that time when you really wanted to speak up for right, but didn't? Conscience is a mighty good thing to have. It'll keep a feller from destroying his character and witness. But it's got to be heeded. Someone asked a man once, "Did you mother's prayers keep you from sinning?" The man answered, "No, but they sure kept me from enjoying it! "And so will your conscience ...if it's in good working order.

* * * * * *

BLIGHT or BLESSING...which are you? Joshua 22:20 "Did not Achan the son ofZerah commit a trespass in the accursed thing, and wrath fell on .all the congregation of Israel? And that man perished NOT ALONE in his iniquity. "Someone says,"If sin, it will hurt no one but me. "But it does! Achan's sin caused a BLIGHT on Israel. It even cost lives of innocent men. Conversely, Genesis 39:5 "Bandit came to pass from the time that he had made him overseer in his house, and over all that he had, that the Lord BLESSED the Egyptian's house for JOSEPH'S sake; and the blessing of the Lord was upon all that he had in the house and in the field." Our own lives can be a blight or a blessing. But someone has rightly said,"We cannot be a BLANK. "

* * * * * *

Quote: "It's a wise man who knows whether he's fighting for a principle or defending prejudice."

* * * * * *

"One loving wife." In the constitution and by-laws of Madison County (Missouri) Quarterly Meeting there's an article which makes a declaration to this effect: "Every minister in good standing shall be the husband of one loving wife." Now everyone knows that was meant to read, "The husband of one LIVING wife." The good folks don't take too kindly to their preachers having plurality of wives.

No one knows how or when the "loving" translation got inserted. Most likely it was by way of typographical error. Over the years the Madison County faithful have refused to tamper with the "loving" rendition. And so that's the way it stands.

As this sojourner pauses to ponder in the twilight, a glance to my side reveals the presence of that one "loving wife." This journey together began on October I 0, 1948 when Gene lie Smith, the prettiest girl in the county held this young preacher's hand and pledged her life-long love and devotion. Through the ensuing six pastorates in three states, she has made the parsonage a home; a true haven of peace and security. Countless numbers have found in her a friend, a wise counselor, a confidant, and a shoulder on which to lean.

My daddy used to preach a Mother's Day sermon on the text given by King David, "As is his part that goeth forth to battle, so shall his part be that tarriethby the stuff. They shall part alike." As far as this preacher is concerned, a faithful preacher's wife is much more than half the battle. May God bless those special women who are known simply as the pastor's wife?

Now if I'm ever again a member of Madison County Q.M. I think I'll vote to keep that article in the By-laws just the way it's been for all these years ..."One LOVING wife!"

* * * * * *

I think most of us know that a good black preacher is endowed with a natural eloquence that is so neat. The following is a black preacher's description of the MARRIAGE of the LAMB.

Soon, and very soothe joy bells are gonna ring. The trumpet is going to sound, and it will be wedding day. The clouds are going to roll back on either side and form little chiffon bows at the base of the blue firmament.

An angel will be dispatched from the bosom of God. He will penetrate the atmosphere and he will announce, "BEHOLD THE BRIDEGROOM COMETH!" The church standing in all the freshness of a spring-time morning will at last extend her hand and say, "Come, Lord Jesus" and the wedding will begin. Gabriel is gonna play the music. David's gonna sing the song..."The Lord is my Shepherd, I shall not want. "Angels are gonna be the ushers. God the Father's gonna perform the ceremony. His great throne will be the altar, and John the Baptistes gonna be the best man.

All the prophets are gonna be the groomsmen. Faith, Hope, and Virtue are gonna be the Bridesmaids. This is gonna be a wedding to behold! Mercy is gonna be the ring-bearer, and the everlasting Light is gonna be the ring.

We look at the bride in our society, but on that day all eyes will be on the Bridegroom. He will step out in the midair robed in RIGHTEOUSNESS, and adorned in GRACE. The Father will join our hands and announce that the waiting is over. We will take the chalice oflove.We'll drink the cup of joy. We'll toast in the triumph over sin. We'll have no more sadness. We'll have no more sorrow.

In just a few days the wedding is gonna begin and we are gonna be part of that Bride that's gonna meet the Bridegroom coming out of glory. It's time to look up. It's getting ready to happen!

April 29, 2002 ...Mrs. Scott and I just made our annual trip to Possum Creek in Texas County, Missouri. This has been a ritual for several years. We joined with kinfolks and enjoyed a wonderful, invigorating experience. The hills and hollers in those South Missouri Ozarks are at their most gorgeous, glorious beauty during the spring turkey season.

Since turkey hunting triggered this annual tradition, it seems logical to insert a report on that part of the trip. Monday, April 22 ...Temperature just right. No wind. Heavy dew. Since our son No. 3 had already "harvested" two gobblers in Tennessee, he accepted the challenge of taking are of"Pa." He did right well. He put this clumsy, tottering elderly man in a good location on a slope facing the north and looking in the direction of some rowdy gobblers. Few things come close to perfection down here. However, any turkey hunter I've known would have settled for what was about to transpire. No. 3, known to some as L.B. (Len Bruce) used his skills at turkey calling, and at 6:30 here came two gobblers, almost running over each other to get to our location. Pure perfection! In reasonable shooting distance, they stopped. Sticking their heads up and stretching their necks, they seemed to say, "Here we are."

Old Betsey boomed! That three inch magnum, fired from a light weight 12 gauge single barrel bounced this old body off a stump which was three sizes too small, to the floor of the forest that was, thankfully, well-padded with leaves, accumulated from several seasons. Perfection took off as fast as two turkeys could run. How could I have missed? You'll never know 'til you're 78 and out there amongst the wild trying to recapture some of the abilities you had at 40, or 50, or 60. At this stage in life, I'm not inclined to spend much time apologizing or explaining how and why I missed putting a No. 6 pellet or two in a turkey's slender neck.

To make this part of the story short, Tuesday morning was, impossible, more nearly perfect than Monday. Only this time it was three Toms that responded to LB.'s imitation of a lonesome hen. One of the three must have been the biggest gobbler on the ranch. Once again, perfection prevailed, 'til this old preacher pulled the trigger. If I do any more preaching, 1 sure hope I shoot straighter from the pulpit than I did at those grinning gobblers. By now they may be more than grinning. They might be laughing out loud. Just for the record, history records that fourteen of those elusive birds have met their doom at the end of this preacher's gun barrel and have helped supply a delicious meal at Genelle's dining table. History might also recordth: 1tseveral of those magnificent birds have been shot at and have troned off to ponder the question, WHAT KIND OF THUNDER WAS THAT?? March, 2002

* * * * * *

My most favorite cartoonist one which I've never actually seen, but I've heard it described. A sheep is traveling a treacherous mountain path. An ll around there are many dangers. As the sheep rounds a bend in the winding path, he comes face to face with a lion, a wolf, and a serpent. Each is poised to pounce on that defenseless sheep.   Just off the path in the shadows is an image of the "GOOD SHEPHERD."

In quiet confidence the sheep tilts his head toward the Good Shepherd and says to   the   lion,   the wolf,   and   the   serpent,   "I'm   with   Him." In the past couple of years I've had occasion often to rely more than ever on the presence, protection, and promises of our Good Shepherd. Since June, 2000, I've had what has become a familiar experience; that of being carted through double doors into an operating room for procedures ranging from brain operation to heart cath, stint implantation, and other procedures. Each time I go through those double doors (they're usually painted a dull gray) I confidently, quietly declare, "I'm with Him."

There come times when our faith is put to the test. For nearly 58 years I've had the blessed privilege of preaching the sacred truths of God's Word. In recent months and weeks, I've rested my head on the comforting pillow of His precious promises. The lion, the wolf, and the serpent have hunkered down and stepped aside without a whimper.

While spending some days and nights recently in ICU, I found special strength and comfort in some of the old-fashioned things that never go out of date. Things like family, friends, and of course, FAITH. How precious is the touch of a loved one, and how sweet the sound of a familiar voice.

In those hours when neither family nor friends could be present, I drew strength and comfort from two familiar sources, verses of Scripture and verses of songs. It's amazing how many "Fear nots" there are in the Bible. And there are quite a few "be of good cheers." When life is at a low ebb, it's pretty important to be able to hang your faith on some bedrock eternal truths.

Besides Scripture verses, familiar lines and lyrics of old songs afforded lots of comfort. Over the years of a lifetime, I've stored lots of songs and hymns in memory's bank. The two that kept coming to mind over and over were, "When through fiery trails thy pathway shall lie, my grace all sufficient shall be thy supply." And the words from that old song, "O come angel band" kept coming to mind. "I know I'm nearing the holy ranks of friends and kindred dear; I brush the dew on Jordan's banks; the crossing must be near. "

In Scripture, Song, and Sermon death has been likened to crossing a river, even a river at flood stage. Now a river overflowing its banks can look pretty boogerish. Maybe it's time to draw from that sheep cartoon. If I'm conscious and alert when death prepares to pounce, I hope to give a tilt and a nod toward the Great shepherd and with confidence affirm, "I'm with Him."

* * * * * *

THE FINAL CHAPTER ...its mid-September, 2002. Now if my .figurin's correct, that puts this plodding pilgrim up there on the pinnacle of three score and eighteen. The sojourn that began in a holler up from the Ratterree place in Texas County, Missouri on February 23, 1924 has had its share of ups and downs, but a LOT more ups than downs. The blessings have far outweighed the burdens. The privilege of pastoring for more than fifty years is totally undeserved. This ministry has brought Genelle and me into close contact with the greatest folksong earth. So many have touched our lives in so many ways. To have served the Master in the capacity founder-shepherd is a blessing of the highest calling. And one more time, THANKS to every church congregation that trusted this team and took us into your hearts. And THANKS to every pastor and church who allowed this undeserving preacher to fill your pulpit as a visiting revival evangelist. I've had the honor of preaching in places far and wide. From California to the Carolinas. From Michigan to Mississippi. Mrs. Scott and I both feel that we've received abundantly more than could be deserved. So many have done so much! GOD BLESS!

* * * * * *

A couple of years ago while participating in the 501 anniversary celebration of the church which we pastored in the mid-fifties in Oilton, Oklahoma a 93 year old deacon recited the following poem. It impressed me that one so aged could memorize and recite like he has done. I secured a copy and now this mere child in his upper seventies is writing it from memory. Here 'tis.

"I've never made a fortune, and it's probably too late now; But I don't worry 'bout that much; I'm happy anyhow.

Asia go along life's journey, I'm reaping better than

I've sowed. I'm drinking from my saucer, "cause my cup has overflowed.

Haven't got a lot of riches, and sometimes the way gets rough;   But I've got a wife and kids who love me, and that makes me rich enough.

So I thank God for His blessings, and the mercy He's bestowed... I'm drinking from my saucer, 'cause my cup has overflowed.

I remember times when things went wrong, and my faith got a little thin.

But then all at once the dark clouds broke, and the sun came shining in.

So Lord help me not to grumble about the tough rows I've hoed...

I'm drinking from my saucer, 'cause my cup has overflowed.

If God will give me strength and courage when the way gets steep and rough, I won't ask for other blessings, I'm already blessed enough. And may I never get too busy to help another bear his load,

Then I'll keep drinking from my saucer, because my cup has overflowed. "

* * * * * *

From my own experiences and from personal observation, I've compiled my list of SURE SIGNS of advancing age...

l. You repeat yourself a lot.

2.   You've got at least one toenail that looks terrible! And probably a toe or two that don't look so good.

3.   You take lots of naps, like during the noon news, during the evening news, mid-afternoon, and at other times.

4.   You get insomnia lots of nights between 12 midnightand4 a.m.

5.   You repeat yourself a lot.

6.   You bump your head a lot! On things like low shelves, raised car hoods, on low-hanging plants, open cabinet doors, and lots of other things.

7.   You look forward to the third of day of each month. (Soc. Sec. Check).

8.   You repeat yourself a lot.

9.   You learn to live on a fixed income and catch yourself wishing they'd let you help more when they fixed it.

10. You try to count your blessings and decide that truly "You're drinking from your saucer, 'cause your cup has overflowed. "

Billy Sunday said it: "The kiss of reunion at the gate of Heavens as certain as the good-bye kiss when we drift out with the tide.

On a "fixed" income, I'm paying for the printing of

these lines by the page. I could probably scrape up the funds for a few more pages, but let's see how these go. GOD BLESS YOU, EVERYONE! I hope you've found some pleasure and blessing from these few BISCUITS from BEN'S BAKERY.

* * * * * *

Following ministers and wives that are apart of the greater family and their burial location and brief biography.

Foster Flemon "Dock" Scott
Birth: Mar. 2, 1860
Ozark County, Missouri
Death: Sep. 12, 1927
Burial:
Prairie Gardens Cemetery
Liberty
Tulsa County, Oklahoma

Son of Flemmon and Phebe (James) Scott. Wife Nancy Howe Wilson, d/o Tanna Wilson -- Britanna Jane Smith.

Children:
George William Scott
 (1890 - 1957)*
Lewis F. Scott
 (1907 - 1975)*

Rev George William Scott
Birth
:   Dec. 18, 1890
Huggins
Texas County, Missouri
Death:
Mar. 7, 1957,
Springfield
Greene County, Missouri
Burial:
Hillcrest Cemetery

Mountain Grove
Wright County, Missouri
Plot: SE 1st 29-5

George was the son of Foster Flemon and Nancy Howe Wilson Scott. He married Oma Lucinda Tanny Ratterree on September 21, 1910. To this union 10 children were born.

Parents:
Foster Flemon Scott
1860 - 1927)
Nancy Howe Wilson Scott
(1867 - 1946)

Spouse:
Oma Lucinda Tanny
Ratterree Scott (
1891 - 1982)*

Children:
Stillborn Son Scott
(1911 - 1911)*
Ina Isabelle Scott Edwards
(1912 - 1999)*
Bessie Jane Scott
Vandivort
(1913 - 2002)*

Samuel Don Scott
(1915 - 1915)*
Adam Scott
(1917 - 2004)*
Mary Ann Scott
Halliburton
(1918 - 2011)*
Agnes Scott Smith
(1921 - 1987)*
Benjamin Randle Scott
(1924 - 2010)*

Sibling:
George William Scott
(1890 - 1957)
Lewis F. Scott
(1907 - 1975)*

Oma Lucinda Tanny Ratterree Scott
Birth:
Nov. 25, 1891
Texas County
Missouri
Death:
Dec. 6, 1982
Springfield
Greene County
Missouri
Burial:
Hillcrest Cemetery
Mountain Grove
Wright County
Missouri
Plot: SE 1st 29-6

Oma Lucinda Tanny Scott was the daughter of David Lewis Gipson and Minerva Zirschky Ratterree. Oma married George William Scott on September 21, 1910 in Graff, Mo. To this union 10 children were born.

Parents:
David Lewis Gibson Ratterree (1849 - 1930)
Manerva Zirschky Ratterree (1852 - 1928)

Spouse:

George William Scott
(1890 - 1957)

Siblings:
Sarah Margaret Ratterree Maxwell (1872 - 1954)*
James Daniel Ratterree (1873 - 1949)*
William Alexander Ratterree (1876 - 1935)*
Mary Jane Ratterree Brooks (1878 - 1966)*
Thomas Jefferson Ratterree (1880 - 1949)*
Josie Ann Ratteree Wilson (1883 - 1951)*
John Learner Ratteree (1885 - 1962)*
Andrew Jackson Ratterree (1888 - 1966)*
Joseph Ratterree (1890 - 1924)*
Oma Lucinda Tanny Ratterree Scott (1891 - 1982)
Lola M Ratterree (1895 - 1983)*

Children

Ina Isabelle Scott Edwards
Birth:
Jan. 30, 1912
Huggins
Texas County
Missouri
Death:
Jul. 28, 1999
Mountain Grove
Wright County
Missouri
Burial:
Hillcrest Cemetery
Mountain Grove
Wright County
Missouri
Plot: SE 1st 149-1

Ina Isabelle Scott was the daughter of George and Oma Ratterree Scott. She married Elzie Edwards on February 12, 1930 in Mansfield, Mo. To this union 5 children were born.

Family links:
Parents:
George William Scott
(1890 - 1957)
Oma Lucinda Tanny Ratterree Scott
(1891 - 1982)

Spouse:
  Elize Foster Edwards
  (1905 - 1994)

Children:
Tharold Eugene Edwards
(1934 - 1999)*

Bessie Jane Scott Vandivort
Birth:
Dec. 24, 1913
Huggins
Texas County
Missouri, USA

Death:
Jun. 12, 2002
Edgar Springs
Phelps County
Missouri, USA
Burial:
Hillcrest Cemetery
Mountain Grove
Wright County
Missouri, USA

Bessie Jane was the 3rd child of Rev. George W. and Oma Lucinda Tanny Ratteree Scott. She married Herbert Vandivort on February 28, 1934. To this union 3 sons were born. They lived on the family farm for 68 years.

Family links:
Parents:
George William Scott
(1890 - 1957)
Oma Lucinda Tanny Ratterree Scott
(1891 - 1982)

Spouse:
Herbert Steaven Vandivort
(1909 - 2002)

Samuel Don Scott
Birth: Oct. 11, 1915
Death: Oct. 17, 1915
Burial:
Union Chapel Cemetery
Wright County
Missouri

Samuel Don Scott died at 6 days old. He was the son of George William and Oma Lucinda Tanny Ratterree Scott.

Inscription:

Sons of Geo. & Oma Scott.

Note: Shares stone with stillborn son Scott

Rev Adam Scott
Birth:
Jan. 23, 1917
Texas County
Missouri
Death:
Mar. 26, 2004
North Carolina
Burial:
Knollwood Memorial Park
Clayton
Johnston County
North Carolina

Adam was the son of George W. and Oma Lucinda Ratterree Scott. He was a Free Will Baptist minister. He married Mildred Nadyne Brown on September 21, 1938. This union was blessed with a son, Duane.

Parents:
George William Scott
(1890 - 1957)
Oma Lucinda Tanny Ratterree Scott
(1891 - 1982)

Spouse:
Mildred Nadyne Brown Scott
(1918 - 2000)

Mary Ann Scott Halliburton
Birth:
May 8, 1918
Wright County
Missouri
Death:
Mar. 27, 2011
Tennessee
Burial:
Stubbs Cemetery
Texas County
Missouri

Mary was the daughter of George and Oma Lucinda Tanny Ratterree Scott. She married Burl Halliburton on September 21, 1938.Seven children were born to this union.

Parents:
George William Scott
(1890 - 1957)
Oma Lucinda Tanny Ratterree Scott
(1891 - 1982)

Spouse:
Burl Ralph Halliburton
(1916 - 2002)

Children:

George Marion Halliburton
(1939 - 1939)*
James Ralph Halliburton
(1951 - 1951)*

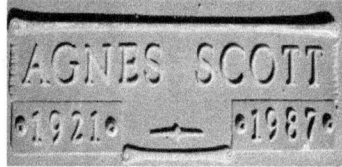

Agnes Scott Smith
Birth:
Aug. 13, 1921
Huggins
Texas County
Missouri
Death:
May 26, 1987
Tennessee
Burial:
Hermitage Memorial Gardens
Old Hickory
Davidson County
Tennessee

Agnes Scott Smith was the eighth child of George and Oma Ratterree Scott. She was married to Rolla Darrel

Smith on April 6, 1941. To this union two children were born.

Family links:
Parents:
George William Scott
(1890 - 1957)
Oma Lucinda Tanny Ratterree Scott
(1891 - 1982)

Spouse:
Rolla Darrell Smith
(1920 - 2013)*

Rev Benjamin Randle "Ben" Scott

Birth:
Feb. 23, 1924
Mountain Grove
Wright County
Missouri
Death:
May 20, 2010
Pocahontas
Randolph County
Arkansas
Burial:
Sutton Cemetery
Pocahontas
Randolph County
Arkansas

Ben R. Scott, 86, of Pocahontas, passed away Thursday, May 20, 2010, at his home. Bro. Scott was born in Mountain Grove, Missouri, the son of George and Oma Scott. He was preceded in death by his parents, three sisters, Ina Edwards, Bessie Vandivort, and Agnes Smith, and one brother, Adam Scott. Bro. Scott was a member of Sutton Free Will Baptist Church in Pocahontas. He was a life-long Free Will Baptist minister, serving as full time pastor for more than 50 years. His early pastorates were in the states of Oklahoma and Missouri. In Arkansas, he pastored First Free Will Baptist Church in Pocahontas, First Free Will Baptist Church in Jonesboro, and for twenty-four years, the First Free Will Baptist Church in North Little Rock. In semi-retirement, Bro. Scott served as interim pastor for First Free Will Baptist Church in Myrtle, Missouri, United Free Will Baptist Church in Walnut Ridge, and First Free Will Baptist Church in Jonesboro.Bro. Scott is survived by his wife of 62 years, Genelle Smith Scott; by three sons and their wives, Randy and Debbie Scott of Pocahontas, Fred and Terry Scott of Garner, N.C., and Len and Aimee Scott of Clarksville, Tennessee. He also leaves behind seven grandchildren, Jason Scott, Amy (David) Carson, Bethany (Josh)

Owens, Kailey Scott, Kaitlen Scott, Benjamin Scott, and Claiborne Scott; and two great granddaughters, Lauryn and Annalyn Carson. Also surviving Bro. Scott are three sisters, Mary Halliburton, Daisey Lindsey, and Leah Postlewaite. Funeral Services were held at Sutton Free Will Baptist Church in Pocahontas. Pastors Randy, Fred, Len, and Jason Scott will officiate. Burial was in Sutton Cemetery.

Family links:
Parents:
George William Scott
(1890 - 1957)
Oma Lucinda Tanny Ratterree Scott
(1891 - 1982)
Inscription:
Married Oct. 10, 1948
(Genelle Smith)

Henry Jasper Smith
Birth:
Jun. 30, 1839
Sullivan County, Indiana
Death:
Jul. 28, 1907
Wright County
Missouri
Burial:
Broyles Cemetery
Talmadge
Wright County,
Missouri

Family links:
Parents:
William Smith (1801 - 1868)
Kesiah H Eades Smith
(1809 - 1854)

Spouses:
Thirsah Woodward Smith
(1847 - 1890)

Matilda Fredrick Smith
(1835 - 1866)*
Elzone Turner Smith (1859 -
1947)*

Children:
Amanda A Smith Burton
(1859 - 1937)*
Josiah H Smith
Maurice L Smith
(1863 - 1865)*
Matilda Alma Smith Young
(1870 - 1959)*

Inscription:
Henry J Smith
Pvt Co C 59th Ind Inf
Civil War
Jul 30 1839 Jun 28 1907

Josiah H Smith
Birth:
May 8, 1861

Sullivan County Indiana
Death:
Mar. 31, 1931
Norwood
Wright County
Missouri
Burial:
Broyles Cemetery
Talmadge
Wright County
Missouri

From death certificate:
Josiah Smith ~ Residence: Norwood, Wright County, MO, Rt 2.~ Farmer
Family links:
Parents:
Henry Jasper Smith (1839 - 1907)
Matilda Fredrick Smith (1835 - 1866)
Spouse:
Mary Elizabeth Butcher Smith
 (1865 - 1950)

Children:
Lora A Smith (1884 - 1906)*
Henry Harrison Smith (1886 - 1952)*

Lloyd Coy Smith (1895 - 1955)*
Homer Basil Smith (1898 - 1971)*

Rev Homer Basil Smith
Birth:
Feb. 10, 1898
Wright County
Missouri
Death:
Jan. 19, 1971
Missouri
Burial:
Hillcrest Cemetery
Mountain Grove
Wright County
Missouri
Plot: SE 1st 77-4

Homer Basil was the son of Josiah and Mary Butcher Smith. He married Verba Mae Carter on March 16, 1920. To this union 5 children were born. Homer taught school before entering the ministry. He was an ordained Free Will Baptist minister for nearly 40 years. He ministered to various congregations and served as pastor of the Mtn. Valley Free Will Baptist church for 17 years.

Family links:
Parents:
Josiah H Smith (1861 - 1931)
Mary Elizabeth Butcher Smith (1865 - 1950)

Spouse:
Verba Mae Carter Smith (1898 - 1971)

Children:
Rolla Darrell Smith (1920 - 2013)*
Infant Smith (1923 - 1923)*
Genelle Smith Scott - Living

Verba Mae Carter Smith
Birth:
May 17, 1898
Wright County
Missouri
Death:
May 16, 1971
Missouri
Burial:
Hillcrest Cemetery
Mountain Grove
Wright County
Missouri
Plot: SE 1st 77-3

Verba Mae was the daughter of Jerry L. and Laura Long Carter. She was united in marriage to Homer Basil Smith on March 16, 1920. To this union 5 children were born. She was a devoted companion and mother. As a wife of a minister her life was a source of blessing and inspiration to many.

Family links:
Spouse:
Homer Basil Smith
(1898 - 1971)

Children:

Rolla Darrell Smith
(1920 - 2013)*
Infant Smith (1923 - 1923)*
Genelle Smith Scott (Living)
Wife of Ben Scott.

Rev Rolla Darrell Smith
Birth:
Dec. 29, 1920
Norwood
Wright County
Missouri
Death:
Mar. 15, 2013
Nashville
Davidson County
Tennessee
Burial:
Hermitage Memorial
Gardens
Old Hickory
Davidson County
Tennessee

SMITH, Rolla D. – Age 92, Nashville, March 15, 2013.

Preceded in death by wife, Agnes Smith; daughter, Linda Underwood. Survived by wife, Helen Ketteman Smith; daughter, Beth Whaley (Vernon); grandchildren, Laurie Whaley Roe (Jeremy) and Jeremy Whaley (Kenya); great-grandchildren, Carter, Luca and Noah; sister, Genelle Scott; step-children, Greg Ketteman (Jill), Carol Reid (Garnett) and Joy Corn (Randy); 11 step-grandchildren and 5 step-great-grandchildren. He pastored at Hazel Creek Free Will Baptist (FWB) Church (MO), Fellowship FWB Church (Flat River, MO), Donelson FWB Church (Nashville), First FWB Church (Savannah, GA) and Grant Avenue FWB Church (Springfield, MO). He was a man of ordinary means yet rich in what matters most...love for God, love for family and love for friends. He was the General Director at FWB International Missions Department from 1960-1962 and 1975-1986 and Missions Instructor at Welch College from 1987-1989. Honorary Pallbearers were missionaries and staff members from the FWB International Missions Department and members of the Harvesters Sunday School Class at Cross Timbers FWB Church.A life celebration service was held at Harpeth Hills Funeral Home with Dr. Paul Harrison officiating.

Family links:
Parents:
Homer Basil Smith
(1898 - 1971)
Verba Mae Carter Smith
(1898 - 1971)

Spouses:
Agnes Scott Smith
(1921 - 1987)
Helen Louise Johnson Smith
(1924 - 2015)*

Rev Herbert Steaven Vandivort

Birth:
May 20, 1909
Texas County
Missouri
Death: Nov. 16, 2002
Phelps County
Missouri
Burial:
Hillcrest Cemetery
Mountain Grove
Wright County
Missouri
Plot: S.E. 1st 76-6

Herbert Steaven Hadley was the son of William Warren and Rosa Bell Meadows Vandivort. He married Bessie Jane Scott on February 28, 1934. To this union 3 sons were born. He became a ordained Free Will Baptist minister Sept. 27, 1935. For 21 years from 1937 to 1958, he served as a bi-vocational minister, pastoring rural churches in Texas and Wright counties.

Family links:
Parents:
William Warren Vandivort
(1871 - 1950)
Rosa Belle Meadows Vandivort
(1872 - 1950)

Spouse:
Bessie Jane Scott Vandivort
(1913 - 2002)*

Siblings:
William Hiley Vandivort
(1897 - 1973)*
Vasa Lee Vandivort
(1898 - 1993)*

Homer Harrison Vandivort
(1900 - 1985)*
Weaver Warren Vandivort
(1902 - 1993)*
Florence M Vandivort Jones
(1904 - 1991)*
Ira Elmer Vandivort (1907 -
1998)*
Herbert Steaven Vandivort
(1909 - 2002)
George Robert Vandivort
(1911 - 2000)*
Alla Dora Vandivort Cox
(1912 - 1989)*
Roy Dean Vandivort
(1916 - 1995)*

**Rosa Belle Meadows
Vandivort**
Birth:
Jan. 1, 1872
Wyoming County

West Virginia
Death:
Dec. 14, 1950
Texas County
Missouri
Burial:
Hillcrest Cemetery
Mountain Grove
Wright County
Missouri
Plot: SE 1st 29-2

Rosabelle was the daughter of Elijah Preston and Dicie Jane Reed Meadows.In October, 1892 she married William Warren Vandivort. To this union 12 children were born. Rosa and Warren moved from West Virginia to Texas County in 1904. She was a charter member of the Oak Grove Free Will Baptist Church in Texas County.

Family links:
Parents:
Elijah Preston Meadows
(1846 - 1932)
Dicey Jane Reed Meadows
(1852 - 1888)

Spouse:
William Warren Vandivort
(1871 - 1950)*

Children:
William Hiley Vandivort
(1897 - 1973)*
Vasa Lee Vandivort
 (1898 - 1993)*
Homer Harrison Vandivort
(1900 - 1985)*
Weaver Warren Vandivort
(1902 - 1993)*
Florence M Vandivort Jones
(1904 - 1991)*
Ira Elmer Vandivort
(1907 - 1998)*
Herbert Steaven Vandivort
(1909 - 2002)*
George Robert Vandivort
(1911 - 2000)*
Alla Dora Vandivort Cox
(1912 - 1989)*
Roy Dean Vandivort
1916 - 1995)*

Siblings:
Rosa Belle Meadows
Vandivort
(1872 - 1950)
Ballard W Meadows
(1872 - 1947)*

Alla Dora Meadows Graham
(1875 - 1967)*
Elias Richard Meadows
(1876 - 1883)*
James Preston Meadows
(1876 - 1961)**
Susan Meadows Farmer
(1878 - 1972)*
Leora Angeline Meadows
(1880 - 1882)*
Harrison Theodore
Meadows
(1882 - 1946)*
Ferdinand Meadows
(1884 - 1974)*
Manerva J. Meadows
Fleshman
(1898 - 1994)**
Florida Faye Meadows Clay
(1902 - 1966)**

Rev John Jefferson Postlewaite

Birth:
May 15, 1890
Death:
Jun. 16, 1960
Burial:
Union Chapel Cemetery
Wright County
Missouri

Spouse:
Lucy Jane Crewse Postlewaite
(1896 - 1991)*

Children:
Leslie W Postlewait (1914 - 1986)*
Harold M Postlewait (1917 - 1987)*
James Leonard Postlewait (1918 - 1982)*
Carl Eugene Postlewait (1921 - 1996)*
Clyde Postlewait (1923 - 1977)*
John Postlewaite (1926 - 2012)*
Freda Pauline Edwards (1930 - 1999)*
Delbert Gene Postlewait (1935 - 2015)*

Sylvia Marie Postlewait (1940 - 1940)*

John Postlewaite

Birth:
Apr. 5, 1926
Death:

Oct. 21, 2012
Missouri
Burial:
Hillcrest Cemetery
Mountain Grove
Wright County
Missouri

He was the 8th son of the late John Jefferson and Lucy Jane (Crewse) Postlewaite. He went to be with His Lord at 86 years, 6 months, and 16 days of age.

John was saved at the age of 12 at the No. 1 Free Will Baptist Church near Huggins, Missouri, when his teacher dismissed school for the students to attend an 11:00 revival service. He answered the call to preach at the age of 19. After attending Free Will Baptist Bible College (now Welch College) in Nashville, Tennessee, he was ordained as a minister of the gospel in 1947.

He married Leah Mae Scott on September 21, 1948 at the home of Rev. Homer B. Smith near Mountain Grove. To this union were born 4 children.

John's first pastorate was at Faith and Hope Free Will Baptist Church near Willow Springs, Missouri. There John and Leah lived in a small log cabin, which was the church parsonage. Throughout the next 53 years, he pastored churches in Oklahoma, Arkansas, Illinois, and Missouri. He planted 7 churches in Washington and Oregon under the auspices of Free Will Baptist Home Missions. He was a well-known evangelist, soul winner, supporter of missions, and mentor to many young people. After moving back to Mountain Grove in his retirement years, he served as Senior Citizens' Pastor at First Free Will Baptist for almost 8 years.

He had a lovely tenor voice and often sang in church and at home. He was also a lover of the Scripture and committed many passages to memory. Even in his last days, he spent several hours a day reading the Bible and could still quote many passages.

He is survived by his loving wife of 64 years, Leah; four children: Joe and Pauline Postlewaite of Florence, South Carolina; Sue and Earl Larson of Brentwood, Tennessee; Sam and Diana Postlewaite of Virginia Beach, Virginia; and Ruth and Donnie McDonald of Tokyo, Japan. Only eternity will reveal how many spiritual children were saved because of his faithful witness.

Parents:

John Jefferson Postlewaite (1890 - 1960)

Lucy Jane Crewse Postlewaite (1896 - 1991)

Siblings:
Leslie W Postlewait (1914 - 1986)*

Harold M Postlewait (1917 - 1987)*

James Leonard Postlewait (1918 - 1982)*

Carl Eugene Postlewait (1921 - 1996)*

Clyde Postlewait (1923 - 1977)*

John Postlewaite (1926 - 2012)

Freda Pauline Edwards (1930 - 1999)*

Delbert Gene Postlewait (1935 - 2015)*

Sylvia Marie Postlewait (1940 - 1940)*

www.ingramcontent.com/pod-product-compliance
Lightning Source LLC
LaVergne TN
LVHW051038080426
835508LV00019B/1579